The
History
of the
World's Greatest
Entrepreneurs

Biography of Success

RONALD SHILLINGFORD

The History of the World's Greatest...

Published by The History of the World's Greatest...

Copyright ©Ronald Shillingford, 2010
The moral right of the author has been asserted

TRADE PAPEBACK
ISBN 9781973268659

CONTENTS

Global Trailblazers

MAYER ROTHSCHILD	Germany	1744 – 1812
JAJA OF OPOBO	Nigeria	1821 – 1891
JAMES J. HILL	Canada	1838 – 1916
CECIL RHODES	Zimbabwe	1853 – 1901
ARISTOTLE ONASSIS	Greece	1906 –1976
DHIRUBHAI AMBANI	India	1932 – 2002
IVAR KREUGER	Sweden	1880 – 1932

Japan's Technology Revolution

TOKUJI HAYAKAWA	1892 – 1980
KONOSUKE MATSUSHITA	1894 – 1989

The American Dream (20th Century onwards)

ASA CANDLER	1851 – 1929
JOHN D. ROCKEFELLER	1839 – 1937
HENRY FORD	1863 – 1947
ELIZABETH ARDEN	1878 – 1966
RAY KROC	1902 – 1985
BERRY GORDY	1929 –
DON KING	1932 –

Criminal Entrepreneurs

LUCKY LUCIANO	Italy/USA	1897 – 1962
GEORGE REMUS	Germany/USA	1876 – 1952
PABLO ESCOBAR	Columbia	1949 – 1993

The Modern-Day Greats

MARTHA STEWART	USA	1941 –
DONALD TRUMP	USA	1946 –
ALAN SUGAR	England	1947 –
RICHARD BRANSON	England	1950 –
STEVE JOBS	USA	1955 –
BILL GATES	USA	1955 –
RICARDO SEMLER	Brazil	1959 –
P DIDDY	USA	1970 –

Acknowledgements

The History of the World's Greatest Entrepreneurs is a book that evolved out of a need to organise my thoughts surrounding the timing of entrepreneurial achievement. Great entrepreneurs, like stars, they shine bright. But, when stars are viewed as part of a constellation they reveal all manner of secrets about our universe time is a tide that brings opportunities to shore. There is a tide in the affairs of men that leads to fortune...Shakespeare. The book covers 1000 years of entrepreneurship revealing waves of opportunities. These guys and girls were fortunate enough to ride them. What I have learned from writing this book can be encapsulated in three famous pieces of writing:

1.
There is a tide in the affairs of men
Which, taken at the flood, leads on to fortune:
Omitted, all the voyage of their life
Is bound in shallows and in miseries.
On such a full sea are we now afloat,
And we must take the current when it serves,
Or lose our ventures.
[Julius Caesar Act 4, Scene 3, lines 218–224.]

2.
"Great men, become great because they have been able to master luck. What the vulgar call luck is a characteristic of genius."

3.
I returned, and saw under the sun, that the race is not to the swift, nor the battle to the strong, neither yet bread to the wise, nor yet riches to men of understanding, nor yet favour to men of skill; but time and chance happeneth to them all.

My first attempt was archived on my computer for over 10 years (to be published 1st Jan 2018) in the form of a compendium which morphed into this book.

I thank entrepreneur and niece Shantelle Shillingford-Golding, whose amazing gift of taking an idea and transforming it to a fully running, fully staffed business is as good as any I've written about. She and her husband Sam Golding have changed the lives and financial futures of hundreds of people through their innovation and dedication to eCommerce. I thank my close friend Michael Morgan, for his constant and consistent support and reliable criticism. Without all your support this book would have remained simply a good idea.

I acknowledge, more than any other my mother Sheila Alleyne Shillingford and her over-arching contribution, rendering all my successes a result of her dedication to me throughout my life and all my failures my own.

I would like to thank Chas Jones of WritersServices.com and author of *Fulford: The Forgotten Battle of 1066*, for his guidance and with whom I enjoyed many interesting discussions. I especially thank Joanne Comerbach of QBBDLL & Co for the tender love and care she provided when viewing my various manuscripts. I also thank Emily Hill of Write My Site expert in the art of prose and helped this novice with much needed technical support.

Although a great deal of time and effort was put into trying to publish my manuscript over the years it seemed rather melodic and appropriate to 'self-publish' a book about the history of great entrepreneurs. I particularly thank James for his faith and belief in the project, which made a difference.

Author's Preface

A business trip to Izmir Turkey gave me the opportunity to visit one of the Seven Wonders of the World, the city of Ephesus. A series of events was initiated that would lead to the writing of this book.

Izmir is also the place where entrepreneur Aristotle Onassis was born in 1906. I knew a little about him, his flamboyance, his virtual ownership of the rich man's playground (Monaco) and his marriage to John F. Kennedy's widow Jackie. As a young kid he had an expectation to be great; he knew he would. I wondered what drove him to become one of the world's richest men. Did the stories about the great city leave an impression on him? Witnessing the hanging of his favourite uncle? Springing his father from jail? His father losing everything after the 1919 Turkish invasion? I was intrigued.

When I arrived back at my apartment from a long day out at Ephesus, I rearranged the furniture so that when I looked up from the book I was reading (a biography of entrepreneur Andrew Carnegie) and paused for thought, I would be met by the amazing sea views directly in front of my apartment. I then had an idea to unplug the TV for over a week, having only the lapping waves breaking on the shore outside as a backdrop. My mind began to wander. I would drift in and out of thinking about Onassis and his tumultuous childhood in Izmir and back to the book and the enigmatic Carnegie, making millions then trying to give it all away. Only the waves and the rustling pages from the book could be heard. Then it hit me. Why not write a complete history of entrepreneurs? Business was good, and I had the time.

The book would not only highlight how the entrepreneurs shaped history, but how history shaped their prospects. I thought that others like me would want to know how the great entrepreneurs became millionaires and what factors and features were common to all of them. What were their relationships with each other like? I came across fascinating men and women, like banker Jacob Fugger whose business scheme and plans so upset Martin Luther he nailed the 95 theses to the Wittenberg Church door and started the Protestant religion. How Mary Ellen Pleasant became a millionaire by operating as a kind of female James Bond, whilst in the bonds of pre-Civil War American slavery. And how former lawyer and immigrant George Remus became one of the richest men in America bootlegging whisky (with the Attorney General on the payroll). He was so emotionally intelligent he was able to get away with openly murdering his wife, after defending himself in court.

Studying an extended history of entrepreneurs over one thousand years provides many insights. It can highlight the connection between entrepreneurs and the political events of their time. The thousand-year study unfolds as a no-holds-barred biography of success.

The book shows how the same opportunities ebb and flow, wax and wane. How political machinations, social and economic events caused winds of change producing tides and waves that are ridden by entrepreneurs who were lucky or savvy (or both) enough keep their sail up when the winds of fortune blew. In the words of Brutus, one of William Shakespeare's most beloved characters:

There is a tide in the affairs of men
Which, taken at the flood, leads on to fortune:
Omitted, all the voyage of their life
Is bound in shallows and in miseries.
On such a full sea are we now afloat,
And we must take the current when it serves,
Or lose our ventures.
[Julius Caesar Act 4, Scene 3, lines 218–224.]

I hope you enjoy reading this book.

All the best,

Ron Shillingford

Foreword

The History of the World's Greatest Entrepreneurs depicts a millennium of enterprise, starting with the 11th Century English tradesman, Godric of Norfolk, and concluding with the African American Sean Combs in the 21st Century. As well as telling the personal stories of the entrepreneurs, this book hopes to illustrate the historical backdrops against which they created their business empires.

The entrepreneurs who feature in this book come from all over the world (there are people from America, Europe, India Japan and Russia amongst other countries) and are from all sorts of backgrounds. The book profiles entrepreneurs who are male, female, black, white, Asian, Hispanic, old and young. The entrepreneurs are from all aspects of the social scale, from penniless immigrants (John Jacob Astor) and slaves (Mary Ellen Pleasant), through to privileged "dandies" like John Law.

The differences don't end there: most of the entrepreneurs in this book appear to have wildly contrasting personalities. On the one hand, there are entrepreneurs like Andrew Carnegie, who believed it was a disgrace to die rich, and therefore worked tirelessly to distribute his wealth amongst the poor. This outlook is in sharp contrast to that of Christopher Columbus, whose methods of controlling other people were so unproductively cruel that Europe's monarchs were reluctant to extend any further funding to him. Even amongst the entrepreneurs of modern times there are not many obvious similarities. The bullish Donald Trump seems to have little in common with the straight-talking Alan Sugar, who in turn appears very different from the zany Richard Branson. And yet, even after all of these substantial differences are taken into account, it's astonishing how many links can be unearthed between the different success stories that feature in this book.

Hopefully this introduction has whetted your appetite for reading *The History of the World's Greatest Entrepreneurs*. Please do take a quick glance at the following Explanatory Notes for clarifications of some of the references to names, numbers and quotes within the book.

Explanatory Notes

•   **Names** – the standard we've adopted for this book is to refer to the entrepreneurs by their surnames, except in the following chapters where the subjects either had more than one surname over the course of their lives or were better known by other names:

•   Mary Ellen Pleasant

•   Madame C. J. Walker

•   Jaja of Opobo

•   Lucky Luciano

•   Martha Stewart

•   P. Diddy

> A further caveat to the surname standard is that we have sometimes used an entrepreneur's first name when describing them in childhood as their stories often involve several other characters with the same surname!

•   **Numbers** – figures that appear in brackets immediately after another figure represent the approximate value of the first amount in today's money [e.g. $75 million ($300 million)]. Where there are dollar signs, they refer to American dollars, unless otherwise specified.

Medieval Entrepreneurs

GODRIC (1070 – 1170)

"In labour he was strenuous, assiduous above all men"
- Source unknown

A Mediaeval social climber

We open our narrative with the tale of Godric of Norfolk, an entrepreneur from mediaeval England who achieved the unachievable: social mobility.

If you were a mediaeval Joe Bloggs from an indebted English family you ran a high risk of being sold into slavery as a means of settling your family's debts. Your likely destination would be Ireland. If you were female and beautiful you stood an even greater chance of being enslaved (the favoured marketing strategy was to get you pregnant and then offer you up as a two-for-one deal).

Godric was born a few years after the 1066 Norman conquest of England. He was the first of three children to his father Ailward and his mother Edwenna. The family were of Anglo-Saxon peasant stock living to a simple prescription; be born poor, live poor, and die poor. The feudal system in place at the time meant there was no such thing as upward mobility.

Godric didn't read the script; he *refused* to follow in the footsteps of his father, who had toiled the land for the benefit of the landowner. From Reginald of Durham we learn of Godric's love of study and self-education (an autodidact). As a teenage freeman living in an economic and military superpower, Godric chose to trade for a living instead. The Norman Conquest brought great change with great benefits. England now belonged to a more orderly and major power. Men like Godric had opportunities to roam into newly conquered Norman lands, gaining access to a flow of goods and knowledge to and from territories seized from the Saracens.

Godric the tradesman

Godric began his career as an entrepreneur by making very small but profitable trades. As his confidence grew, so too did his sales territories. The distances that limit a less daring boy were overcome by Godric's sense of adventure. He got on his proverbial bike, assiduously going from farmstead to farmstead, village to village, and fortress to fortress, selling all manner of goods and always turning a profit. He initially travelled the length and breadth of Lincolnshire and then up to St Andrews in Scotland. Godric developed into an experienced peddler and traveller, entering foreign markets where barriers were lowered by the Norman takeover.

Reginald described Godric as, "…vigorous and strenuous in mind, whole of limb and strong in body. He was of middle stature, broad-shouldered and deep-chested, with a long face, grey eyes most clear and piercing, bushy brows, a broad forehead, long and open nostrils, a nose of comely curve, and a pointed chin. His beard was thick, and longer than the ordinary, his mouth well-shaped, with lips of moderate thickness; in youth his hair was black…"

Expanding the empire

Godric was on the up, becoming not only an accomplished merchant but a decent sailor too. The world had become a smaller place, and he ventured into trading on the high seas in markets that lay around the coastline of the British Isles and Scandinavia. Godric traded not only with ordinary men but also among nobles, selling ornaments and tapestries. His system was to identify rare and therefore more precious wares, and take them to faraway markets where they were less available and therefore highly coveted. Locals would often pay over ten times their cost price.

He continued this cycle of buying goods cheaply in their local market and selling or exchanging them abroad. Each trip saw a steady improvement in Godric's ability to buy and sell. Godric's success enabled him to expand vertically. He took the opportunity to collaborate in joint ventures, purchasing a 50 percent interest in a merchant ship. This boosted his wealth, allowing him to acquire a further 25 percent interest in another vessel. His skill as a navigator on the high seas and his adventurous entrepreneurial spirit meant he could not resist the opportunity of becoming a pirate. Godric was now rather more than the chap who had travelled around Lincolnshire; he was a man of means, and no longer at risk of ending up a slave in Ireland. The gifted negotiator, international merchant and millionaire were now worth more than £3000 (£1,500,000).

Godric's spiritual calling

In 1101 Godric went to the Holy Land (the First Crusade had begun in 1099). The trip to Palestine had a great effect on him. On the return leg he visited the shrine of St. James at Compostable in Galicia, where the remains of the disciple James are said to be laid to rest.

Not unlike the world around him, Godric was a man going through changes. The life of an adventurous travelling salesman, far away from home with no ties, can lead to some of the most indecent excesses. He decided to bring this shameless depravity to an end. Back in England he had a go at estate management, controlling the land of a nobleman, but he gave it up, ironically unable to turn a blind-eye to the degeneracy and dishonesty that took place on the estate amongst the nobleman's young sons and their friends.

Godric returned to the Holy Land in 1102, the year of the Second Battle of Ramleh. King Baldwin of Jerusalem was pummelled, losing most of his soldiers. Baldwin fled, taking refuge in a tower that stood in a small fortress. When the Muslims attacked, the fearless Godric became a hero, rescuing the besieged king. Godric decided to spend time in quiet contemplation with hermits in the desert. He began a new adventure, administering to the sick, injured and dying soldiers of the crusade in a crusader hospital in Jerusalem. After returning to England he travelled to Durham and continued his new adventure. Godric gained a position in charge of sacred objects in the local church and went back to school (at approximately 40 years old) attending with the choirboys of St. Mary-le-Bow church.

The first known millionaire-philanthropist

On a further pilgrimage to Rome and Saint-Gilles in southern France Godric took his aging mother as companion. She made the journey barefoot as a show of humility. Godric continued to struggle with a great sense of remorse and guilt over his previous gambling, womanising, street-brawling (he was quite handy by all accounts) and financial gains. He was so troubled by his past that in 1110 he discarded all his worldly possessions. His pursuit of money was over. .

Godric settled down for good as a Catweazel-like hermit in the woods of Finchale on the River Wear. Bishop Ranulf Flambard granted him land at Finchale near Durham in 1115. There he established a hermitage, at a beautiful spot by the river. His reputation as a great trader was well known and word got out that he was living deep in the forest. The idea that he had given away his entire wealth was met with great scepticism. A group of Scottish soldiers under King David of Scotland thought they could beat a secret location of buried treasure out of Godric. That fact that he claimed to be conversing with animals should have indicated that he was probably crazy enough to give up riches for a life of poverty. Godric fared better with the animals than the humans though. Wild beasts would 'ask' him to shelter them whilst being hunted, and he would agree to do so.

A man of many talents

Godric continued to stretch himself, even becoming a major songwriter in later life. *Cantus Beati Godrici* (which today might attract a parental advisory label) was one of Godric's big successes: in it he asks the Virgin to help him attain ecstasy. Another production was *Cantus Sancto Nicholao* motivated by spring visions of the patron saint of seafarers and pirates. If the modern music charts had existed in the 11th Century, Godric's releases would have gone platinum. His poems make him England's earliest known lyricist in recognisable English. In 1995 a Radio 3 celebration – *The Fairest Isle* – listed Godric as the very first English composer.

Godric's talents were unlimited. The former entrepreneur was revered for having the ability to see into the future and knowing what was going on thousands of miles away. It is not known if he used these supernatural powers to help make his fortune, but his guidance was sought by Pope Alexander III and the martyred Archbishop of Canterbury Thomas à Becket. Prior to the Archbishop's murder by King Henry II he was counselled by Godric. Unfortunately, Godric did not see his murder coming. It is not known how popular Godric's services were following the event, but consultants have had a bad name ever since.

Godric was broad built but small in height (about 5ft) with sharp blue eyes. In old age he was described as having "…[hair] as white as snow [black in his youth]; his neck was short and thick, knotted with veins and sinews; his legs were somewhat slender, his instep high, his knees hardened and horny with frequent kneeling; his whole skin rough beyond the ordinary, until all this roughness was softened by old age.... In labour he was strenuous, assiduous above all men."

Stricken with a long illness, in his little hermit's grotto, Godric died penniless on May 2nd 1170, aged 100. If that weren't remarkable enough, Godric managed to be canonised as a Saint *before* he died.

GIOVANNI de MEDICI (1360 – 1429)

"Lord, who shall abide in thy tabernacle? Who shall dwell in thy holy hill? He that *walketh uprightly*… He that puteth not out his money to usury, nor taketh reward against the innocent. He that doeth these things shall never be moved."

- Psalm 15:1-5

An expanding world

The early part of the new millennium saw a changing of the guard. The former great Muslim power of the West left Europe like a receding glacier. Barriers were removed that had previously prevented European entrepreneurs accessing the exotic and emerging markets of China, Indochina, the Middle East, and Africa.

The Italian Marco Polo had educated Europe about the secluded but advanced empire of China, which established a Bureau of Paper Currency in Kaifeng in 1154, to act as the central agency in charge of all money issues. In 1160 Emperor Kao Tsung reformed Chinese paper currency, improving the economy. The greater trading distances were accompanied by greater risk, and the greater the risk, the greater the opportunity for making large sums of money. The East-West balance of power was changing.

The shifting tectonic plates of empire presented opportunities for Western Europeans to travel and expand their market reach. The waxing and waning fortunes of mediaeval European empires gave rise to a class of entrepreneur like no other: the banker. One such was born two hundred years after Godric's death. His name was Giovanni de Medici – a banker very much on time.

The Bible, the Torah and the Koran all speak against paper money and lending. This barrier slowed the expansion of banking as an expression of entrepreneurship. Nevertheless, the investment community was expanding globally and needed fluidity of wealth. Trying to contain the money trade proved to be like trying to hold back the tides and in 1220 Christendom deemed that interest is not interest, but compensation to the lender for expenses and loss.

By 1338 some 80 banking houses were operating in Florence, with exchanges in every part of Europe. The pre-eminence of Florence in international banking and as a financial centre was based not only on the strength of the gold florin but also on the rationalization of Florentine commerce and industry. The city catered to the international market, especially in luxury goods. The centre of that trade was Rome and ironically the papacy became the foundation of Florentine banking. Europe was in the midst of a cultural and commercial revolution. Ways were found to circumvent the strict regulations of the church. In fact, the main circumventer of the church rules was the church itself. The papacy was the first to insist that moderate interest paid on money invested at a risk to the creditor should not be considered usury. Furthermore, they contended, it was not usury when a charge was made for loans repaid after the promised date of repayment, or if the payment was made in land instead of money. The effects of this sudden shift and change would be felt across the world. Some were aptly placed and well-adjusted to take full advantage of it.

Birth of a banker

The great Giovanni di Bicci de Medici was born in 1360 in Florence, one of five sons. The fledgling money industry was struggling for legitimacy and Medici's hometown of Florence was in the ascendancy.

Prior to the 1390s five Medicis were hanged during a 17-year period. Medici's father Averado died from the plague in 1363. He was an entrepreneur who had made it big but had subsequently lost everything and left his family penniless.

Life in Florence without money was like life without money in any big city today – you were viewed as a nobody; worthless. To be rich you needed an income of at least a few hundred florins a year. A florin at this time was equivalent to £20 today. But a house in the city, a maid and couple of slaves would set you back 200 florins a year. There was a pecking order. How you made your money, where you made your money and how you spent your money (family chapels and lending to the state) determined your status. De Medici was an entrepreneur fuelled by a hunger for the prestige once obtained and lost by his father.

Medici was destined to become a banker. He was the apprentice of banker and distant cousin Vieridi Cambio de Medici who, by 1370, was one of the leading bankers in Florence. The family had branches and business dealings far and wide. In 1385, Medici was entrusted with the opening and independent running of a banking branch in Rome and established commercial relations in Bruges and London. Part of their success was down to a strategy of decentralised banking. His banks were interlocking but independent, meaning there was less risk of them all going down if one bank became affected by economic contagion.

In 1386 Giovanni de Medici married Piccarda Bueri. On September 27th she bore him a son and named the boy Cosimo. He would later become an extremely successful entrepreneur in his own right.

Banker to the Pope

By 1393, Medici was ready to do his own thing, and he established a bank in Florence, ten years before it was ruled legal to charge interest on loans. Clients would often pay in goods (such as cloth) and licences to cloak usurious returns. In 1402 and 1408 Medici established two cloth manufacturing bogettas (workshops) adding even greater profits to the already profitable banking operation.

It was time to expand the operation to Rome. Medici engaged a mover and shaker called Baldassare Cossa. Cossa was a larger-than-life entrepreneur extraordinaire. The former pirate and soldier was widely known as an incurable womaniser. But he had the ability to make things happen. Baldassare helped refine the monetary machine of the Pope in concert with Medici. Cossa improved the Pope's coffers no end. He had field agents monitoring the health and age of incumbents. He then created a market for 'expectations,' as he gracefully put it. He held a Dutch auction for places on a list for ecclesiastical election. Cossa went even further, introducing the sale of 'preferences'. Thus, a man who had paid for the expectation of the parish position might find, when the incumbent died, that it had been sold for a larger sum to someone who had purchased a 'preference'. A later Medici – Giovanni did Lorenzo – is quoted as saying: "How well we know what a profitable superstition this fable of Christ has been for us."

Baldassare Cossa was such an able operator he even wangled his way into the position of Pope itself. Now Medici had the Pope as a client and friend. During 1414 the Pope left for an important mission to Constance. He took a Medici bank rep as an adviser. This signalled Medici as being very much on the up. After Cossa's election as Pope (now one of three Popes occupying the position at the same time) the profits levered from the papal connection rolled in. Fifty percent of Medici's profits came from his two branches in Rome. He knew the commercial value of being indispensable to important people and backed the Pope John XXIII during his war with Pope Gregory XII. In June 1412 Pope John made peace with King Ladislaus, King of Naples and agreed terms. Medici pulled a deal together coming up with the Florins for the payoff. The banker had been able to manoeuvre his way into position with arguably the world's most powerful man. He was also fast becoming one of the world's richest men.

By now Giovanni de Medici occupied the upper echelons of Florentine society and was extremely rich. He lost the account of the Papal Chamber to his competitor the Spini group, although in 1420 Spini suddenly went belly-up and Giovanni de Medici stepped in, dependable as always. Medici had another string to his bow in the form of his son, 30 year-old Cosimo, a banking genius and beneficiary of his father's nurturing as a hunter of opportunity. Medici went from strength to strength, becoming the most successful business in Italy and then the most successful in Europe.

The 61 year-old Giovanni de Medici established a family chapel and had four terms as one of the seven priors who make up the Signoria (chief legislative body of Florence). But public office was not one of his ambitions. Public office was bad for business, attracting envy and creating rifts between him and other power brokers. Maintaining the status quo was paramount. Medici was made Count of Montverde but refused the title, choosing to remain an ordinary citizen, keeping his eyes firmly on the prize: profit. He was a quiet man, at times witty, with a liking for dry humour. He wasn't a good speaker but gave sound advice with great magnanimity. His deathbed speech to his sons was one of unity. He implored them to practise great caution.

Giovanni de Medici was not the most famous Medici but were it not for his extraordinary success his posterity would likely have become tailors or farmers rather than Dukes, Cardinals, Popes and Queens. On the 28th of February 1429 Giovanni de Medici died one of the world's richest and most influential men.

CHRISTOPHER COLUMBUS (1451 – 1506)

"But in truth, should I meet with gold or spices in great quantity, I shall remain till I collect as much as possible, and for this purpose I am proceeding solely in quest of them"

Waxing and waning of empires

There is a romantic view of Christopher Columbus as a dogged explorer, but in fact he was one of the world's greatest and most ambitious entrepreneurs, the seas for him merely a means to an end. He orchestrated one of the world's greatest ever entrepreneurial ventures, the equivalent of an immigrant charming the US government into allowing NASA to provide him with spaceships, convicts from the penitentiaries and funding to find oil on the moon.

Columbus was born in 1451, the oldest son of Susanna Fontanarossa and Domenico Colombo, an entrepreneurial weaver, cheese trader, wine and wool merchant. He had one sister and four brothers, one of whom – Bartolomeo – would become a mapmaker in Lisbon, the principal centre of cartography. As a teenager, Columbus's father sent him to the University of Pavia. While there, he studied geometry, astronomy, grammar, geography, the Latin language, and navigation. Columbus gave up life as an apprentice to his father in 1465 and went to sea as a professional seaman. He gained experience both as a pirate and as a victim of piracy. By now Columbus was a fully-fledged businessman, working for the Centurione family and René I of Naples, and travelling as far and wide as Iceland and Guinea, negotiating, purchasing and delivering goods. There was always adventure for the young man and he was developing fast out of necessity. His first brush with death came when he was 25 years old, having to swim ashore when his ship (part of a convoy bound for England) sank after being hit in a battle with pirates near the coast of Portugal. Columbus was not a particularly talented sailor; he had never discovered anything before, or led a group of men in anything other than business.

By 1453 the Ottomans, the emerging superpower, seized control of Constantinople. This development meant Western entrepreneurs required new routes to Eastern markets. This exacerbated economic competition between the European imperialist nations vying for control of such businesses as the lucrative spice trade. The change in geopolitics would influence Columbus's prospects. Columbus had big ideas and knew how to impress. He cooked up a story about himself as a descendant of Colombo, who in turn was a descendant of an emperor of Constantinople. Armed with this credibility he now pitched for the funding of a new and high-risk venture.

Developing the business plan

In 1484 Columbus put a business proposition to John II, King of Portugal. It was not unlike Richard Branson and Burt Rutan's scheme for Virgin Galactic to travel beyond this world into 'the great unknown.'

Columbus proposed a scheme where he and the king would become two of the world's richest men. The project was an alternative route travelling the globe West, instead of East, to

Asia, avoiding Muslim-controlled territories and hazards. Columbus was to pocket ten per cent of all the trade between the two trading spheres in perpetuity with the title of 'Grand Admiral of the Oceanic Sea' thrown in for good measure. A Royal Commission rejected the proposal. There was anticipation that a less risky alternate route, with greater immediate benefits, lay in an opportunity to round the Cape of Good Hope to the East. On the East coast of Africa there was a vast trading empire. The predominantly Muslim, Swahili-African brokers were hooking up Indian, Chinese and Arabian traders in their local markets with the 'Great Zimbabwe' stone-built empire in the African interior. (Archaeologists have since discovered Roman coins there.) The Portuguese would eventually get around the Cape and usurp the Swahili trade before pushing on to India.

Fundraising

The following year Columbus' wife died and he decided to move to Spain. His new targets were– Queen Isabella and King Ferdinand of Spain. The Queen heard his pitch but decided to pass.

Her hands were full handling the Moors (Muslims) who had been in control of the Iberian Peninsula for 800 years. But by 1492 the last Moor was packing his bags, booking a one-way ticket to Morocco. King Ferdinand and Queen Isabella also managed to raise some extra money the following year by increasing the confiscation of Jewish property.

Columbus laid on the charm thick and fast, visiting the palace as often as he could. The anticipated 'inheriting' of Jewish property and the end of proceedings with the Moors eased the Queen's financial demands. The sovereign was now in a much better position to fund the Columbus venture, which at the behest of Ferdinand, she promptly did. Before he met with Ferdinand and Isabella, Columbus drafted a document regarding his business plan for the future colonization of the new-found lands. Nearly two-thirds of the document was concerned with how to handle the gold obtained and certainly not with discovery, science or religion. They drew up the contract and he was off.

Columbus departed Palos, Spain, in August 1492. He offered a cash reward of more than 10,000 maravedis (a year's pay) for the first man to spot land. On October 12th a sailor sighted the land known to us today as the Bahamas. Columbus argued he had seen the lights on the island several nights before, so he paid himself the cash instead.

Discovering America

Columbus thought he had reached an island off the coast of Asia, near Japan and the advanced Chinese Empire and entered it into to his log as such. He was in fact in the Caribbean and landed at an island he called San Salvador (Bahamas). He sent out not geologists and surveyors but gold-hunters, who came up short. Columbus then continued sailing along the coast of Cuba, certain that he had finally reached the continent of Cathay. He searched in vain for the magnificent cities Marco Polo had described, hoping to deliver a letter from the Spanish monarchy to 'the great Khan,' the Chinese emperor. Afterwards, Columbus wrote on October 21st, "I shall set sail for another very large island which I believe to be Cipango [Japan was described by Marco Polo as a sort of El Dorado] according to the indications I receive from the Indians on board." Columbus' island proved to be the island of Hispaniola. On the subsequent journey the Santa Maria ran aground and not all of the men could fit onboard the remaining Niña. So, Columbus left 40 of them behind in a fort on Hispaniola, the largest island in the Antilles East of Cuba.

On January 16th 1493 Columbus departed Hispaniola for Spain in the Niña, laden with exotic goods, including slaves. Travelling farther, sending out parties to survey the land, and pushing on to discover more was not the game plan. Columbus arrived back in Spain in March to a hero's welcome. King Ferdinand and Queen Isabella were captivated by the show of pineapples and parrots but the pièce de résistance was the couple of islanders that Columbus threw in. He had named the main island Hispaniola (modern Haiti and the Dominican Republic) and described it as a paradise, with hardworking natives *dying* to work for their new lords and masters. And of course, Columbus kept the King and Queen on the hook, selling them the promise that copious supplies of gold were lying just around the corner. The Spanish monarchs added a noble title and other honours to those already guaranteed by Columbus's business contract. He was now a celebrated success. Though Columbus never did set foot in what is known as America today, he had nevertheless arrived in Spain in more ways than one.

In September 1493, a grand fleet of 17 ships departed Cadiz for what would be Columbus' second voyage to the 'Indies.' The first Spanish colony to be developed by Columbus was Santo Domingo (modern Haiti). He battled with the natives there, eventually overwhelming them and taking control.

He returned to Hispaniola in November to find his sailors dead and the fort destroyed. The lads had got bored, got hammered, and then got laid, raping, murdering and stealing everything they possibly could. Half his crew were the dregs from Spanish jails and many were condemned men. They fought among themselves, vying for women and gold. The native men were not impressed and slaughtered them.

HOMELAND SECURITY

Fighting Terrorism Since 1492

Columbus' ships later ran aground, and a friendly local village came to their rescue and unloaded the sinking vessels. Columbus was amazed at the helpfulness of the natives and assured his king and queen that, "not even a shoe string was lost!" The Cacique (chief of the tribe) Guacanagari, welcomed the stranded sailors. The natives' reward for their hospitality was Columbus scaring them into servitude by firing a Lombard and musket in a demonstration of power.

After sailing along the Cuban coast for a month in June 1494, Columbus compelled his crew to swear in a notarised statement that Cuba was not an island but "the mainland of the commencement of the Indies." He threatened his crew with a "penalty of 10,000 maravedis and the cutting out of the tongue" of each one that hereafter should say anything to the contrary. Even today, people of the Caribbean call themselves West Indians, despite West India being halfway across the world.

Gold was in short supply and the imperative to keep stakeholders happy required desperate measures. So, Columbus stole what the natives wore as casual jewellery. He hurriedly shipped it, along with the expedition's first dividend of slaves to Spain. Twenty-six of them (less than half the cargo) survived the trip to Spain. In February 1495 business was much better. Columbus shipped 550 natives to Spain for the slave markets and this time 350 survived the voyage. The art of shipping humans as chattel cargo was improving. Later the hardier black African cargo (1511 Ferdinand II of Aragon observes that "one black can do the work of four Indians") would prove more cost-effective with less 'natural wastage.' Nevertheless, Columbus made a smashing return on the Taino Indians from the island of Hispaniola he crammed into his ships, which he sold into slavery in a Seville market in 1495.

Columbus' business continued its precious metal exploration. He struck gold in the Caribbean mountains in 1499 (during the third voyage), making him a rich man. It stimulated the development of capital and foreign exchange markets and the use of bills of exchange among Europeans. The pooling of resources to reduce trade risk with faraway destinations led to the development of new experimental forms of equity capital from which the joint-stock companies would eventually evolve.

Destruction of an ancient culture

Columbus overestimated his financier's support for the venture. Ferdinand and Isabella were hearing a lot of criticism of Golden Boy's methods. Moreover, he had not fulfilled his projections on their earnings. So, the monarchs decided to send in an investigator (auditor) with absolute authority. His name was Francisco de Bobadilla and when he arrived at the settlement he took one look around and had Columbus clapped in irons and out on the next ship to Spain. Columbus had decimated the native population in an attempt to get them to mine for precious metals. It could never work over a long and sustained term and Columbus was ordered never to set foot on Hispaniola again.

Columbus spent the next year pestering the monarchs, begging them, in a persistent stream of letters, to give him permission to travel to the Indies again. There were enough people in the Caribbean to find new lands. But Columbus was a salesman, always promising big money returns. With permission from the King and Queen, Columbus departed from Cadiz, Spain, with four ships in May 1502. When he arrived, the colonists wouldn't allow him on to the main island, so he sailed West and landed in present-day Panama. Gold was located and a trading post established; however, the natives grew restless and Columbus bolted.

In January 1503, Columbus established a garrison at Río Belén, Panama. The garrison was attacked by the indigenous natives, so in March he again had to flee. Columbus now had to cope with unfriendly waters. The ship limped as far as Jamaica with Columbus and his crew stranded hundreds of miles from the nearest Spanish settlement. In desperation, a few individuals were sent out in canoes to cover more than a hundred miles of open sea to seek aid. They made it to Hispaniola in August, but the Governor there despised Columbus so much it was almost a year before a vessel was dispatched to rescue them.

Columbus had devised an ingenious plan to ensure his survival in Jamaica. He threatened the natives that his God will destroy the moon at his behest if they did not submit to his authority. The natives laughed. Columbus disappeared into a hut armed with a timing device. Getting the timing just right he reappeared and said he'd give them one last chance. They declined. Columbus with pomp and theatre ushered their eyes to the skies. The moon turned blood red and appeared it had part of it broken-off. The natives begged Columbus to give it back. He did so, and the frightened natives brought food and supplies for Columbus and his crew. Of course, it was simply an eclipse of the moon on February 29th 1504. Columbus had a copy of Regionmontanus' *Ephemerides astronomicae*, which predicted the exact time of the event.

Columbus's methods were undoubtedly cruel and often unproductive. His entrepreneurial ambitions blinded him to the plight of others and he often caused chaos, creating many enemies. On May 2nd 1506, the great Columbus died at home surrounded by his family, friends and his seven servants, in Valladolid, Spain. He wanted his titles to be passed to his son, Diego. Queen Isabella had died two years earlier and Diego was now in the king's favour, eventually gaining his father's title, Governor of Hispaniola. Columbus's cousin explorer Rafael Perestrello, commanded an expedition from Portuguese Malacca (Malaysia) to land on the shores of mainland southern China, and trade with Chinese merchants at Guangzhou, during the Ming Dynasty.

The life of Columbus before and after 'discovering the Americas' was dedicated to making it in business. The drive, resilience and vision produced by his entrepreneurship were the only way the great discovery of the Americas was going to happen. The funds needed to take on such a financially risky venture were enormous, but Columbus sold the idea by promising unimaginable riches to his benefactors, investors and sponsors. His achievement changed the world forever: the modern world's richest nation traces its great rise on the world stage back to Columbus's entrepreneurial feat.

JACOB FUGGER (1459 – 1525)

"I wish to make a profit for as long as I can."

The birth of modern banking

In 1545 a Spaniard called Diego Gualpa fell from a hill in Potosí (modern Bolivia) snatching at grass on the way down in an attempt to halt his fall. One clump of earth had silver ore attached at its base. The Spanish invaders wasted no time in mining silver from the region with a view to shipping it to Europe in vast quantities. The combination of a surfeit of silver and improved transportation and navigation was to trigger the onset of a world economy.

Fortunately, the formation of the modern banking system was well underway, largely thanks to an entrepreneur called Jacob Fugger, who died two decades before Gualpa's discovery. Cantillon, a banker who coined the term 'entrepreneur', wrote in his treatise that banking served as an intermediary to reduce the risk and transportation costs of shipping large amounts of money and valuables over great distances.

Banking grew out of the need to provide fast cash to merchants and entrepreneurs (so long as suitable security could be provided). A banking system also offered the ability to transact business over long distances using bills of exchange.

The new climate for international trade in the late 15th Century affected all levels of society in all of Europe, from merchants to aristocrats. Ships had improved in design: they could go further and faster, and they could carry more cargo. Exotic goods from new markets in far-off lands were imported, and finished goods were exported. Opportunities were plentiful for those who had the initiative and were prepared to inconvenience themselves to seek them out.

Jacob Fugger was one of the few. He was born in Augsburg, Germany in 1459, the latest in a long line of entrepreneurs. However, Fugger was about to dwarf the rest of his family's achievements.

As a student (his mother sent him to be educated in Venice) Fugger showed great aptitude for business arithmetic, banking, double-entry book-keeping and finance. In 1487, at the age of 28, the entrepreneur founded Fuggers Bank in his hometown of Augsburg.

The entrepreneur did loan deals with dubious power-brokers and questionable nobles who were now in his debt. He acquired the rights to various mines which produced strategic metals, and this allowed him to influence political policy, including war. Now in possession of the copper mines Fugger decided to double-up on the bounty. He began his monopolistic ambition to control copper, forming a cartel with two other suppliers. Their resources now pooled enabled them to lower cost and increase prices. All copper was sold at one price in Venice where margins could be greatly increased and protected. By 1501 increased revenue and expertise saw Fugger and his brothers operating mines in Germany, Austria, Hungary, Bohemia and Spain. By 1511, Fugger was so invaluable and effective as a financier that he was made a Count by his client, Emperor Maximilian I. The relationship was solid, allowing Fugger to negotiate another major deal in 1515. It resulted in all the output of Maximillian's silver mines belonging to Fugger for the next eight years and that of the copper mines for the next four.

Triggering the Protestant Reformation

As though founding the modern banking system wasn't enough, Jacob Fugger was also potentially responsible for the onset of the Protestant Reformation! In 1517 Pope Leo X (who happened to be a descendant of Giovanni de Medici) decided to announce an indulgence. He wanted cash to finish the refurbishment of St Peter's Cathedral. Count Albrecht, who already had two archbishoprics, wanted a third. The Vatican was fine with it but Albrecht needed to stump up the extra cash needed to buy the third position. Fugger offered to lend Albrecht the money needed to buy the diocese. Fugger planned to launch an indulgence campaign on behalf of St Peter's project for the Vatican. Half the cash raised would go to the Vatican and the other half would pay back his loan provided for the securing of the diocese in favour of Count Albrecht. Fugger hired Johann Tetzel to sell the scheme to the public.

JOHANN TETZEL

SELLING INDULGENCES

Tetzel had the gift of the gab and was adept at separating believers from their money. He raised the required cash by marketing letters of forgiveness granting full or partial remission for sins. Some rigorous buyers did their work with due diligence, taking letters to the Professor of Theology at the University of Wittenberg, one Martin Luther. Luther was not impressed and spoke out against Fugger and Tetzel. Tetzel replied by ridiculing Luther. Martin threw a fit and nailed his 'Ninety-Five Theses' to the Wittenberg church door. Protestant Christianity had made its debut.

When Fugger's client Maximilian I died, his six year-old grandson Charles inherited the throne. The death of Charles' father, Philip of Hapsburg, also entitled him to the crown of the Netherlands. At 16, the death of his maternal grandfather Ferdinand II of Aragon (married to Columbus' sponsor Queen Isabella I of Castile) made him King Charles I of Spain. All

Spain's dependencies in Italy and the new territories of America were now his. Charles I's European holdings were to grow further still: at 19, the death of his paternal grandfather Maximilian brought him all the hereditary lands of the Hapsburgs and now the possibility of being elected Holy Roman Emperor.

This was not so good for Fugger. Charles sacked him in favour of a rival banker and he was out in the cold. But Fugger was terrifyingly cool under pressure. Charles had major competitors challenging him for the title of Emperor of the Holy Roman Empire, including Francis I of France and Henry VIII of England and then there was the ever-present Saracen (Islamic) threat. Fugger started spinning 'wheels within wheels.'

Two great powers were emerging in Europe at this time: France under Francis I and the Habsburg Empire. England was a lesser power and was courted as an ally by the two major players. The 1518 Treaty of London, a non-aggression pact between major European powers to help resist the Islamic expansion into South-Eastern Europe, had just been signed. Whilst they all still competed, co-operation was required to deal with bigger common enemies (mutuality). Fugger told Charles that without serious money behind him he would never become Emperor. Charles knew that serious money came only from the Fugger or Medici banks.

Fugger went to work making approaches to the electors. They got the picture and in turn counselled Charles in his favour. The Margrave of Brandenburg held the pivotal vote. Frances offered the Margrave a wealthy French wife plus large dowry. Fugger countered, offering Maximillian's granddaughter as a bride with the added weight of a third in cash up front and two-thirds after the election. It was game over. Charles re-hired the supreme strategist Jacob Fugger and in 1519 he became Emperor Charles V. Jacob Fugger was now financier to the world's richest and most powerful man.

More than a banker

Fugger's interests expanded far beyond banking. He also made money from commodities, metals, spices, art, food, pepper, medicine, silks, brocades, herbs and jewels. His most important product was fustian (a blend of wool and cotton). He reduced the timelines for transactions, operating a reliable courier service covering 85 miles a day. He cleverly couriered news, including political and economic messages, to an increasingly complicated, unpredictable and ever-expanding commercial world. It was a precursor to the *Reuters* service founded by Paul Julius Reuter in 1851. Besides this, Fugger produced a financial newsletter in various languages.

With 18 business branches Fugger was the heavyweight champion of German business. Now he wanted a shot at the European title. He began by taking papacy accounts from the Germans, then the Scandinavians, next the Hungarians and finally the Poles. By 1525 he was undisputedly the most powerful heavyweight financial force in the world. Fugger was so powerful that Charles V ordered an anti-trust prosecution of the Fugger Bank because he was concerned about their control of metal ore. The ore had military implications –it was a strategic metal. Fugger's power was checked when he was charged with running a monopoly. But the entrepreneur went to work protecting his business empire, and Charles eventually relented.

During Jacob Fugger's time Columbus reached America and the last Moor was expelled from Spain. Columbus had brought back gold and all manner of exotic goods from America that could be traded around the world. Europeans had rounded the Cape of Good Hope, opening up access to the rich and commercially driven black African Swahili civilizations of modern day Kenya, Mozambique and Tanzania. This in turn gave Europe access to the rich stone-built empire of Zimbabwe. In 1531 European explorer Vicente Pegado, described Zimbabwe saying: "Among the gold mines ... is a fortress built of stones of marvellous size ... and one of them is a tower more than 12 fathoms [22m] high." Fugger's bank helped this trade development to take place, mitigating and safeguarding the increased transaction risks that were brought about as a result of the expanded trading landscape.

Emerging from the Dark Ages

Europe was going through its rebirth. Gold and global trade opportunities poured in. Fugger oiled the wheels of this great expansion with financial liquidity. He affected the amount of money in circulation and could influence day-to-day prices as well as the selection of monarchs, bishops, and even the Pope. The year Fugger died – 1526 – Nicholas Copernicus wrote his portent for banking, the "Treatise on Debasement." Both Luther and Calvin would approve usury (with qualification). An unnamed writer summed up the Protestant stance thus: "It took with the brethren like polygamy with the Turks."

Jacob Fugger the Rich, as he became known, had clearly arrived on time. When he died he was one of the richest men in the world and his profits averaged in excess of 50 percent during the last two decades of his life. Despite his advancing years Fugger had no wish to retire. What typified him was his statement "I wish to make a profit for as long as I can." He ensured the success of his posterity by having his sons will their property to the business. Fugger understood power below is scene depicting Fugger burning the debt papers of Emperor Charles V in 1535.

Renaissance Entrepreneurs

HENRY MEDILLO (1650 – 1756)

"Nothing endures but change" – Heraclitus

Piracy in the Caribbean

Pirates are great romantic figures of legend and fable – and were long before Johnny Depp delighted female audiences with his portrayal of Captain Jack Sparrow in the hit movie *Pirates of the Caribbean*. The terms 'buccaneering' and 'entrepreneurship' have always been closely associated. 'Buccaneer' originated from settlers on Hispaniola who first arrived with Columbus. The first Europeans in the Americas began hunting wild pigs with long-barrelled muskets. The name was derived from the special wooden huts called 'boucans' where the men smoked their meat (inheriting the name 'boucaniers').

The rise of the great entrepreneur Henry Medillo, who was born in 1650, coincided with the Golden Age of piracy. If one were to take a map of the world and plot the locations of where great fortunes were made it would reveal one of the big secrets to creating great wealth – location, location, location. A great location affected by or undergoing momentous change is the place to be. Henry Medillo's spot on the map was 1600s-1700s Caribbean. Merchant princes like Jacob Fugger and Giovanni Medici fostered the circulation of capital for speculation over great distances. The formation of joint stock companies coalesced with banking to release the genie of entrepreneurship into the world of sea faring trade. This boded well for Europeans.

Spain the superpower

More than a century after Jacob Fugger's demise, change had swept through Europe again, producing new winners and losers. Catholic Spain was the superpower of the 17th Century and large Spanish galleons began to sail between Europe and America, loaded with precious cargos. Moreover, Spanish rule had been established over the very profitable business of buying and selling African slaves, providing the new American economies with powerful free labour. Spanish entrepreneurs produced both staple and luxury crops for export, such as tobacco, sugar, and leather. The Iberian monopoly on overseas riches was a threat to competing European nations, particularly the British. The rise and rise of Spain had to be checked.

Violence and war erupted as a matter of course between commercially competing nations. Every European nation with the means to steal land from either natives or each other did so. The biggest theft of the time was the theft of Jamaica, taken by England from Spain during Cromwell's colonial war. The Spanish had previously wrestled it from the Arawak.

Enter the entrepreneur Henry Morgan and his apprentice Henry Medillo who were to take full advantage of the chaos. Contrary to popular opinion, Captain Henry Morgan was not a pirate but in fact a privateer (legal pirate) – an entrepreneur of the high seas. In 1630, the first buccaneer colony was set up on the island of Tortuga, North of what is present-day Hispaniola (Haiti). It became a prosperous settlement and the headquarters for all sea-rovers of the Caribbean. Adventurers of all nations began to flock to the so-called West Indies to seek their fortunes privateering against the wealthy Spaniards. The Dutch called them 'zeeroovers'; the French 'filibustiers'; the Spanish 'piratas.'

In the Caribbean the use of privateers was especially popular. These men invested their capital in ships and personnel. The cost of maintaining a fleet to defend the colonies and harry the enemy was beyond the capabilities of any national government. Private vessels would be commissioned into a 'navy' with a letter of marque, along with a substantial share of whatever the privateer could capture from enemy ships and its settlements. The King or Queen would get a cut after expenses. These ships would operate independently or as a fleet. If successful, the rewards were great.

Famous buccaneers

When Francis Drake captured the Spanish Silver Train at Nombre de Dios (Panama's Caribbean port at the time) in 1573 his crews were rich for life. This substantial profit made privateering potentially a lucrative business. Wealthy businessmen and nobles got in on the action, financing 'legitimised' piracy in return for a share of the proceeds. It was similar to the legitimate funds that would flow into Columbia four centuries later to finance the illegal drug-trade deals during Pablo Escobar's reign which would prove so beneficial to the Columbian economy.

The captured booty was a boost to colonial economies. Buccaneers were extending their influence all over the Indies and the mainland, but as they did so they found resistance to their attacks strengthening, both on sea and on land. It became increasingly necessary for them to form fleets under the command of an 'Admiral.' One of the first to command a fleet of mixed nationalities, including black Jamaicans, was Dutchman Edward Mansveld. He sailed from Jamaica with a privateer's commission as Admiral. The venture was to establish a privateering entrepreneurial base on the route of the treasure fleets from Portobello, a town on the Isthmus of Panama. In August 1667 the Spanish recaptured the island and Mansveld was taken to Portobello and executed. His second-in-command, waiting in the wings, was Henry Morgan, who took over the title of Admiral. Later he'd become Admiral Sir Henry Morgan, Justice of the Peace, Judge of the Vice Admiralty Court, Custos Rotulorum (Latin meaning 'Keeper of the Rolls') and the richest plantation owner in Jamaica.

It was Henry Medillo who was destined to take over from Morgan. By 1668 the teenager had risen to be one of Captain Morgan's most trusted lieutenants. The early days of Henry Alfonso Medillo are unknown. He is believed to have been born in the Canary Islands in the mid 1650s and went to sea aboard a British warship as a cabin boy at the age of eight. In 1672 he participated in the bleak but triumphant assault on Panama City. Medillo gained his commander's undying comradeship when the jungle-weary force sacked the rich town, scattering the much larger Spanish army. The city was the repository for all the gold and silver brought up the coast from Peru. It was also a haven for goods and supplies that came every year from Spain to the colonies. The buccaneers set about its plunder. Morgan's forces left Panama with a booty estimated at 400,000 pieces of eight (£1,800,000). Though his courage was impressive what endeared him to Henry Morgan was getting more than a hundred mules from monks at a monastery to take the booty back to the waiting pirate ships. Unfortunately, there was great discontentment when it was divvied up amongst the men. They received a mere 40 apiece (£180).

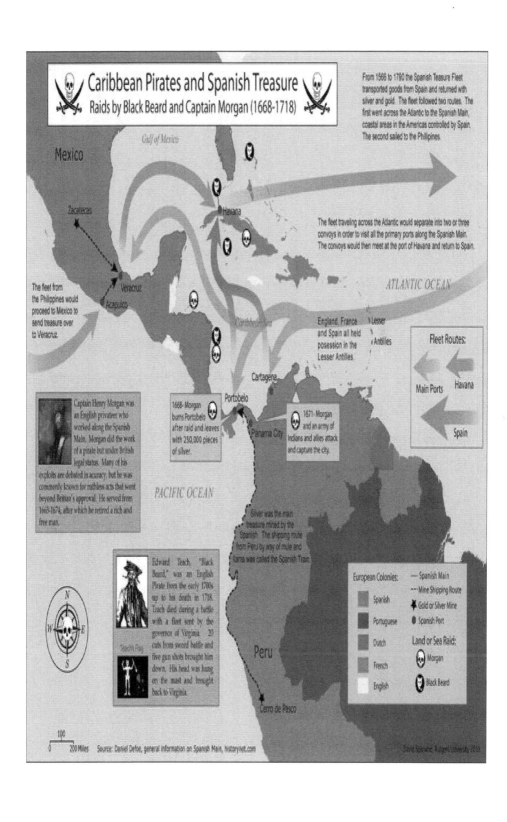

Caribbean Pirates and Spanish Treasure
Raids by Black Beard and Captain Morgan (1668-1718)

From 1566 to 1790 the Spanish Treasure Fleet transported goods from Spain and returned with silver and gold. The fleet followed two routes. The first went across the Atlantic to the Spanish Main, coastal areas in the Americas controlled by Spain. The second sailed to the Phillipines.

The fleet traveling across the Atlantic would separate into two or three convoys in order to visit all the primary ports along the Spanish Main. The convoys would then meet at the port of Havana and return to Spain.

Mexico

Gulf of Mexico

Zacatecas

Havana

ATLANTIC OCEAN

The fleet from the Philippines would proceed to Mexico to send treasure over to Veracruz.

Veracruz

Acapulco

Caribbean Sea

England, France and Spain all held possession in the Lesser Antilles.

Lesser Antilles

Fleet Routes:

Main Ports — Havana

Spain

Cartagena

Captain Henry Morgan was an English privateer who worked along the Spanish Main. Morgan did the work of a pirate but under British legal status. Many of his exploits are debated in accuracy, but he was commonly known for ruthless acts that went beyond Britain's approval. He served from 1663-1674, after which he retired a rich and free man.

Portobelo

1668- Morgan burns Portobelo after raid and leaves with 250,000 pieces of silver.

Panama City

1671- Morgan and an army of Indians and allies attack and capture the city.

PACIFIC OCEAN

Silver was the main treasure mined by the Spanish. The shipping route from Peru by way of mule and lama was called the Spanish Train.

Edward Teach, "Black Beard," was an English Pirate from the early 1700s up to his death in 1718. Teach died during a battle with a fleet sent by the governor of Virginia. 20 cuts from sword battle and five gun shots brought him down. His head was hung on the mast and brought back to Virginia.

Teach Flag

N W E S

Peru

European Colonies:
- Spanish
- Portuguese
- Dutch
- French
- English

— Spanish Main
--- Mine Shipping Route
🗡 Gold or Silver Mine
● Spanish Port

Land or Sea Raid:
- Morgan
- Black Beard

Cerro de Pasco

100
0   200 Miles   Source: Daniel Defoe, general information on Spanish Main, historynet.com

David Spickler, Rutgers University 2010

Retention of profits

Medillo was shrewd. Following his first time "on the account" as it was called, he carefully invested his earnings with his trusted financial adviser and broker Moishe Feinbind, a Danish-born Jewish banker stationed in Jamaica. If his share of the booty was not satisfactory he could get Feinbind to grow it on the Dutch stock market. The financial planner had sugar plantations and rum distilleries in play on the advanced Dutch Amsterdam bourse. This became a central plank to Medillo's business strategy. He continued raiding as a privateer and then moved into self-financing his own crew with his own resources. He attacked everything that he could overcome without too great a threat of loss, regardless of the ship's colours. Anything too big he let go. He was now simply a pirate. All his revenues were invested on the Amsterdam bourse, apart from the funding required to run the operation.

By 1700 Henry Medillo realised that the mid-to-long-term market conditions were weak and projections discouraging. This was heralded by the arrival of a new British warship sent to protect their now-burgeoning American colonies. The elimination of piracy from European waters expanded to the Caribbean in the 1700s. The decline of piracy in the Caribbean paralleled the decline of mercenaries and the rise of national armies in Europe. Medillo only took calculated risks. He wasn't a gambler – time was up and a change was about to begin. He was prepared to bow out.

Exit strategy: retire to a Caribbean island

Medillo had come across an island in his early pirating days. The jungle-like rolling hills and mountains radiating inland from its perfect harbours were excellent places for battle-weary, wealth-burdened nautical entrepreneurs to recover, recuperate and do some much-needed book-keeping. He began plans for a permanently settlement on Poco Cabesa's lush North-East coast in the Caribbean Sea, with his extended family and dozens of his closest compatriots, including his accountant and consultant Moishe. Among them was his close and trusted team member the famous Anne Bonny.

Anne was an adventurer and wanted to continue the pirating game. Medillo was by now quite elderly and advised her that the world had changed and the Golden Age of pirating was over. He counselled both Anne Bonny and notorious 'Calico Jack' Rackham about the risks posed by the new British Navy. They weren't to be discouraged, and Anne left with Rackham. Medillo eventually allowed the two to anchor and re-supply at Medillo Grande for a sizable fee, in cash. After Bonny's capture by the British, Medillo, risking his own life and safety, in 1720 joined with other reformed pirates to travel to Jamaica and arrange for the young pregnant woman to be pardoned. She went on to marry a respectable doctor in America.

In 1756 Henry Medillo died, over 100 years old (longevity ran in the Medillo genes). His extensive family surrounded his bed, weeping. Henry Medillo's three wives bore him 14 innately intelligent and attractive daughters. His descendants still enjoy royal status on the spectacular paradise island called Medillo Grande today. Henry Medillo took risks at the right time and got out of the game at the right time when the risk/benefit ratio shifted negatively. He went on to enjoy a life of great civility in 'paradise,' dying in his bed, a rich old man.

WILLIAM PATERSON (1658 – 1719)

"The bank hath benefit of interest on all moneys which it creates out of nothing"

Early life in a Scottish farmhouse

William Paterson was born in 1658 in a farmhouse in Dumfriesshire, Scotland. At the age of 17 he set off on a great adventure. His first stop was England, but he was soon lured by the call of the Caribbean. Like Medillo before him, Paterson was tempted by the array of opportunities offered by an entrepreneurial lifestyle but, unlike Medillo, Paterson was a very decent and upright young man.

The Caribbean was a land of pirates, privateers and buccaneers, filled with reprobates, villains and good-for-nothings. This inspired the highly principled Paterson to begin preaching to his devious and fallen brethren. He stood out like a sore thumb, his intellectual strength and character made him the natural choice for the motley crew's spiritual guide. It was an unlikely start to the career of the man who would one day become the founder of the Bank of England.

Scottish empire in the Caribbean

Buccaneers were frontiersmen. As the 20th Century economist Joseph Schumpeter put it, they were men prepared to "to act with confidence beyond the range of familiar beacons." William Paterson had that spirit, which eventually took him to the capital of piracy – Port Royal, Jamaica – in 1675. It was there that Paterson's mind fermented, formed and marinated his first business idea. Unfortunately, like many first business ideas, it was bunkum.

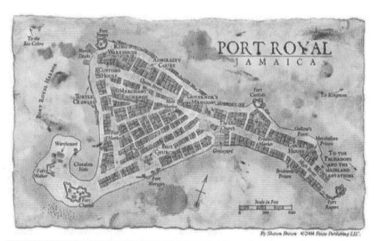

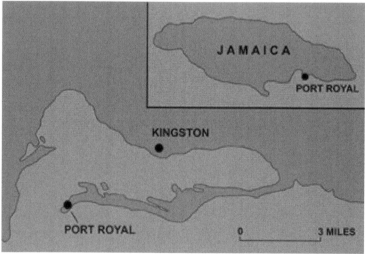

Upon returning to England Paterson was unable to persuade the government of James II to invest in his scheme to create a colony on the Isthmus of Panama with a view to dominating the strategically important maritime region. Paterson took the germ of his idea to the continent, pitching it without success in Hamburg, Amsterdam and Berlin.

Like all true entrepreneurs he knew when to call it a day, so Paterson let it go and took a job with a firm of merchant tailors. He moonlighted as a trader of products he'd collected on his travels and amassed an impressive amount of money in the process. But he still dreamed of a great scheme to make himself and Scotland rich beyond measure.

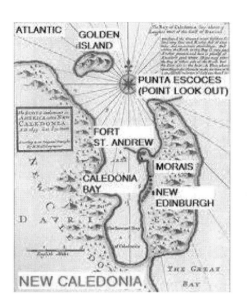

The big idea

In 1690 Paterson formed the Bampstead Water Company. The world continued to get smaller and that meant increased trade. Currency issues, along with the funding of ventures and deals, were in greater and greater demand. Paterson rampaged through Europe, trying to expand and consolidate his business empire. This again required funding, and money was in short supply. The penny finally dropped: the country needed a national bank; a ready source of capital for large projects. In 1694, Paterson founded what was to become the world's greatest institution – The Bank of England. The subscribers lent their money to the nation and this debt became the bank's stock. The subscribers numbered 1,520 raising £1.2 million (£168 million). However, his fellow directors saw Paterson and his methods and ideas as a danger to their own ambitions and distrusted the recalcitrant Scot. Though he was one of the original directors, it took him less than a year to wind up his colleagues to such a degree they threw him out. Paterson, a serial entrepreneur, was working on a new idea which invoked the ire of his fellow directors at the Bank of England (capital was already in short supply). It became known as an 'orphan bank' because it was to use the debt due to the city orphans, from the corporation of London, for capitalisation and to form the bank stock. It didn't work out but Paterson did not give up.

Whilst in Jamaica he had met William Dampier, a British buccaneer who had worked with Henry Morgan and his trusty lieutenant Henry Medillo to defeat the Spanish in the Caribbean. In the process Morgan had crossed the Isthmus of Panama, and had done so quite easily. In 1679 Dampier achieved the crossing. This meant one could travel from the Atlantic Ocean to the Pacific in mere days. Despite Paterson's earlier, unsuccessful, attempt to make his fortune from the Isthmus of Panama, Dampier convinced him of the area's significance.

WILLIAM DAMPIER REACHES AUSTRALIA

The Darien Company

In 1695 Paterson unveiled the Darien Company. His scheme offered Scottish merchants the opportunity to control the invaluable Isthmus. On November 13th in London Paterson began taking in money for the Company of Scotland Trading to Africa and the Indies (Darien Company). However, the activities of the Darien Company in London amounted to an infringement of the monopoly rights granted to the Bank of England and the (English) East India Company. The bottom line was that money in Scottish pockets meant money out of English pockets and that wasn't on.

On December 17th the Lords and Commons went to King William III (William of Orange), to present an address of protest against the Scottish company. William III declared himself "ill-served in Scotland." By January 1696 the London directors of The Darien Company were under examination by the Committee of the House of Commons. The House demanded their impeachment and subscribers dropped the company like hot coal. The English arm of the venture collapsed. Paterson and the other principal promoters bottled it and made a run for Scotland.

The company opened a subscription book in Edinburgh on 26th February 1696. The proposed amount of capital to be raised was £300,000 (£42 million). Scottish investors bought the entire issue. Half the total capital available in Scotland was now virtually in Paterson's hands. The Scots were turned on by the prospect of their beloved country moving out of the shadow of England and onto the world stage, trading to Africa and the Indies.

Paterson was highly trained in advanced Dutch methods of commerce, trade and stock market management. His push-push style and familiarity with exotic fundraising methods were a threat to the monopolies held by the Bank of Scotland. They correctly judged that the Darien Scheme was a Trojan horse, a bank veiled as a trading company likely to destroy their legal monopolies.

William Paterson left for Amsterdam in 1696, with colleagues Erskine and Haldane. However, he failed to interest any major Dutch players in the offering. Paterson entrusted some of the company funds to James Smith, his friend and fellow director, who promptly stole the lot. During September 1697 Paterson was dragged in and interrogated by a special committee of the company; he was eventually exonerated and acquitted of complicity. It later emerged that nearly half of their subscription funds had disappeared and couldn't be accounted for. As a consequence, the company stripped its founder of his office. It was at this point that The Company of Scotland (as it became known) began to focus on colonisation rather than banking.

Paterson's grand scheme was Scottish trading to Africa and the Indies. This was coupled with a dream of establishing a settlement on the Isthmus of Darien, a free trade zone, with ships of all nations allowed to find shelter in its harbours. Differences of race or religion were to be ignored. From this strategic geographic location, Scotland would become key to world commerce. In one supreme stroke, Scotland was to be converted from one of the poorest nations in Europe to one of the richest.

AN ISTHMUS CONNECTING NORTH AND SOUTH AMERICA

In July 1698 the first ships of the Darien Scheme expedition set sail. Twelve hundred settlers were invited to participate in one of the greatest entrepreneurial schemes ever undertaken. Dogged by continuous rumours of his financial impropriety, Paterson was prevented from being nominated to a post of importance for the expedition. Instead he travelled as a private individual. His ambitions would cost him dearly. Paterson's wife and child fell ill aboard the ship destined for Panama. He watched helplessly as they both died.

They finally landed on November 3rd 1698 at Acla, which was renamed Caledonia. A site for a fort was chosen and named St Andrews, and a town, New Edinburgh, was established. But right from the beginning the voyagers were beset by immense problems. Mistakes were made, and they suffered from pestilence and disease. The company underestimated both the size of the Pacific and the difficulty of crossing the Isthmus in the absence of a canal.

The settlers made treaties with the indigenous people, but both superpowers – the Spanish and the English – made themselves a nuisance. Spain was already in the area at Cartagena, Columbia, and began mobilising against the settlers. A royal proclamation forbade the

English (now thriving and in control of Jamaica since 1655) from trading with them. One of the Darien Scheme's ships was taken. Desertions and death from disease weakened the colony daily.

Shaping the future of finance

By June 1699 they had had enough. A proposal to abandon was unanimously accepted with only one objector – William Paterson. He was at death's door, too ill to do anything for himself, and was quite literally carried aboard on a stretcher. As they bore him onto the deck he continued his protestations but could do nothing to stop them. The return leg was another disaster. Out of the 900 people who had survived the initial journey, another 150 died on the way back. They had to abandon ship in both Jamaica and New York. In the end only one ship, the Caledonia, made it back to Scotland in December 1699.

Paterson soon recovered his strength and immediately went to work on a new venture. He prepared an elaborate plan for developing Scottish resources by means of a council of trade and then tried to induce King William, with whom he had frequent interviews, to invest in a new Darien expedition. But it wasn't to be.

In 1701 Paterson opened a new chapter in his life. He started lobbying various statesmen, promoting the union between Scotland and England. Rather than competing against each other the two entities would compete with the rest of the world. In 1704 Paterson's vision of a credit-based economy began to take shape when promissory notes were declared legal tender by statute in England. The quixotic entrepreneur was engaged by the establishment in settling financial relations between the two countries.

One of the last acts of the Scottish parliament was to recommend William Patterson for consideration to Queen Anne (first sovereign of the newly united Great Britain) "for all he had done and suffered." The Act of Union was negotiated in 1707. The new parliament paid compensation to all those who had lost money in the Darien scheme. William Patterson made a major contribution to the forming of the Union. He was returned as a member for the Dumfries burghs, though he never took his seat. Parliament decided that his claim should be settled, but it was not till 1715 that an indemnity of £18,241 (£2 million) was ordered to be paid to him. Even then the battler found considerable difficulty in obtaining it from the government.

Paterson selling the Darien Scheme

Vindication of a dreamer

William Patterson died on the January22nd 1719. His dream of controlling a key geographic location was vindicated by countless successful entrepreneurial adventurers after him. The Panama Railroad project completed a rail link in 1855. In 1904 the United States Federal Government purchased it from the French Canal Company. In 1914 it opened the Panama Canal. The infrastructure helped ensure US emergence as a world superpower. The US only handed back control of the Isthmus to Panama in 1999.

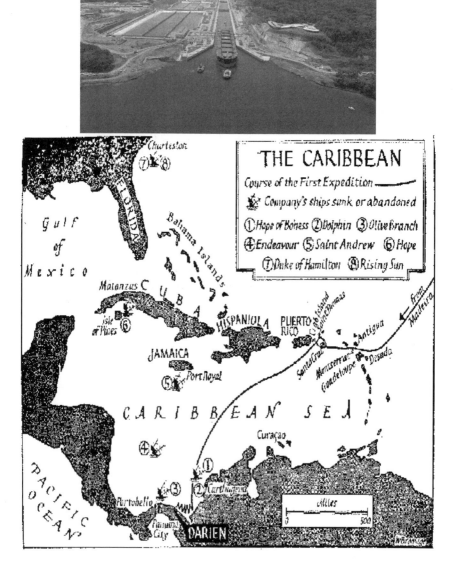

JOHN LAW (1671 – 1729)

"There are several Proposals offer'd to Remedy the Difficulties the Nation is under from the great Scarcity of Money."

A dandy is born

John Law was born in Edinburgh in 1671 – four years before fellow Scot William Paterson packed his bags to seek his fortune abroad. Law's father, Mr. Law Sr., had his own goldsmith and money-lending business. His net worth of £29,000 (£3,700,000) was primarily made up of outstanding debt.

The Law family lived and operated in Fife, where Mr. Law Sr. had purchased an estate at Cramond on the Firth of Forth (which included Lauriston Castle) a major river estuary in Scotland. When Law's father died, his mother took over the business.

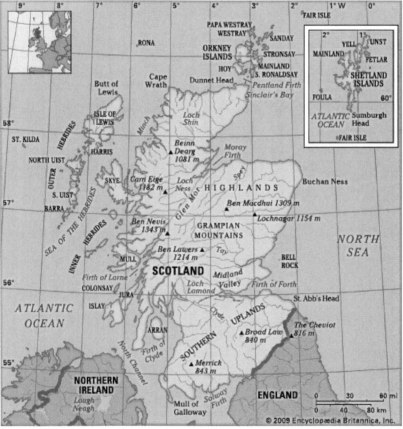

Promissory notes

In Europe modern banking grew out of the goldsmith trade. The goldsmith was essentially a repository for gold, an accepted standard of value. Goldsmiths could offer a secure place (a 'safe') for depositing gold, and they soon noticed that only a small percentage of the gold on deposit was withdrawn at any one time. They realised that if they simply printed promissory notes or receipts (paper money) they could loan it out. That is, they could lend illusory money and be paid back in gold plus interest. Goldsmiths didn't have to own any gold themselves; yet they could make money out of others who needed it. In theory, if any of the promissory note holders tried to cash their notes in for gold, there should always be enough on deposit to satisfy demand. By exploiting this systemic quirk a banker would effectively have 'a licence to print money' or 'make a mint.'

Europe's trading footprint grew wider in the 17th Century, with shipments destined both for the East and the West (Americas). Doing business over long distances was a time-consuming – and expensive – affair. Speed became an entrepreneurial weapon in the hunt for wealth. The goldsmith trade facilitated the speeding up of transactions by offering merchants the 'readies.' A small-time entrepreneur (merchant) awaiting a shipment from abroad could now put up some jewellery as collateral, receiving a paper note or receipt accounting for his deposit, in exchange for a loan to tide him over until he sold off a portion of the delivery. Entrepreneurs started using receipts for deposited gold to pay off suppliers and creditors. So long as there was confidence in the market's ability to redeem the promissory note, the method worked well.

It was in this environment that John Law cut his teeth, working for his father when he turned 14. It kept him focused and attentive for three years. It was when he turned 17 that he fell in love – with himself. He was tall, good-looking and well built, as well as being intelligent and commanding money, a good name, and prestige. Law thought he had it made.

The goldsmith's son

Great change was taking place in Europe – and particularly within the British Isles – at the turn of the 17th/18th Centuries. In 1688 William III (also William of Orange) was installed on the throne of England alongside his wife, Queen Mary II. In 1704 promissory notes were declared legal tender in England. The Bank of Scotland was the first European bank to circulate paper currency successfully, redeemable for cash on demand.

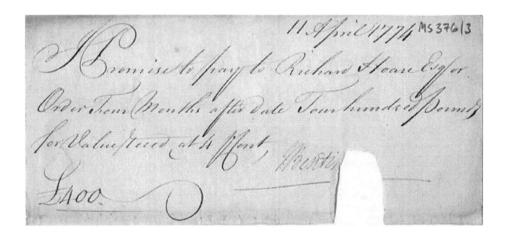

John Law, the eldest son of the Law family, left Edinburgh for London in 1689. He led the life of an exhibitionist dandy, funded by his inherited wealth, and was given the nicknames Beau Law and Jessamy John by his envious male detractors. After a number of years in London, Law had burned through his inheritance with ruthless efficiency. His 'gambling system' and speculating on government bonds in the city could not compensate for his squandering. He then began working through borrowed funds in pursuit of fame, fortune and licentiousness. Fortunately, Law's mother was always on hand to bail him out.

A fatal duel

During 1694 John Law had a set-to with rival dandy Beau Wilson over Elizabeth Hamilton, the countess of Orkney (and mistress of William III). They had a duel at Bloomsbury Square, London on April 9th 1694. Law killed Wilson and was arrested, tried and sentenced to hang. Whilst he was on 'death row' his sentence was commuted to manslaughter and a fine. Wilson's family appealed, wanting Law dead, so he organised an escape to the continent via Amsterdam. A boat was waiting for him at the Thames, to whisk him away after he broke out from the Old Bailey jail. In 1695, just as the Bank of Scotland was being created, The London Gazette advertised a reward for the return of the fugitive. The paper described him as, "well shaped, above six foot tall, large pock holes in his face, big high nose, speaks broad and loud. He's a recognised athlete, a London dandy, dedicated to gallantry."

John Law slipped back into Scotland ten years later, still an outlaw. The adversity in Law's life put him in the right place in the right time. The Netherlands had the most advanced financial system in Europe. In the Dutch capital Law had noticed that bank withdrawals were much less frequent than deposits. One could use depositors' money in the confidence there would always be enough cash to cover withdrawals. Whilst the money was unused it could be invested in all manner of schemes. Moreover, one could print and issue promissory notes and use them to pay bills, invest, and start up companies. All things being equal there should always be enough to satisfy depositors' withdrawals and allow them to share in the profits. Banking seemed right up John Law's street. It was a mathematical confidence trick par excellence.

Scotland was in the midst of an economic depression. Law proposed the issuing of interest-bearing paper notes, which operated as currency underpinned by land. It was referred to as a land bank. The money would fund Scottish development of fisheries, minerals and foreign trade. The Scottish parliament dismissed the idea. Law later wrote his treatise *Money and Trade Considered with a Proposal for Supplying the Nation with Money*. He received tacit support from some quarters for his idea of currency notes backed by land instead of gold, but not enough to convince parliament. The looming union between Scotland and England would likely result in Law being hung, so he fled back to the continent and where he continued his truculence by snatching another man's wife, one Lady Katharine Knollys (daughter of Earl of Banbury) and had children with her.

Insatiable gambler

Law had roamed Europe for a decade observing the various banking systems. Amsterdam in particular was an entrepreneurial nirvana, and the penny dropped for Law. Like a cub learning to hunt he observed the antics of the East India Company, the banks, the stock exchange and the gamblers who sought to manipulate the stock market. He pitched his idea for a new bank and banking system to influential individuals. Along with his friend and partner the Earl of Islay, Law was successful on both the London and Amsterdam Stock Exchanges. In addition to this he traded in foreign exchange in Genoa and speculated on the French-Dutch exchange rate. He made a lot of money. Law teamed up with Lord Islay again, opening an account at a goldsmith's bank with a view to get involved with lottery tickets in England. A scheme to insure lottery ticket holders was hatched in Amsterdam.

Law was fast and expert in mathematical computations, gambling at the. He would turn up to a game with a sack of gold in each hand, claiming the position of banker, so he could influence the odds in his own favour. The game was kind to Law. With stockpiles of cash at his disposal, he bought 'letters of introduction', allowing him to hobnob with nobility.

Everywhere Law roamed in Europe he caused a stir. Some cities had him closely watched; others insisted on his leaving the city, in fear of his ideas and practices corrupting its inhabitants – particularly the young, and other individuals who were susceptible to ideas that would disrupt the status quo. He was settled in Paris by 1715. Victor Amadeus, Duke of Savoy had advised him to have go at pitching the French King, after passing on the opportunity himself. France was in an economic mess and on its knees. The royal budget was out of control and the debt obscene. The five year-old great-grandson of King Louis XIV had just ascended the throne.

At the Faro Tables Law was always waxing lyrical about his theories on money, wealth creation and his financial and economic system. His scheme had lately been turned down by the finance minister of Louis XIV, Nicolas Desmarets, shortly before the monarch's death. One of Law's regular companions at the gambling table was the Duke of France, regent to the new infant king. The Duke was so disaffected by France's predicament he turned to John Law for assistance. Law proposed the establishment of a state-chartered bank with the power to issue un-backed paper currency and the securitisation the national debt with a form of bond. He cited the advantages of paper-based systems such as those in Britain and Holland.

A French national hero

In 1716, with the aid of his brother William, John Law founded The Banque Générale as a private company, and France responded by granting him citizenship. In 1718 Banque Générale was chartered and became the Royal Bank of France; 75 percent of its capital consisted of government bills, and it was tied from the beginning to the national debt. That same year Law floated a joint stock trading company called the Compagnie d'Occident, which was granted a 25-year trade monopoly of the West Indies and North America. Law expanded the company by acquiring the Compagnie des Indes Orientales, the Compagnie de Chine (China), and other French trading companies. He bought the tobacco monopoly, and absorbed the slave-trading Company of Senegal and the French India Company. This conglomerate (generally known as the Mississippi Company) became a super-company.

The Mississippi Company was granted the right to mint and issue coinage by the French government in 1719. John Law now controlled the mines, the public finances, French banking, French sea trade, tobacco revenues, salt revenues and all commerce in Louisiana. Louisiana's most famous city New Orleans was founded by John Law and named in the honour of The Duke of Orleans.

Law announced he would buy the entire debt of France for shares in his Mississippi Company. He issued shares from a small office on a tiny street called Rue de Quincampoix. The road became a de facto stock exchange; outhouses became waiting rooms. Usurers with nearby offices offered 'clock loans' at 25 percent per quarter-hour.

La rue Quincampoix à Paris, en mars 1720, après la panique déclenchée par les ennemis de Law qui réalisèrent brusquement leurs actions et leurs billets. Gravure d'Antoine Humblot. (Bibliothèque nationale, Paris.)

Counterfeiters with false certificates confused investors. Murders, robberies and fatal accidents took place. Men and women both noble and plebeian became paper rich overnight, and some cashed in their paper for gold and coin. One servant was sent on an errand to cash in the stock of his master. The master was in the black and wanting to realise his profits. The savvy servant, upon learning that the price had risen still further, promptly pocketed the difference, handed over the balance to his master as expected, and bolted. In an attempt to regulate the market Law was forced to buy the Hôtel de Soissons. Investors were forbidden from buying stock from anywhere other than this new headquarters. Within a short time over 500 tents were pitched in the gardens of the hotel by stock jobbers and the like. As Niall Ferguson put it in his book *The Ascent of Money*, "It was as if one man was simultaneously running all five hundred of the top US corporations, the US treasury and the Federal Reserve System."

Aristocrats were prepared to wait slavishly for several hours outside Law's office for a few minutes of time – a fact which Law was happy to take advantage of. They even came up with elaborate schemes to get an audience with him. One woman, aware of his reputation for chivalry and gallantry, sought her driver's help in orchestrating the overturning of her carriage, planned to coincide with Law's arrival. Another hoax involved a fire at a venue where Law was to known to be.

By 1720, John Law was considered a national hero in France. The entrepreneur converted to Catholicism, neatly circumventing the law against Protestants occupying public office in France, and was appointed France's Comptroller General of Finances (a role akin to prime minister). Now he was in prime position to make a strike. He acquired palaces and great tracts of land and part of country estates. His company's value was measured in hundreds of billions. At the height of his wealth, Law was personally worth approximately £13 billion today's money. His reputation was further enhanced by his enormously generous nature. He supported anyone who lobbied him after falling into poverty. It was in French the term 'millionaire' first appeared and it was John Law who it first described.

Causing a revolution

One investor, who had been slighted by Law in an investment opportunity, tried to create a stampede by withdrawing such a quantity of cash that it took three wagons to deliver the money to its owner. Some clever stock jobbers slowly and methodically traded in their paper for bullion coins of gold and silver. The shrewd understood the fragile nature of the financial bubble Law had created and knew it had to burst sometime. As a result, Law's meteoric rise was short-lived. A run on the bank plunged France, and the rest of Europe, into a severe economic crisis. It has been argued that shockwaves from the collapse ultimately triggered the French Revolution.

In May 1725, the French government issued an edict devaluing the company's notes and shares and fixing their prices; shares were reduced by half. Confidence in Law's company was completely destroyed. The effect of the edict was so devastating that it was repealed within a week. However, the damage was done, and Law resigned as Comptroller General. The bank closed, unable to cope with the crowds looking for their money. Many people were crushed to death in the mêlée.

The Madness of Crowds by Charles Mackay, first published in 1841, described the affects John Law was having on the French populous. In one incident fifteen people were crushed and suffocated to death in a bank's doorway. Some of the bodies were taken by the indignant depositors to the Palais de Justice to demonstrate the true cost of the economic mess the government had presided over. Men were shot by regiments of the royal army, sent in to keep order. Entrepreneur Samuel Bernard, who was involved in farming as well as banking, was sentenced to death for his chicanery, eventually bribing his way out of a 'municipal lynching.' The French parliament, always envious of Law's sudden rise to power and influence, sought his trial with a view to a public hanging at the gates of the Palais de Justice in the centre of Paris, to appease the masses.

Elsewhere, a guy was boxed in the face during a road range incident on a Parisian street, involving two carriages. He saw another guy, who he didn't realise was the master of the servant who had hit, purely out to restore order. The approach of the master spooked him. The master realised the two drivers were causing a crowd to gather and creating a scene. But the poor guy who had been struck thought 'to hell with this there's two of them!' and cried out that John Law and his servant were trying to murder him. On hearing this, the crowd turned into a mob, causing both servant and master to flee into the nearest church for refuge, pursued by the horde.

Leaving France

On December 13th 1725, two days after fleeing Paris, Law gained permission to leave France. He eventually returned to England (after brief spells in Rome and Copenhagen) where he had received a formal pardon in 1719 for the murder he had committed nearly a quarter of a century earlier.

Law eventually left Britain for Venice, where he died of pneumonia in 1729. An inventory of his wealth showed he owned furniture, sculptures, musical instruments and a collection of 480 paintings, including works by Titian, Raphael, Michelangelo and Leonardo da Vinci. As an entrepreneur Law was untarnished by ultimate failure. Despite being a fugitive for most of his life Law ended up owning a world superpower's economy. He could have easily stashed away wealth in the form of gold on his travels through Europe. He could have bought land in far-off places but despite his flaws, it was generally agreed that he wasn't a swindler. The Duke of Orléans (the stand-in king of France) protected him and ensured he left the country in safety, despite the episode triggering the downfall of the French monarchy – France became a republic by the end of the century.

Today, John Law's banking methods are standard global banking practice and have helped to secure the West's stranglehold on global wealth. The benefits of John Law's methods have been learned but the accompanying risks and lessons of his demise have been overlooked. As Mark Twain puts it: "History doesn't repeat itself – at best it sometimes rhymes."

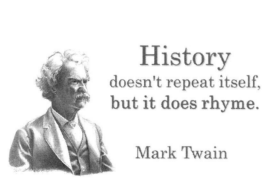

History
doesn't repeat itself,
but it does rhyme.

Mark Twain

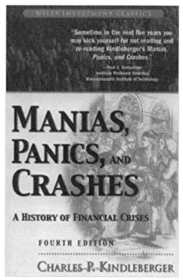

MATTHEW BOULTON (1728 – 1809)

"I sell here, sir, what all the world desires to have - power!"

Matthew Boulton was a key instigator of the Industrial Revolution. During the course of his life, the entrepreneur made three unaligned world-class fortunes and changed the industrial face of Britain – and arguably the world – forever.

A head start

Boulton was born in Birmingham, England. His father (also named Matthew Boulton) was an entrepreneur, manufacturing toys, metal articles, buttons, and buckles. Boulton senior enjoyed reasonable success and his son shared his enthusiasm for manufacturing.

At the age of 17 Boulton the younger helped expand his father's business still further, after developing a rather interesting buckle. He was made a full partner when he turned 21 and the entire management of the business was turned over to him. His father consolidated the family success by marrying his son to a distant cousin, Mary Robinson, in 1749. She was the daughter of Luke Robinson, a wealthy Lichfield mercer with a substantial fortune. Young Boulton not only acquired Mary but also her £14,000 (£1.4 million) inheritance to boot. This eased the pressure on the business after he embarked on a process of vertical expansion –

hankering after a business big enough to encompass the whole process from manufacturing through to sales, as well as catering to his lofty ambitions. He was one of the first entrepreneurs in Europe to divide the labourers of a workshop into specialist tasks, increasing production one thousand-fold. Mass production had arrived.

Fortune number one: Jewellery

After running his father's business successfully for more than five years, Boulton decided it was time to up his game. During 1755 he acquired an existing plant at Sarehole Mill in Hall Green, near Birmingham. He took full control of the business after his father died in 1759. Within two years the Sarehole Mill was too small for the expanding business. He purchased land and property, including a mill, at Soho in Hockley Brook in the Midlands, very close to Birmingham's Jewellery Quarter (which still prospers today). Around this time Boulton entered into partnership with John Fothergill, a specialist in the jewellery business. Fothergill brought with him a wide range of experience in European markets, which were very important to the city of Birmingham's trade. Now Boulton had all he needed to enact his grand vision of building a great 'manufactory.'

At Soho, Boulton fused together all the distinct elements of the manufacturing process. The town's skilled craftsmen were all brought under one very large roof. All the functions of a modern business, including design and marketing, were now under Boulton's masterly control and direction. His secret was to equip workers with all manner of labour-saving devices, thus enabling them to become more productive. His overall strategy was to build a reputation on the highest quality jewellery, silverware and plated goods. To this end he recruited the country's best designers. Matthew Boulton was now building quite a reputation and had an extraordinary talent for developing alliances with influential people. In 1758 he met entrepreneur and statesman Benjamin Franklin, who later visited his manufactory.

However, Boulton found himself having to perform amid personal disaster. Business was great but in 1759 his wife Mary died. She was always sickly and during their four years of marriage she had had three children who all died in infancy. Boulton, having lost Mary, now sought another mate of equally suitable stock – his dead wife's sister Anne. This had the in-laws up in arms, given that Boulton already had his hands-on Mary's inheritance (under the law of the time a woman's wealth automatically reverted to her husband). Her family didn't want Boulton to siphon even more of their wealth. Nonetheless, the couple were married on June 25th 1760 at St Mary's Church Rotherhithe. She came with the same sort of money his first wife did. His father had also died the previous year so death brought a serious increase in his wealth.

Fortune number two: Steam engines

During 1766 Benjamin Franklin was in London on behalf of the colony of America. He wanted to rid the colony of the Stamp Act, a small but offensive tax on paper and paper products, including playing cards. The tax had fuelled the growing revolutionary movement in the American colonies. Boulton and Franklin were in constant correspondence with each other. In their letters they discussed the applicability of steam power to various useful purposes. Both of them were unaware that James Watt had already invented a steam engine when they came up with their own design. Boulton constructed a model and sent it to Franklin, who in turn exhibited it. Boulton actually met James Watt whilst the inventor was en route to London to patent his steam engine invention.

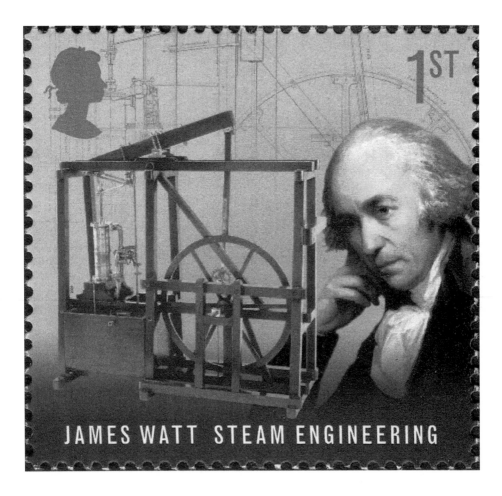

JAMES WATT STEAM ENGINEERING

The entrepreneur snared Watt by baiting him with the Soho Manufactory as a base to work from. Before moving to Birmingham Watt had his engine dismantled and sent on ahead of him. On arriving he found not only the machine working but also its problems resolved by Boulton and his men. The problem that Watt had struggled with for years had been solved by Boulton's team in a matter of weeks. Thus, began the association of Matthew Boulton and

James Watt. There were obvious reciprocal benefits. Scientists dream of finding a financial benefactor. Entrepreneurs dream of finding the next big thing. For this entrepreneur steam power was it. Boulton now had one of the age's greatest scientific inventors in his armoury, along with his father's business, some of the country's best craftsmen, Mary's inheritance and Anne's 'income' (and future inheritance). But having all the right ingredients is nothing without a great chef.

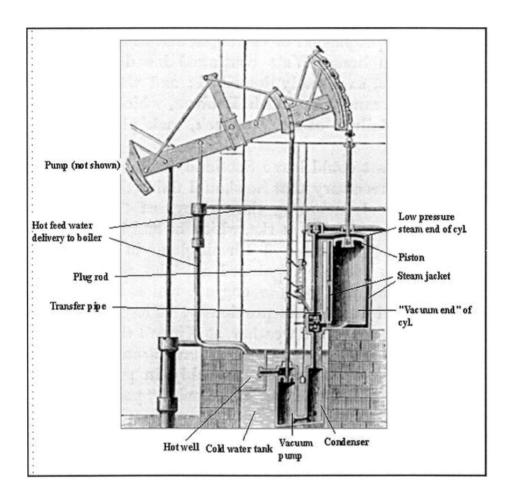

Pump (not shown)

Hot feed water
delivery to boiler

Plug rod

Transfer pipe

Low pressure
steam end of cyl.

Piston

Steam jacket

"Vacuum end" of
cyl.

Hot well   Cold water tank   Vacuum   Condenser
                               pump

Boulton and Watt were bang on time with a solution for the age. The world was shrinking, and industry was expanding at its fastest rate since Roman times, with entrepreneurs like Richard Arkwright in the driving seat. New machines were being invented that could only benefit from the addition of steam power. James Watt's invention was as essential to manufacturing then as electricity is to computing today.

In 1775 Boulton and Watt formally entered into partnership. Boulton devoted all the capital he possessed and could borrow to fund the invention. It was a gargantuan decision. He had experienced many failures and setbacks as well as successes. He was already rich and had everything to lose. He financed all the experimenting and patents without any assistance from James.

After six years of fruitless endeavour it took James Watt less than two years after meeting Boulton to solve the problems associated with the machine's design. In 1782, Watt patented a rotary motion, which enabled the engine to drive machinery. Boulton coined the term 'horsepower' to indicate the engine's comparable power.

Although capital and labour were still difficult to obtain, Boulton refused to employ young children He introduced a very early form of social insurance scheme, funded by workers' contributions of 1/60th of their wages. It paid benefits of up to 80 percent of wages to staff that were sick or injured. Furthermore, the workplace was required to be clean, well lit and well ventilated at all times. From 1775 to 1800 Boulton possessed and protected a monopoly on steam engine construction. Practically all the steam engines that were constructed in Great Britain before the year 1800 were produced by his manufactory.

Fortune number three: Minting coins

By now Boulton's manufacturing plant was the most famous factory in the world, visited by living legends such as the enlightened Catherine the Great of Russia and Lord Nelson. He had become a celebrated entrepreneur and an exceedingly rich man. However, it was not enough. At the age of 59 he embarked on his third great enterprise: minting coins. Matthew Boulton became the main supplier of coinage in the country and supplied many countries abroad including the territories of the expanding British empire. He in fact created modern coinage.

Boulton was a man's man. In 1792 he was involved in a hands-on battle (not for the first time) with rioters. He deployed a cannon and brandished the equivalent of a baseball bat to protect his factory.

He died in Birmingham on August 18th 1809 and was buried at St Mary's, in Handsworth. Business partners James Watt and William Murdock would later be laid to rest alongside him. Boulton's net worth at time of death was £150,000 (£130 million). The proud city of Birmingham have erected many monuments to the great entrepreneur.

The American Dream (Pre-20th Century)

JOHN JACOB ASTOR (1763 – 1848)

"Serve the classes, live with the masses. Serve the masses, live with the classes."

Johann Jakob Astor I was a major player in the real life drama of the making of America, becoming the country's first genuine millionaire.

This son of a German butcher was born in Waldorf, <u>Baden,</u> and would go on to make many independent fortunes that even today continue to earn billions for his posterity. The ambitious young boy went to work in London as an apprentice to his brother, studying how to run the business, which manufactured musical instruments. It was here that he learned to speak English.

Making money from fur

As soon as America's War of Independence came to an end Astor seized the opportunity to start building his fortune. He regularly visited the harbour, desperate to find a ship bound for the New World.

He arrived in New York Harbour, the immigrant drop-off spot, in March 1784, with six flutes and very little money. Astor was not only a foreigner to the natives of America but also to European Americans (colonists) in their newly-won home land. Johann Jakob anglicised his name to John Jacob in order to fit in, but he would retain a strong German accent all his life. On the voyage to America he had listened to journeymen speak of their exploits trapping game and trading with the natives. Not long after his arrival Astor was earning a living beating furs.

Fur beating was nasty – blood and guts everywhere. The hardy, sharp-minded young man soon acquired an eye for a good fur deal. Within a year of his arrival the entrepreneur was up the Hudson River and off into the American great outdoors. Soon afterwards, he was back on the streets of London with a ton of furs and boots still damp from the Hudson. The profits acquired were used to obtain various products locally to sell in America.

In love with money

John Jacob Astor began an intense love affair – his mistress was money. Less romantic was his marriage to widow Sarah Todd. His new mate was no oil painting, but voluptuous, with a great big pair of assets: $300 ($6,000) dowry and a boarding house. Conversations among her lodgers centred on the politics of the old countries and shipping. These were exactly the types Astor wanted to surround himself with and learn from. They knew their way around and had contacts. Young Astor paid close attention to their conversations.

He and Sarah opened a store in New York selling furs and musical instruments, giving them yet another source of income. The store's management was down to Sarah. Within four years of his landing in New York Harbour he was doing well enough to purchase $3,000 ($60,000) worth of furs in Montreal, the centre of the fur trade. These were shipped to traders in various European cities. The trip from New York to Montreal crossed serious frontier territory, and Astor did it alone.

The following year John Jacob Astor bought five times the inventory he had previously acquired. He then joined forces with a Canadian establishment called the Northwest Company, just after founding the Southwest Company. Each party held a 50 percent share in the other. The coalition required both entities to operate strictly within the confines of their respective geographic areas. Astor would try to extend his 'hunting territory' by snatching as much area as he could get his hands on, which often meant getting into a competitor's patch. When a law preventing Canadians from involvement in the American fur trade was introduced, Astor jumped at the opportunity to make his partners an offer they couldn't refuse. His partners had their hands tied and Astor landed himself the whole concern at a bargain price.

Profits from his fur trade were used to finance property acquisitions. In 1789 Astor bought his first piece of land in Bowery Road, New York, from his brother Henry. He spent $7,000 ($145,000) acquiring more over the following two years.

In 1795 Britain signed a trade agreement, the Treaty of Amity, Commerce and Navigation, with the newly formed coalition of the United States of America. The British moved their troops out of Northwest Territory, leaving it open to US citizens. Astor instinctively declared he'd "now make a fortune." Over the next five years he did just that, establishing himself as America's number one fur merchant.

Astor stuck to knitting, importing musical instruments, selling furs and guns, including cannons. Like many traders he profited from selling guns, bullets and whisky to Native Americans. In return the traders were paid in valuable fur pelts.

Trading with China

By the late 18th Century, Europe was keen to boost imports and exports with China. World demand for Chinese exports was as strong then as it is today. Europe also wanted to stem the outflow of silver, which was being given to Chinese opium growers as payment for the drug, a situation that would eventually lead to the Opium Wars. China was not keen on doing much business with the West. The Chinese emperor even sent a message to George III of Britain which read thus: "As your ambassador can see, we possess all things … there is therefore no need to import the manufacturers of outside barbarians in exchange for our own produce."

Eventually, the Chinese fielded four 'gilded' merchants authorised by the central government to trade with Western merchants at Canton. One of these merchants was the wily John Jacob Astor. His Chinese import and export business mushroomed, helping to boost his net worth by millions.

ASTORIA IN 1813.

John Jacob Astor was making so much money and such a reputation for himself that a number of silly claims were being made on his fortune. One such attempt was to the tune of over $5 million ($83 million). The suit against him argued that Astor had found Captain Kidd's treasure. It proved to be a hoax. John N. Emerick, a junior partner on an early voyage, claimed he had schooled Astor in the trade of furring. Tens of millions of dollars were claimed for Emerick's heirs. They failed too.

The West won its trade war with China. Astor was by now a very rich man, and used money from his mounting cash pile to invest in a trading ship called Severn. The vessel carried a variety of goods to China and on the return leg, carried tea and silks for distribution to various international ports. Astor became a megalomaniac, with delusions of grandeur. He began to see his success as karma and believed he was destined to bridge the East-West trading antagonisms. The entrepreneur went from being a heavyweight trader on the London market to an international mega-mogul, with China as his most important market.

The path to unimaginable wealth

Ships travelled to Asia and Europe, delivering goods and returning with an embarrassment of riches. Astor was at a loss as to what to do with his cash mountain. High-risk and management-intensive opportunities didn't appeal to him. He ran his business from the equivalent of a two-bed flat with a dozen people involved. Land appeared to be the best repository for his surplus funds. Astor bought himself 243 lots of backwater marshland in an overlooked area of New York called Manhattan.

On May 24th Peter Minuit buys Manhattan from a Native American tribe (Lenape or Shinnecock) for trade goods, valued at 60 guilders ($24.00). They had then swapped it with Britain in exchange for a nutmeg producing island in Indonesia

The Manhattan land was virtually unused and unwanted. It was populated with a few farms and retreats for escaping the hullabaloo of the New York metropolis.

"This beautiful pond, occupying the site of the present great gloomy pile of prison buildings known as The Tombs, was the scene in 1796 of the first trial of a steamboat with a screw propeller. It was the invention of John Fitch." (Page 454)

The land did include a mansion, which Astor leased to the State Governor, George Clinton. Astor could always use a favour from a high ranking official, so he scratched a lot of political backs expecting reciprocation. In 1803, an indebted Vice President Aaron Burr (who lost the presidency election by one vote) gave up Manhattan land to Astor in exchange for ready cash. As Burr fell further into debt his political career fell apart, and after a dirty campaign with long standing political rival Alexander Hamilton, he shot Hamilton dead in a duel. Burr was subsequently charged with murder in 1804. He sold Astor another lease in Greenwich Village, Manhattan for $8,000 ($130,000), then disappeared. Major swathes of Harlem and other parts of the island of Manhattan were bought up by Astor from old-money folk. The timing could not have been better. New York was destined to become the centre of the commercial world and Manhattan was to be its epicentre. In 1808 Astor established the American Fur Company. The entrepreneur now had access to an unbelievable trading domain, bigger than many of Europe's leading countries.

By 1812, Astor and a syndicate saved the bankrupt American government by negotiating a very profitable war loan. Secretary of War Munroe got his own personal loan – some $5,000 ($56,000) –from Astor in 1814. Munroe became Secretary of State and Astor found this lofty post very advantageous. Diplomats had advance knowledge of international machinations about to break. In a world of competitive states vying for territory and position, knowledge is power. Advance warning meant reduced risk. What better than to have the Secretary of State, to whom all diplomats are beholden, in one's debt? Moreover, awareness provided great opportunity for profit. So, Astor always maintained a generous relationship with the Secretaries of State.

The first US monopoly

In 1822, Astor received another godsend. The US government closed a government trading post deep in Indian territory, removing his biggest competitor. By 1830, yet another company – the Columbia Fur Company – was absorbed. Astor now had supremacy in Michigan as well as Wisconsin, and was uncontested along the tributaries of the lower Mississippi River. John Jacob Astor had created the first monopoly in US history. He was a supreme and unassailable entrepreneur.

Astor sold the American Fur Company in 1834 (the industry's best days were behind it) and along with it went all his other non-property-related businesses. This was part of a disposal strategy. Astor was now arguably the richest man in America and indeed one of the richest in the world. The game was well and truly won and he began focusing his attentions on social concerns. He matriculated all his children into old-money aristocracy by way of marriage. This ensured his progeny stood the greatest chance of success.

Even today, John Jacob Astor's Manhattan real estate holdings continue to make billions for several generations of his descendants. From an uncouth butcher emerged one of the most aristocratic families in America. The means was entrepreneurship. Ironically, Astor's posterity would eventually try to obscure their humble origins and distance themselves from the "old German butcher", even removing their ancestor's portrait from public view.

Money on the brain

John Jacob Astor passed away on March 29th 1848. It was said that "few grieved." Before the entrepreneur died he sighed and murmured his regret in not buying the whole of upper Manhattan. Even as he prepared to meet his maker, the entrepreneur's mind was on the hunt. Astor has gone down in history as one of America's top five richest men (based on share of US GDP): far richer even than Bill Gates.

SAMUEL COLT (1814 – 1862)

it is said that God made all
men, but Samuel Colt made
all men equal.

EB1870.ORG

"It is better to be at the head of a louse than at the tail of a lion! If I can't be first I won't be second in anything"

Gun ownership

Abraham Lincoln may have freed America's slaves, but Samuel Colt made them equal. He redressed the balance of power by putting a gun in the hand of all adversaries who could afford one. Today there are 80 million gun owners in America. The embryonic USA was a dangerous, competitive and desperate place in the early 19th Century, with communities desperate to keep what was theirs, and others desperate to take it. And Samuel Colt helped shape this violent gun-toting country. Gun makers benefited from industrialisation like any other business. He who could create an efficient killing tool, and 'machine' it economically would be richly rewarded – since human nature would provide the demand.

In human society competition takes place on numerous levels. Samuel Colt seemed to have tapped into this need to compete. It manifested itself in his lifelong quest to produce a killing machine, designed to improve the possessor's odds of success in a battle. But it was also evident in his drive to make not only *good* guns but the *best* guns. Moreover, he also competed personally, trying to outsell every last competitor.

Colt was clearly competitive by nature and this competitiveness was hardened by adversity. He wanted to be recognised as the best. It dominated his life and thoughts. He experienced waves of tragedies and failures that would put an ordinary man on his back, or worse underground. But Colt was a different sort of animal: relentless, single-minded, a megalomaniac. However, from the age of seven to 14, young Colt observed that the world was born to fall apart, and he was helpless to do anything about it. Soon after he would take control of his own fate and, in doing so, influence the fates of millions of others.

Samuel Colt was born in Hartford, Connecticut. His father Christopher Colt, an entrepreneur, was originally a farmer who had moved his family to Hartford and opened a textile mill. Sam Colt's mother, Sarah Colt née Caldwell, died when he was eleven and his father's business failed soon afterwards. Two years later, his father was remarried to a woman called Olive Sergeant.

Colt had four brothers and three sisters. Two of his sisters died in childhood and the other committed suicide in later life. Colt's brothers would become an important part of his business. After the unrelenting series of tragedies Colt ended up as an indentured servant on a farm in Glastonbury aged eleven. It was a means of receiving an education.

Fascination with mechanics

Colt use to love observing the efficiency of the machines in his father's dye and bleaching factory. He undertook various chores there. It was later, whilst working on the farm out in the great American outdoors, that he realised how important guns were in feeding oneself, dealing with the threat of hostile native Americans and outlaws, and defending oneself against wild animals. When Colt finished his farm chores for the day he would often spend time looking at an old gun he brought with him. He would try to work out how he could increase the guns number of barrels without significantly increasing the gun's overall weight.

At school, Colt's fascination with science and mechanics grew when he read the *Compendium of Knowledge*, a scientific encyclopaedia. This book caused young Colt to neglect his bible studies and he didn't shine at school. The adventurous young boy left school at the age of 15 to become a sailor. On a voyage to India, Colt studied with interest the 'turning and locking' action of the ship's capstan. He had an epiphany. Colt would later write: "Regardless of which way the wheel was spun, each spoke always came in direct line with a clutch that could be set to hold it... the revolver was conceived!" Applying the same principle to a gun, he imagined how many rounds one could get off at the enemy in short succession without having to reload. Colt had stumbled across an idea that he would one day turn into a world-famous brand.

Upon his arrival back to the US in 1831, Samuel Colt spoke with Henry Ellsworth, Commissioner of the United States Patent Office, who encouraged him to obtain a patent for the model he had created whilst at sea. Colt's design was not much different from the standard front-loading flintlock pistols, except for the introduction of a 'revolving chamber'. The chamber rotated automatically on firing. 'The Colt' could hold five or six shots in its chamber at the same time. The technology didn't set the world on fire but a 'self-loading gun' quite literally *would.* He convinced his father to fund some prototypes that he'd commissioned a local gunsmith to produce it in 1832.

Eighteen year-old Colt travelled the country trying to earn the money to launch his gun business. A chemist at his father's factory had introduced him to laughing gas (nitrous oxide), so he travelled as far as Canada to put on demonstrations in museums, lecture halls and town halls. Young Colt was a very able showman (the act was called Doctor Coult) and promoted the gas successfully enough to procure the funds to help with the prototyping of the pistol and foreign patenting. He was on the road for four years.

Eli Whitney, a gun inventor of a previous generation, lost a fortune to imitators. In 1836, Samuel Colt received a European patent for his new 'revolver'. He had already secured patents in England and France. The registration put him in good stead. Colt was not inventing exactly but was simply improving designs such as Elisha H. Collier's revolving Flintlock. With cash from family in New Jersey, Colt opened the Patent Arms Manufacturing Company.

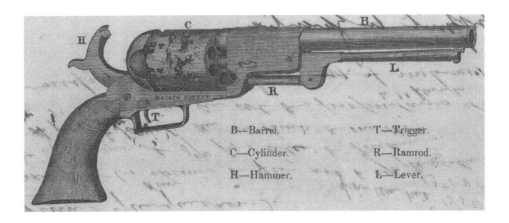

B—Barrel.   T—Trigger.

C—Cylinder.   R—Ramrod.

H—Hammer.   L—Lever.

Bankruptcy

Colt formed the company with the help of an uncle who was himself a successful local entrepreneur. New Jersey was the place to be in America for manufacturing. The city was the one of the fastest-growing manufacturing centres in the country. It was there in 1836 that 22 year-old Colt built his first factory. But he was forced to go back on the road fundraising after being let down by co-owners of the business. Monies were needed to develop new machinery to make the guns' interchangeable parts. Dudley Selden, Colt's cousin who was responsible for overseeing the finances, accused the young entrepreneur of reckless spending, saying: "You use money as if it were drawn from an inexhaustible mine."

A letter from John Pearson, sent around the same time in 1836, palpitates with the pressure of the business and conveys how many involved in it must have been feeling: "I worked night and day almost, so I would not disappoint you and what have I got for it … why vexation and trouble ... The manner you are using us is too bad ... Come up with some money."

On March 5th the first production models of Colt revolvers were produced. In 1842 the entrepreneur developed a range for the pocket, belt and holster, along with two types of long armour rifle; one cocked by a hammer, the other by a finger lever. In all cases, gunpowder and bullets were loaded into a revolving cylinder while the primer was placed into a nipple located on the outside of the cylinder, where it would be struck by the hammer when the trigger was pulled. Despite the revolver's obvious ability as a hunting or killing machine, sales were sluggish. The Government bought a few, but no queues formed outside the factory. After the production of 5,000 pistols and rifles Colt had to file for bankruptcy. The difference between great success and great failure is often a matter of luck and timing. In Colt's case the launch within months of the Bank Panic of 1837 was bad luck. The bad *timing* was; there weren't any major wars being fought in America at that time. But Samuel Colt was soon to come back, more forcefully than ever before.

Strategic alliance

The entrepreneur was down but not out. He formed an association with the inventor of the telegraph, Samuel F. B. Morse, and tried to get the government to buy into a new invention. The pair began marketing waterproof ammunition; underwater mines for harbour defence. Success was limited. Colt began promoting the telegraph companies, widening the market for his waterproof telegraph cable. He made $50 (£20) per mile.

The US annexed Texas in 1845, precipitating the Mexican-American War. Units of the US Dragoon forces and Texas Rangers were engaged in fighting horse-mounted Apache, Comanche, and Cherokee in Texas. War meant a change of fortune for Colt. The natives, armed with bows and arrows, could shoot a batch of arrows faster than their European invaders could shoot a batch of bullets.

By the end of the campaign the US soldiers were celebrating 'the Colt' as being largely responsible for their success in defeating native forces in the competition for land – and indeed for their very existence in America. The US soldiers could now reload as fast as the Native warriors. From 1831 to 1838, Cherokee, Choctaw, Creek and other South-Eastern nations were removed to the so-called Indian Territory, now Oklahoma, on the Trail of Tears. An estimated 100,000 people were moved West, driven out by the revolver.

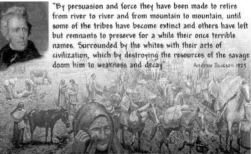

"By persuasion and force they have been made to retire from river to river and from mountain to mountain, until some of the tribes have become extinct and others have left but remnants to preserve for a while their once terrible names. Surrounded by the whites with their arts of civilization, which by destroying the resources of the savage doom him to weakness and decay" Andrew Jackson 1829

The US War Department loved it too. Capt. Samuel H. Walker of the US Army travelled east to look up Sam Colt (who was no longer fettered by the spectre of debt liability and could now think more clearly and creatively). The two knocked heads on the design of a new, improved and more powerful revolver. Within a week (with Captain Walker providing an inside track) the US Ordnance Department had ordered a thousand new 'Walker Colts' (the order was worth $25,000) – now the largest, most powerful black powder handgun ever made.

Samuel Colt was back, but without a factory. Nevertheless, greatness attracts money and money attracts greatness. Colt turned to Eli Whitney, Jr. (son of the late entrepreneur and inventor of the very firearm that Colt had sought to improve) who had a factory in Connecticut.

Jesse James

Litigation against Samuel Colt relating to his bankruptcy had come to an end in 1846. He resurrected his patent rights the following year. Colt launched the .44 calibre, the 'Six-shot Walker,' using the Whitney factory. The government order was completed and shipped the year outlaw Jesse James was born.

As an adult Jesse James would carry Colt's .36 calibre 'Navy Colt'. Smaller and lighter, it allowed the outlaw and his brother Frank to carry up to six guns at a time – a veritable two-man platoon. In 1946 Walker wrote to Colt praising the killing machine: "The pistols which you made ... have been in use by the 'Texas Rangers' for three years ... the only good improvement I have ever seen ... summer of 1844, Col. J.C. Hayes, with fifteen men, fought about 80 Comanche ... Without your pistols we should not have had the confidence to undertake such daring adventures." Sam Colt was good at eliciting such letters for the promotion of gun sales as we shall see later.

US land grab

The .44 calibre 'Six-shot Walker' gun was the difference in the USA's war with Mexico which broke 30 years of peace. Half of Mexico's territory, including Arizona, New Mexico and California, fell into US hands. Mexico's territorial losses signified the rise of the United States as the predominant power in North America. US land-grabs and hungrily competing immigrants fuelled the domestic market for guns.

In 1848, Samuel Colt established his own factory to churn out the killing machine. It was Colt's 'peacemaker' that settled many an argument in the wild wild West. There was a steady demand for guns and the new factory kept up. The plant was based upon the 'American system' of manufacturing observed at Eli Whitney's plant (interchangeable parts). Whitney had created an advanced method to build the first industrialised firearm factory in the world. Everything was based on standardised interchangeable components.

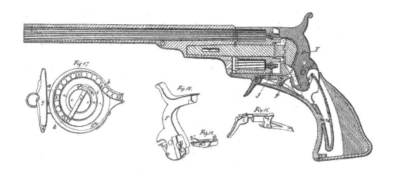

In 1851, Colt began buying up property in the South Meadows that fronted the Connecticut River, close to his birthplace. He dreamed of constructing the world's greatest civil armoury there. The land acquired was swampy lowland, exposed to flooding. As a result, it was undervalued. He acquired 250 acres at a cost of $60,000 ($1,200,000), built a dike two miles long, and planted French Osiers to prevent soil erosion. The whole thing took two years and $125,000 ($2,500,000) in additional investment. There he established employee housing, a ten-hour day for employees, washing stations in the factory, a one-hour lunch break entitlement, and built the Charter Oak Hall, a club where employees could enjoy games, newspapers, and discussion rooms.

European fame

Colt leapt on an opportunity to exhibit at London's legendary 1851 Great Exhibition at Crystal Palace in Hyde Park. Soon afterwards, he became the first American manufacturer to open a manufacturing plant in England, thereby solidifying his reputation in international markets. Colt's products were patented throughout Europe and if there was an infringement on his patent he sued. Generally, the courts ordered that royalties be paid to him on each gun sold. This would often cause the competitor to go bust, leaving Colt with a virtual monopoly.

Colt made a fortune in Europe because of the many wars taking place there. Even if no war was actually going on, the perceived threat of it caused European countries to spend large amounts of taxpayers' money on armaments, including Colt's revolvers. Colt made sure of this by going around telling each nation's government that their rivals were buying his pistols. This allowed him to procure large orders from many countries who feared falling behind in the arms race.

Colt, a self-proclaimed genius, was relentless in self-promotion. He even caused the introduction of anti-lobbying regulation in 1876 after spending more than $100,000 ($2 million) in bribes trying to get an extension on his revolvers' patents. Colt would wine and dine anyone who had the clout to influence buying decisions on gun procurement in Congress or the War Department. Decision-makers would be given gifts in the form of expensive ornate guns. Journalists would be wooed with dramatic and entertaining news stories from the war fronts or amusing stories involving his guns. Colt wrote: "I am noticing in the newspapers occasionally complementary notices of the Sharps Burnside rifles and carbines, anecdotes of their use upon grizzly bears, Indians, Mexicans, etc., etc. Now this is all wrong – it should be published Colt's Rifles, Carbines, etc. When...there can be made a good story of the use of a Colts Revolving rifle, carbine, shotgun or pistol ... upon Grisly Bears, Indians, Mexicans, [sic] ... for publication ... the opportunity should not be lost ... Send me 100 copies ... give the editor a pistol."

Colt's firm was incorporated in Connecticut as the Colt's Patent Fire Arms Manufacturing Company in 1855, with an initial issuance of 10,000 shares of stock. Colt held 9,996 shares and dished a few out to his associates, which included business associates and trusted factory superintendent E.K. Root, an important inventor in his own right. That year the New Hartford factory was completed. The factory was equipped with the most up-to-date metalworking machines, capable of turning out 5,000 finished handguns in its first year of operation, some 80 percent of which were turned out on precision machinery. Typically, the metal parts of a Colt revolver were designed, moulded, machined, fitted and stamped with a serial number, hardened, then assembled: all of them with uniform with interchangeable parts. Colt is reported to have said: "There is nothing that can't be produced by machines."

Samuel Colt was an unmitigated success and it was now time to 'show and tell'. He put a huge, conspicuous dome on top of his factory roof. It was like a king placing a crown on his own head. By 1856 (the year he married a local reverend's daughter, Miss Elizabeth Jarvis), Colt's methods allowed him to produce 150 weapons a day, ten times more than the previous year's production rate. What's more, the product was extremely well made. Thousands of people up and down America were firing Colt's weapons at each other with ever greater ease and efficiency. As the guns became cheaper Colt was able to widen the market, giving poorer people the ability to compete with their richer rivals on more equal footing. Colt was soon featured on the top ten rich-list of US entrepreneurs.

The American Civil War

During a vacation in Cuba in early 1861, as news of an imminent American Civil War broke, Samuel Colt wrote back to his managers instructing them to "run the Armoury night and day with a double set of hands ... Make hay while the sun shines." Sales quadrupled. Interestingly, Colt was opposed to slavery on the grounds it was inefficient rather than immoral. He supported the Union but, like Rothschild before him, supplied both sides. During wars between natives and his own European settler faction, Colt sold firearms to both sets of protagonists.

Samuel Colt's influence on democracy was more far-reaching than Abraham Lincoln's, since he ensured that the enforcers of the ideal were equipped with the right tools. He also provided ordinary men and women with the means to involve themselves personally in the protection of their own civil and human rights in the competition for scarce resources. Guns were firmly ingrained in the American way of life.

Samuel Colt was world famous by now. The honorary title of Colonel was bestowed upon him by the Governor of the State of Connecticut for his political support. In 1847 when Colt reopened after his bankruptcy his employee headcount was 47. By 1861, the first year of the American Civil war, with his armoury running at full tilt, it was more than 1,400 employees, with annual earnings of about $250,000 ($4.5 million).

Colt's health began to fail in late 1860. Gout had caught up with him two years earlier. He was always driving himself and pushing the boundaries. As ill health set in, Colt was in the process of doubling the size of the armoury, which was already running 24 hours a day. He died on January 10th 1862, aged only 47 years old. He produced more than 400,000 weapons in his lifetime. He was worth $15 million ($270 million) at the time of his death. Control of the company remained in the hands of the Colt family until 1901, when it was sold to a group of investors.

Samuel Colt changed the world forever. Handguns like the Colt .38 Special continue to be used today by police forces throughout the world. But it is Hollywood that has given the infamous Colt revolver a cult all of its own, as an ominous settler of differences.

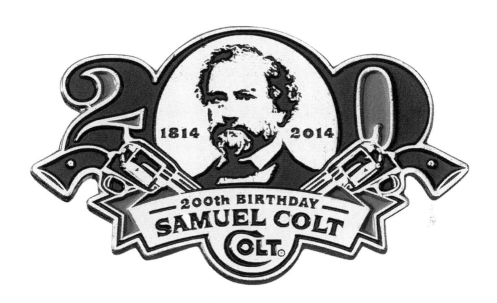

CORNELIUS VANDERBILT (1794 – 1877)

"I don't care half so much about making money as I do about making my point, and coming out ahead."

America's population distribution

Though Columbus had conquered the crossing of the Atlantic more than three centuries ago, the crossing of America from East to West remained a barrier. The result was that most European immigrants settled on the East coast.

The Homestead Act of 1862 (the great land give-away) was the result of years of agitation for free land that started in 1844. It was introduced with the hope and expectation that it would relieve the concentration of immigrants that flooded the Eastern cities, and act as a safety valve to relieve the pressure of unemployment and the competition for jobs.

The Pacific Railroad Act, passed in the same year as The Homestead Act, and the completion of coast-to-coast telegraph in 1861 helped settlers create more than 372,000 farms. By 1900, the settlers had filed 600,000 claims for more than 80 million acres (320,000 km²) of land in the West under the Homestead Act. It enabled nearly a million and half people to acquire farmland. In 1861, for example, Kansas entered the Union. After the Civil War, the population of Kansas exploded with wave after wave of immigrants seeking opportunity.

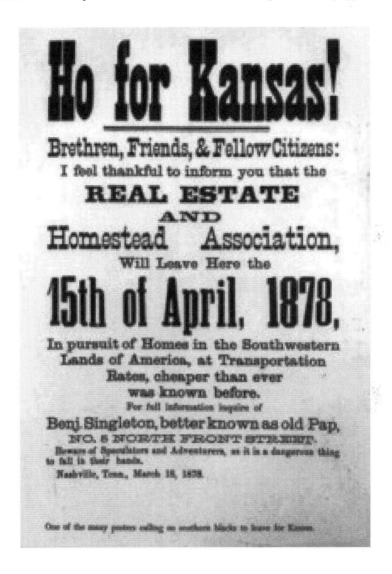

In 1871, 29,000 claims were made in Kansas under the Homestead Act. By 1885–1886, this number had leaped to 43,000 claims. The population of San Francisco in the West exploded after the discovery of gold in California from a mere 1,000 in 1848 to 20,000 full-time residents a mere two years later. Steam power would provide a solution to the problem of crossing the country from East to West and offer immense opportunity for entrepreneurs like Cornelius 'The Commodore' Vanderbilt.

Technological advancement

Humphrey Gainsborough produced a model condensing steam engine in the 1760s, which he showed to James Watt of Scotland, the inventor who would enter into life-changing partnership with one of our other great entrepreneurs, Matthew Boulton. In 1769 Watt patented the first significant improvements to the engine and in 1775 his business – spearheaded by Boulton – was up and running.

The increased efficiency of the Watt engine finally led to the general acceptance and use of steam power in industry. 1802 William Symington built the first 'practical steamboat', and in 1807 Robert Fulton used the Boulton Watt steam engine to power the first commercially successful steamboat.

'Mr. Symington's New Steam Boat.

Cornelius Vanderbilt was born on Staten Island, New York. His father operated a ferry in between the Island and the New York harbour. The young Vanderbilt was itching to get stuck into the family business and left school at the age of eleven.

By the time he was 15, Vanderbilt's mother was sufficiently concerned that he would run off to sea that she struck a deal with him: she would pay him $100 ($1700) for clearing and planting an eight-acre field.

Vanderbilt cleared the field, received his payment, and immediately re-invested his profits into a small two-mast flat-bottomed boat. He began ferrying freight and passengers between Manhattan and Staten Island at 18 cents ($15) a throw. His core customers were commuters. It was then he had his first and only scare, nearly sinking whilst out on the river. It didn't stop him though. After this incident his transport was renowned to be as safe as houses and as dependable as rain in Manchester.

They called him 'Cornele, the boatman'. He took any job, anytime, anywhere, come hell or high water. As a competitor he was hard to live with, undercutting everyone he came up against. His secret weapon was brinkmanship and pushing the stakes higher than his competitors could stomach. The business was the Easy Jet of the seas and Vanderbilt was a kind of bad-tempered truculent Stelios.

The fledgling entrepreneur's business was taking place against a backdrop of strife between Britain and America over trade shipping rights. This could have made life difficult, but war was often good for business. Vanderbilt made sure it was. In addition to his regular business he secured an army contract to supply six posts around New York Bay. Money was made on the side bringing food down to New York City from the farms up the Hudson River, circumventing the British blockade of New York City. Vanderbilt ploughed his profits into a part-interest in two other boats.

After the war the young entrepreneur went coastal, carrying oysters, watermelons, whale oil, and shad (river herrings) up and down the coast between Chesapeake Bay and New York. The boy was a grafter and when he wasn't transporting he was selling. The day he got married (to his first cousin Sophia Johnson in 1814) he went back to work as soon as the service was over.

Staying ahead of the curve

At the age of 23 Vanderbilt had a stash of $9,000 ($89,000). This figure didn't include his sailing vessel interests. However, he decided not to swim against the tide when steam-propelled boats invaded Staten Island. Vanderbilt was belligerent but not stupid; he sold up and got a job with Thomas Gibbons, owner of a small steamboat. He didn't hang about, convincing Gibbons immediately to build a steamboat designed by him.

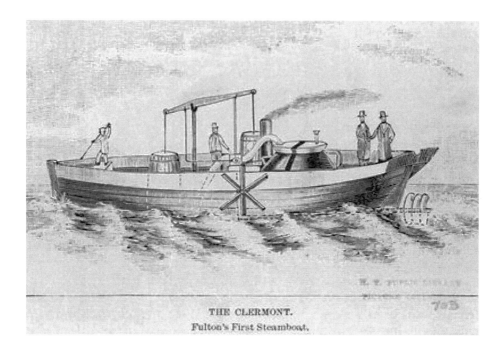

THE CLERMONT.
Fulton's First Steamboat.

The New Jersey to Manhattan route was subject to a legal monopoly but Vanderbilt didn't care. He ferried passengers in direct violation of the law, knocking spots off the monopolists and undercutting them (four times cheaper and below his own cost-price). He made up the difference by loading food and drink prices at the bar. Passengers could choose whether they wanted to eat or not. Vanderbilt made it difficult for the authorities to catch him. He built a secret compartment on the vessel where he hid to avoid arrest. In 1824 the monopoly was removed, prices plummeted, and Vanderbilt welcomed competitors to his arena like a matador. 'Low Cost' was his middle name. Vanderbilt was quick to adapt in a fast-changing world. He adopted new shipping technologies; specifically, tubular boilers and the use of anthracite coal.

In 1829, Vanderbilt used the $30,000 ($655,000) he had saved as the start-up fund that took him into the steamboat business, beginning with the New York City to Philadelphia run. He undercut everyone in sight. The following year he entered the Hudson River market and squared up to the Hudson River Steamboat Association. He cut fares from $3 ($65) to $1, then to ten cents and then made them free of charge. It was sheer brinkmanship. Increased food prices offset the losses. The Steamboat Association blinked first, offering him a one-off payment of $100,000 ($2,100,000) and $5,000 ($105,000) a year for the next ten years to stay away from their territory. It was money for old rope.

Vanderbilt now had the Long Island Sound market (an estuary of the Atlantic Ocean) and coastal trade in his sights; he soon had control of them. In 1844 Cornelius Vanderbilt was elected as a director of the Long Island Railroad, which at the time provided a route between Boston and New York via steamboat transfer. He could see changes on the horizon, and the railway was the future.

Vanderbilt was six feet two inches and as hard as nails. When he spoke it was loud, rough, and suffused with sea-fearing colloquialisms. His message was driven home with unfettered profanity. By the age of 40 he was worth $500,000 ($11 million). He had been working like a man possessed since he was a teenager. The multi-millionaire announced in 1853 that he would take the first break of his life. He needed it. Cornelius Vanderbilt got married at 19 years old and had 13 children. He built himself a whopping great yacht, naming it 'The North Star,' and toured Europe like a Roman General returning from a successful foreign campaign. Whilst the cat's away the mice will play and Vanderbilt was betrayed by a couple of colleagues who gained control of one of his companies. But with some nifty footwork (stock trading) it didn't take the entrepreneur too long to regain command and control.

The Californian Gold Rush

In 1848 the great entrepreneur Sam Brannan (who is profiled in the following chapter of this book) announced the discovery of gold in California and set off a stampede of adventurers heading for California from the East coast. Steamships via Panama instead of Cape Horn knocked 69 days off the journey. Vanderbilt formed the Accessory Transit Company in 1851 to take gold prospectors to California. He paid $10,000 ($200,000) to the Nicaraguan government for a charter to cross their country, charging half the cost of the Panama route. He raised cash by issuing bonds.

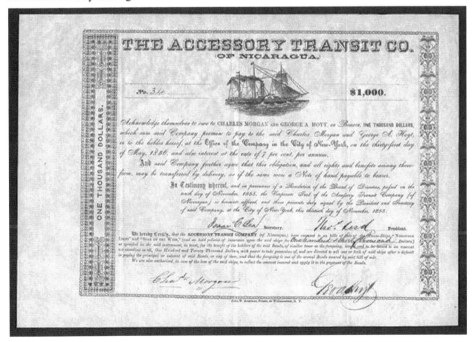

Locals said couldn't be done. Fearless Vanderbilt personally took a small steamboat up the San Juan River to test the route. He had the river cleared of obstacles, built a road from the West shore of the lake to San Juan del Sur and constructed a port on the Pacific coast. He placed a steamboat on Lake Nicaragua and knocked six hundred miles and two days off the trip to California, reducing fares from $600 ($11,000) to $400 ($7,500) and eventually to $150 ($3,000).

Eliminating the competition

Vanderbilt offered the US Government free transportation of their mail, taking away $500,000 ($10 million) worth of subsidies from a couple of competitors. Freight and passengers were previously crossing the Isthmus of Panama on mule-back to get from East to West. In 1855 William Walker took over the country using a mercenary army, acting as the self-installed President of Nicaragua.

William Walker was a US physician, lawyer, journalist, adventurer, and soldier of fortune (of Scottish descent) who tried to conquer numerous Latin American countries in the mid19th Century. He held the presidency of the Republic of Nicaragua from 1856 to 1857. He formed a coalition with officers of the Accessory Transport Company to take it from Vanderbilt, and was ousted in 1857 by mercenary forces supported by Vanderbilt, who organised five Central American countries to cooperate in the removal of Walker. William Walker was executed by the government of Honduras in 1860.

Having regained control of the ATC, Vanderbilt approached the Pacific Mail Steamship Company and the United States Mail Steamship Company, which operated routes across Panama, and offered to stop running the Nicaragua route in return for cash. His subsidised rivals knew they were on a hiding to nothing competing with him. They were all too well aware he played by a different set of rules (rules too risky to compete with). His rivals got together and paid him $672,000 ($1,300,000) to clear off and do business elsewhere. A year later, when he threatened to reopen (re-enter their territory), they increased the $40,000 per month stipend to $56,000.

Vengeful, ruthless and relentless

Vanderbilt entered the Atlantic steamship business in 1855. The UK and US governments subsidised their own home-grown companies, which left Vanderbilt out in the cold – but he was quick to adapt to the new trading climate. He resumed normal service, cutting fares for both passengers and mail, going for volume with second and third-class passengers.

Vanderbilt built a steamship, the 'Vanderbilt', to compete with the British Cunard Line, spending $600,000 ($110 million) creating a magnificent structure. It was largest vessel on the Atlantic. It was so fast it set a new speed record from Sandy Hook, USA, to the Isle of Wight, UK.

Vanderbilt had benefited from the growth of the steamboat business, but now the industry had peaked. In 1857 he became a director of the New York and Harlem Railroad, despite harbouring a personal antipathy towards rail travel. Two decades previously, in 1833, Vanderbilt was involved in one of the earliest train disasters in America. He suffered two fractured ribs and a punctured lung. In the front car was ex-President John Quincy Adams, who was not injured, but whose son was killed.

The steamboat business may have been on a downward curve, but Vanderbilt still managed to sell his Atlantic line for $3 million ($53 million) in 1861. He retained the 'Vanderbilt' steamship, later gifting it to the US government.

Photo # NH 60881   USS Vanderbilt. Artwork by Clary Ray

Vanderbilt was so powerful that, in 1863, the entrepreneur positively influenced the election of President Erastus O. Haven. Ruthless, with few friends and a wealth of enemies, Vanderbilt was a true entrepreneur. Though fabulously wealthy he lived modestly. The public found him a turn-off, which did not bother Vanderbilt. He said women bought his stock because his picture was on the stock certificate; he also pinched the backsides of curvaceous female servants and cursed like a sailor in public. He was known to have spat chewing tobacco on a host's carpet. When his first wife died he married a woman 43 year his junior. In his will, Vanderbilt gave a paltry one 1 percent to charity and disowned all his sons except William, who was a chip off the old block. William got 95 percent of his father's $40 million ($700 million) estate, making him the richest man in the country.

SAM BRANNAN (1819 – 1889)

"You go back and tell Brigham Young that I'll give up the Lord's money when he sends me a receipt signed by the Lord, and no sooner"

Mormonism in America

America had a reputation of being a refuge for Europeans suffering religious persecution during the 16-19th Centuries. During the early 19th Century the Mormons had 20 thousand members scattered across the US and had to endure great persecution. The Mormon leader at the time, Brigham Young, did a deal with the US government: in exchange for helping defend the US Western frontier during their war with Mexico, the Mormons would be provided with migration assistance to settle in that region.

The Mormons did a great deal of construction work during and after the war with Mexico, which ended in January 1847. On July 4th of that year, the Mormon battalion raised the US flag over Los Angeles. Shortly afterwards they were discharged from the army. Soon a historic Mormon migration would take place to the West of America.

Sam Brannan was born in Saco, Maine, a thriving coastal village 14 miles South-West of Portland. In 1832 Brannan's favourite sister, Mary Ann, converted to Mormonism whilst in Boston, along with her husband Alexander Badlam. Brannan was present during their first Mormon gathering, held in Ohio. He travelled there with his sister and her husband to set up home. An association with Joseph Smith (founder of Mormonism and considered by his followers a prophet) began in the state. Brannan and Smith lost money on land speculation in 1837, when the former was still only 19 years old.

Brannan began an apprenticeship, working in the church's printing office publishing the *Evening and Morning Star*, the *Messenger* and the *Advocate*. Brannan was a man on a mission, he bought out his apprenticeship after only three short years. America at that time was experiencing 'get rich quick' hysteria. Brannan watched with interest, as he observed the power of the press to influence the masses.

Whilst in Indianapolis the emerging orator worked on the anti-slavery publication the *Indianapolis Gazette*. During his travels he established some major political connections with the Democratic Party. By December 1843 he was a missionary and leader of men in southern Ohio. He was soon on the move again, leaving Ohio in favour of New York City, in search of opportunity. There, Brannan began gathering souls.

Many Europeans who had left their homelands for America in order to escape religious persecution witnessed Christians burning fellow Christians on American soil. Bigotry was rife. Brannan along with his fellow Mormons had to flee the Eastern seaboard to evade the new religious bigots of America. He chartered and financed a sailing ship called the Brooklyn, taking everything he required to build a community from the ground up – books, printing press, farming equipment, tools and firearms – arriving in California on July 31st 1846, a couple of weeks after the state ratified its inclusion in the union.

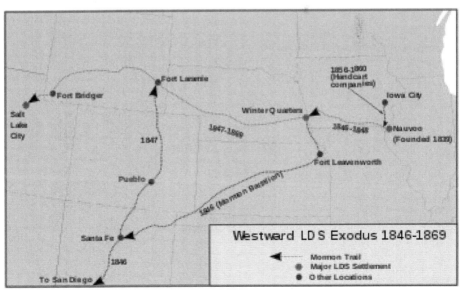

Pioneering leadership

The treacherous journey was over 20,000 miles, circumnavigating the American continent, because a land route hadn't been effectively established yet. Sam Brannan, now the leader of a Mormon colony of 238 followers, dragged them around Cape Horn and back up above the equator. They were at sea for five months and 27 days. Many didn't make it; six children, four adults and one crew member died en route. Sam Brannan was young and strong and came through unscathed. What he didn't know was that he was destined to make the sea route redundant.

When he arrived he immediately launched a publication called the *California Star*. The paper became known later as *The Alta Californian*.

Alta California (or Upper California) was formed in 1804 as part of the Spanish colony of New Spain, one of the territories of the independent United Mexican States following its War of Independence. During the Mexican-American War of 1846 John Drake Sloat declared Alta California part of the United States. They officially ceded to the US under the 1848 Treaty of Guadaloupe Hidalgo.

Cashing in on dreams

Brannan had promoted California to his followers as the Mormons' promised land. However, Salt Lake City emerged as the preferred Mormon state and it remains so to this day. During the return leg of a journey from Salt Lake City Brannan and his fellow Mormons stopped over at Fort Sutter, California. A Swiss/German man called John Sutter, a great social visionary, owned the fort there. He was a man with a plan – to create a rural utopia in the congenial climate of California. But one of Sutter's workers, James W Marshall, changed all that: in early 1848, he found gold on Sutter's land, which would lead to the Great Gold Rush of 1849. Stephen Cooper, who had recently sold Brannan a horse, made $980 ($25,000) in three days. It was Brannan who turned him on to the opportunity. Brannan was interested in gold too, but he had no intention of digging it out of the ground.

John Sutter knew if gold was known to be in the region his dream was over. He sought to keep the whole thing quiet and buy up as much land as possible that encompassed where the gold was thought to be. But the find was leaked. When Brannan heard of the discovery, and Sutter's attempt to keep the whole thing under his hat, he bought every shovel, pan, sieve and wheelbarrow he could find from far and wide. Then, on May 12th 1848, he put a few nuggets of gold in a bottle, and walked down the main street waving it and screaming at the top of his voice: "Gold! Gold! Gold from the American River!"

During June 1848 the *California Star* wrote of towns emptying as their inhabitants rushed to the gold fields. Four days later, the *Star* ceased publication when its staff joined the rush. Such was the euphoria of the Great Gold Rush.

The get-rich-quick brigade leapt on the bandwagon and pandemonium broke out. The price of mining supplies leapt tenfold. Brannan cornered the market in speculator's supplies and sold everything a speculator could ever need, becoming a millionaire overnight. Brannan found mining people's pockets far more dependable and milked the prospectors for all their worth. He knew the gold would not last as long as the dream of finding it. Col. Richard Barnes Mason, who was appointed military commander in California, wrote of Sam Brannan: "The principal store at Sutter's fort is that of Brannan and Co., he had received in payment for goods \$36,000 (\$700,000) worth of this gold from the 1st of May to the 10th of July."

Ships' crews deserted, and some cities witnessed a major drop in population as men rushed to the California hills via his store. Brannan's outlet at Sutter's Fort began taking in \$150,000 (\$3 million) a month. He made another fortune by selling land in San Francisco. He had acquired the land earlier, and now sold it to the new arrivals, attracted by news of gold finds reported in his paper. The cities emptied; the goldfields and Brannan's tills filled up. He utilised his publishing company to exaggerate the gold discovery in the region, reporting that speculators were becoming millionaires in a matter of months and some in weeks. Brannan exaggerated their success stories wildly, and it led to delirium.

Brannan also collected a tithe from his own followers' gold finds to pay for various enterprises. Brigham Young (the new Mormon leader) heard about this and sent a man along to collect God's share. Brannan refused to pay unless God himself issued a receipt. He was eventually excommunicated in 1849.

Brannan had become disillusioned by the church, feeling they had abandoned him earlier when he and the colony were in desperate need. He wrote in a letter: "Within the last year I have Cleard over a Hundred Thousand Dollars and hope to [keep] This from the authorities of the Church. They have forsaken me. I Have Been Here three years and over and Received No acount only What i traveled Clear to the Salt Lake after. No one Ever thought Enough of Me During my Long Stay hear to Wright to Me and in fact i am unable to See What i Was Sent here for unless it Was to Get me out of the Way Suposing it Being a Spanish Country i Would Be Kiled… When the Lord finds out I have Got a Little Money He will Begin to feel after me. I would not have you think that I am making Light of My Creator, for i Still Entertain the Same feelings towards him that I Ever Did and He Has my prayers for Support and Health & Strength" [Sic].

NEXT TIME WHEN I PREACH ON TITHING, DON'T SING 'JESUS PAID IT ALL' AS OUR INVITATIONAL HYMN

A passion for adventure

The entrepreneur was now well on his way to becoming the richest man in California, but money did not satisfy Brannan's passion for adventure, risk and drama. Perhaps suffering delusions of grandeur, he got involved in the political chaos in the Mexican provinces. He also went exploring the wilderness of the Californian interior.

Brannan knew that for the region to continue to be prosperous it needed law and order. The absence of credible law enforcers attracted reprobates such as a group called the Regulators or, as they called themselves, the San Francisco Society of Regulators. Made up of professional killers and criminals, as well as former Mexican-American War veterans, they were popularly known in the press as the Hounds. This group had a notion to bring their own brand of law and order to Brannan's hometown, as well as the goldfields.

The "Hounds" Attacking Little Chile

There were already laws against black people speculating for gold (even though slavery was unconstitutional in California) but the Hounds wanted to go one step further. Their idea was to drive all 'foreigners' from the recently discovered gold fields. In their view, foreigners (including natives and Mexicans) were unworthy of speculating for American gold. The Regulators murdered, maimed and raped these groups wholesale. They virtually took over the town, preying on the townspeople with impunity and creating havoc.

Brannan decided to protect his investments, which were literally the townsfolk and their property. He formed what were effectively vigilante committees made up of townspeople with business interests. These vigilantes wore suits, kept minutes, and above all, 'stretched necks'. He was able to control the Regulators by hanging a few of them after they had massacred some Chileans. Brannan didn't escape from this war unscathed: he managed to get himself shot eight times in one altercation after everyone had had a bit too much to drink.

Developing California

Brannan continued to buy and develop land in California throughout the 1850s, strengthening his political position as he did so. He bought 3,000 acres of land in Napa Valley, hired Japanese gardeners to tend the land and bought 800 horses. He also sank a fortune into the town of Calistoga, populating it and building a railway line to connect it. He created a Hot Springs resort there with a grand hotel as its centrepiece. The resort eventually opened in 1863, complete with vacation cottages, a mansion, a bandstand, a horseracing track and stables, a distillery, pools, cabanas, and a roller-skating rink. Wide circular avenues trellised the 2,000-acre estate.

In 1853 Brannan was elected to the California State Senate and, by 1856, the entrepreneur owned one-fifth of the entire city of San Francisco and Sacramento, earning between $250,000 ($5 million) and $500,000 ($10 million) per year. On October 31st 1857 Sam Brannan opened a new bank, the New San Francisco Bank. The idea was to create a repository for all the money and gold being collected. Once again, he serviced the gold rush rather than participate in it. Much of the bank's stock was to be invested in land.

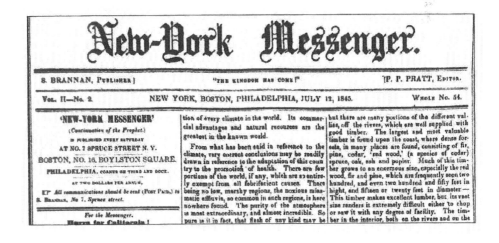

SAMUEL BRANNAN'S BANK.

DEPOSITS SECURED BY

FOUR HUNDRED AND FIFTY THOUSAND DOLLARS

OF PRODUCTIVE REAL ESTATE,

IN TRUST FOR THEIR REDEMPTION.

TRUSTEES:

VOLNEY E. HOWARD,   SAMUEL J. HENSLEY,   ELI COOK.

THE UNDERSIGNED has established in the City of San Francisco a BANK, under the above name, style and title. The object is to furnish a safe place of deposit to all classes of the community, especially to FARMERS, MINERS and MECHANICS. For the accomplishment of this object there has been conveyed to

COMPETENT AND RELIABLE TRUSTEES.

PRODUCTIVE REAL ESTATE,

AMOUNTING TO NOT LESS THAN

Four Hundred and Fifty Thousand Dollars.

Certificates of Deposit will be issued for any amount, from Five Dollars upwards, but no Certificate will be issued bearing interest for a less sum than One Hundred Dollars, nor for a shorter time than six months. The interest paid upon these Certificates will be at the rate of three per cent. per annum.

All Moneys Loaned will be upon First Class Securities,

but borrowers will be required to pay all the expenses of searching titles, drawing mortgages and other papers; the right reserved to the Bank to say who shall search the titles, draw the papers, and the manner in which they shall be drawn.

GOLD DUST will be received and deposited at the United States Mint, or any Assay Office, for assay, and the depositors of the same charged the usual market rates for so doing.

FOREIGN AND DOMESTIC EXCHANGE purchased and forwarded, charging usual commissions in each cases; but no Exchange will be forwarded, without funds or ample satisfactory security in hand.

THE BANK IS SITUATED IN THE

CITY OF SAN FRANCISCO,

On the Northeast Corner of MONTGOMERY and CALIFORNIA STREETS,

And will be open daily, (Sundays and Holidays excepted,) from 9 A. M. until 4 P. M.; on every Saturday evening from 7 to 9 o'clock, and on the night previous to the sailing of the steamers from 7 o'clock until 11 P. M.

SAMUEL BRANNAN.

SAN FRANCISCO, October 31st, 1857.

American history records one of the greatest engineering and entrepreneurial feats of the 19th Century as the construction of the Transcontinental Rail Road. It linked the prosperous East with the developing West. The men who achieved it were known as the four shopkeepers. Former pushcart salesman and now railroad builder Theodore Judah signed up miners' supplies shop owners Collis Huntington and Mark Hopkins, dry goods seller Charles Crocker and miners' general store owner Leland Stanford. All came out to California in search of gold and struck out. Collectively they became worth billions – but the largest shareholder in the Transcontinental Railroad venture was Sam Brannan.

Brought down by alcohol

Brannan was easily the richest man in California – a region spawning millionaires by the week – but, in 1868, his fortunes changed. He had just purchased 160,000 acres of Los Angeles County, California, when his wife sued for a divorce. Suddenly, half of Brannan's wealth was due to be paid to his ex – *in cash*. Since much of his wealth was in the form of land he was forced to sell a significant amount of it. He compounded his misfortune by aiding the Mexicans with money and supplies in their struggle against Emperor Maximilian, ending up on the losing side. After these setbacks Brannan hit the bottle with a vengeance. People began taking advantage of his alcoholism (including his family). As a result, he eventually lost all his cash. Brannan borrowed against what capital he had left and lost that too.

Brannan never really recovered from this setback. In 1879, sickly and partially paralysed, he got married again, to a Mexican. The Mexican government awarded Brannan $50,000 ($1 million) for his past assistance in protecting its people against the Regulators.

The award gained Brannan a financial reprieve, giving him one last hope. He paid off his creditors, stopped drinking and was able to receive treatment for his paralysis. The following year Brannan received a grant of lands in the Sonora colonisation from the Mexican Government. The scheme didn't take off.

By 1887 68 year-old Brannan was selling pencils door to door trying to raise cash for the trip back to San Francisco. The newspapers featured the old lion returning to his former territorial hunting ground. He was described as "old, gray, broken in strength, able only to get about with the aid of a cane. The old keenness of the eye alone shows that his spirit has survived the decay of his body."

Brannan was struck by inflammation of the bowels and was so poor he couldn't pay for treatment. He was dead within a fortnight.

Sam Brannan died broke on a small fruit farm outside San Diego on May 14th 1889. In his will he left each of his three children one dollar, stating: "I gave their mother at the time of my divorce from her, a large fortune of over one-half millions of dollars and she took charge of the children and alienated them from me and since I learned that she squandered it away in gambling and mining stocks which I am sorry to hear."

Brannan's children left his body in the morgue for nine months until his brother-in-law claimed it and brought it back to be buried at Mt. Hope Cemetery in San Diego, California.

MARY ELLEN PLEASANT (1814 – 1904)

The story of 19th Century America is a narrative of freedom, ambition and the Gold Rush. However, there are untold stories, obscured from view by the brilliance of American patriarchs. Scratch slightly below the surface and you'll find tales of women, whose accomplishments ran ahead of society's willingness to acknowledge them. The achievements of Mary Ellen Pleasant were unknown not only because she was a woman but also because she was a slave. This was a woman who would rise from her background of slavery to amass a multi-million dollar fortune – all whilst on the run as a fugitive.

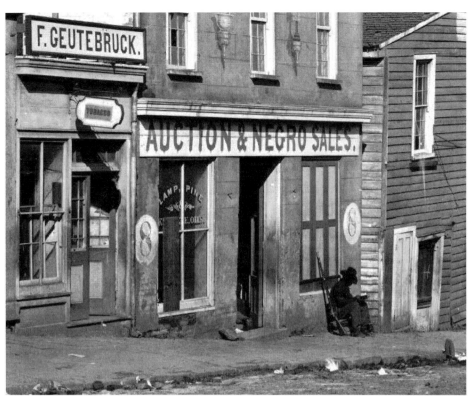

Free African labour

Whilst America was being flooded with European immigrants, another alien population was landing in huge numbers: slaves. Imported from Africa, they were brought to America to provide free labour to white European settlers.

The enslavement of Africans in the West was distinct from all other systems of bondage throughout history. The West's institutionalised 'chattel slavery' system rendered the person non-human by law, merely an asset, like a cart or cow. Family kinship was methodically broken up, and rape was rife along with indoctrinated self-degradation. Lighter-skinned captives were set against the darker-skinned slaves and American-born slaves set against African-born slaves in a pecking order of inferiority. The plight of a female slave was utter misery from birth to death – some even suffocated their children at birth to avoid a life of suffering.

The system was designed to remove hope and gain total submission, like breaking a horse. But now and then a captive rebelled. Mary Ellen Pleasant, born half a century before slavery was abolished in 1863, simply tore it up the script and went after her would-be captors, turning predators into prey. It was this unbreakable spirit that would drive her to net a fortune worth $30 million ($600 million) at its peak.

She started life without a surname. Her birth was the result of the illegal extra-curricular activity of John H. Pleasants, the son of the Virginia state governor, and her mother, who was a Voodoo priestess; a descendant of the 'Voodoo Queens' of Santo Domingo; and above all – a slave.

At the age of nine, Mary Ellen was light enough to pass for white or "crossover" as it was colloquially termed. She was also as cute as a button, attracting another planter who was so taken by her that he bought the enchanting little girl, with a view to freeing her later. He had Mary educated at New Orleans Ursaline Convent and then sent her to work for friend, Louis Alexander Williams, a merchant in Cincinnati.

REBECCA, an Emancipated Slave, from New Orleans.

Photographed by KIMBALL, 477 Broadway. N.Y.

Entered according to Act of Congress, in the year 1863 by GEO. H. HANKS, in the Clerk's Office of the U. S. for the Sou. Dist. of N.Y.

Williams did not pay for the work she did, but offered her freedom if she worked for him over a specified period.

However, his finances were a mess and he grew jealous of Mary Ellen being at the centre of his wife's great affection. So, he cashed Mary in. The transaction landed her back into slavery but this time as a nine-year indentured servant with an old lady, called Grandma Hussey, an abolitionist Quaker.

As Mary Ellen was being passed around, her precocious mind soaked up each new experience and the different philosophies of her contrasting and multiple owners. She had a spell at business management in the Hussey general store. Because she couldn't read or write Mary Ellen learned to memorise all that went on during a day's trading. At the end of an evening Grandma would log every reported item sold, not doubting for a moment Mary Ellen's accuracy and integrity. The mnemonic exercise simply accelerated the young girl's already quite remarkable mind.

At the age of eleven, the maturing young lady was told not to let on about being black. Skin colour and complexion politics determined survival and life chances, and the Husseys wanted the best for her. They had fallen under Mary Ellen's spell (she had the same effect on anybody who spent time in her company). They loved her and she loved them. As she grew, the well-rounded young lady learned a range of skills including the art of enterprise and tailoring. She also became a church soloist in Boston, all thanks to the Quaker family.

The young adult Mary Ellen was a southern belle, a lady with a cultured demeanour. Yet the rose had thorns. In spite of being bought and sold several times, she was her own woman in her mind. Mary Ellen learned early on how to get the measure of people and weigh them up for her own purposes, just as her buyers had done with her, but she had charm and possessed the brilliance of wit.

Despite her upbringing and light hue she had a fierce allegiance to her own race and the plight of the slaves she'd left behind. She spurned the opportunity to go north to Canada or south to Latin America and the Caribbean to enjoy unfettered freedom masquerading as white. Instead, she chose to use her energising sense of injustice to serve the purpose of fighting the battle for freedom.

Marrying James Bond

After leaving the Husseys she met and married a well-to-do Bostonian called James W. Smith, the son of a black mother and a white father. He was an entrepreneur, contractor and merchant who had inherited a plantation from his father. The estate was staffed with a black workforce, all of whom had been liberated from slavery by Smith.

He, like his wife, could pass for white. The illustrious Mr. and Mrs. Smith worked as spies for the famous William Lloyd Garrison's abolitionist movement. Garrison was the publisher of *The Liberator*, founder of the American Anti-Slavery Society and the Underground Railroad. Garrison didn't just believe slaves should be free, he also believed they had a right to full equality.

James Smith operated as a 'slave stealer'. His 'camouflage' allowed him to move in and out of a plantation without suspicion. He would liberate slaves from plantations and bring them back to his own estate. There they'd become part of his financial cooperative. Mary Ellen helped him run the operation, which entailed transporting black captives out of slave-holding territories to free states and countries like Canada or Mexico.

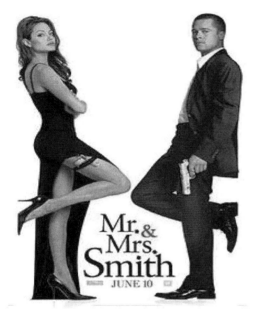

Unfortunately, James died suddenly, leaving Mary Ellen alone but wealthy. She inherited the money earmarked for the freeing and transporting of slaves, some $45,000 ($1 million). Once again, she turned her back on the opportunity of an undemanding life for herself by continuing the struggle against ignominy of slavery.

Being a single woman drew unnecessary attention to herself, so she soon married a man called James Pleasance. She once said that he loved her money as much as he loved her. Mary continued her mission to free as many black captives as possible. Operating like the Scarlet Pimpernel, she disguised herself before moving stealthily onto plantations in a wagon, snatching up slaves before making her getaway. It was an expensive operation, funded with her money. Danger was a close and familiar escort.

During 1850, slave-catchers were known to be closing in on her, and she was forced to hide out with Pleasance's family down in New Orleans. Mary Ellen had always been intrigued by her Voodoo past. New Orleans presented her with an opportunity to become reacquainted with it. Whilst there she spent time studying with Queen Marie LaVeaux, a Voodoo high priestess. The LaVeaux method instructed her in the art of leveraging information (knowledge being power).

Fugitive lost in San Francisco

A scout suggested that Californian Gold Rush country would be a good place for a fugitive to get lost. A bedraggled Mary Ellen arrived in San Francisco on April 7th 1852, a year before Levi Strauss (inventor of Levi Jeans) arrived from Germany and six years after Sam Brannan settled in the state. She arrived with $15,000 ($210,000) in gold coins. In the Gold Rush town there was almost one murder a day; 7000 drinking dens for 40,000 souls; and a 6:1 male-to-female population ratio.

Mary Ellen had to avoid the vigilantes. She wasn't safe in the city but neither was she safe outside it. The ingenious fugitive slave created two identities: Mrs. Ellen Smith, a white boarding-house cook; and Mrs. Pleasant, an entrepreneur and black abolitionist. She had to dance without anyone hearing her steps. Stealth was her middle name. She immediately took full advantage of opportunities to lend money to the miners and other business-folk at a rate of ten per cent interest, becoming a de facto banker.

Mary's strategy was to harvest commercially sensitive information in the booming town of San Francisco. To this end she acquired jobs in the houses and the exclusive haunts of movers and shakers. Mary Ellen possessed a powerful manipulative charm, underpinned by emotional intelligence and beauty. She could charm the birds out of the trees. The birds in this case included the personal secrets of the rich and famous.

She focused on men of power and their finances, influence, wives and mistresses, attacking her prey where they were most vulnerable. She secured contacts running exclusive men's eating establishments, starting with the Case and Heiser club. Case and Heiser were commission agents. There the charmer met most of the city founders as she prepared sumptuous meals for them. Whilst running the club she manoeuvred herself into a position to receive titbits of financial gossip. Additionally, black servants working for her were systematically stationed in locations where they could overhear and gather commercially sensitive information. Deals were casually tossed around the dining tables where she served, listened and learned. She's quoted as saying: "My custom was to deposit silver and draw out gold, by which means I was able to turn my money over rapidly."

Mary used her influence to deploy her freed slaves in the houses of elite families and bachelors. Black people were so unacknowledged that white people spoke openly and unguardedly about their most intimate secrets in front of them as they would in front of the household dog.

Stories of infidelity and illegitimate black children spawned by well-to-do white men were gleaned and leveraged. This phenomenon improved the feed and distribution of commercially sensitive and private information to Mary Ellen. The escapees got jobs; she got the information; it was leveraged in exchange for investment opportunities; money was made; and in turn more slaves were freed – virtuous circle.

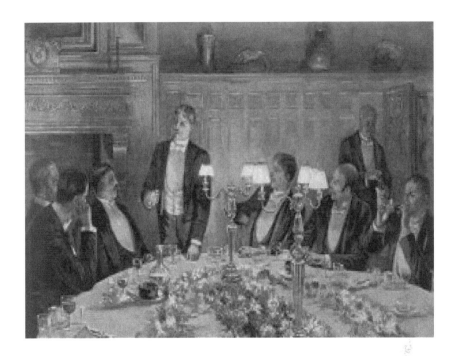

Insider information

Having information on opportunities for investment is one thing – implementation was another. Mary circumvented the racial barriers to entry by snaring a young white clerk, Thomas Bell, at the Bank of California. The Bank of California was owned by William Ralston, who established it as the second richest in America. Mary Ellen gave Tom the instructions and guidance; he did the deals. They both grew rich. The more money she made the more slaves she freed.

Mary Ellen vacuumed the town for secrets, becoming the J. Edgar Hoover of San Francisco. No one wanted to take her on. Being her friend was a safer course of action. The omniscient, bewitching sorceress had San Francisco locked down.

Mary Ellen was very selective about her investments. She created a diverse investment portfolio including mines, transport, farming and ranching. She made significant investments as a property developer and designed the house she and her business partner Tom Bell lived in along with Mrs. Bell, who was thought to be necessary for appearances.

The booming laundry sector was one example of her strategic investment method. It was ideal. The labour-intensive service provided jobs for escapees, who gathered information from inside the homes of the rich and famous, as well as killers and criminals. Throughout the 1850s (the same period in which Sam Brannan was getting rich) she set about buying up laundrettes and starting up new ones in strategic positions such as servicing the Pacific mail steamers. The former slaves would work at very competitive rates. Forty-five percent of women in San Francisco worked as laundresses until desperate and starving Chinese and European immigrants destroyed profit margins. The pressure on profits, and her fugitive status, caused Mary Ellen to head back East in 1858. Staying in one place for too long could be disastrous. Nevertheless, it was a triumphant return. She and Tom Bell had become multi-millionaires.

John Brown's financier

Another reason Mary Ellen moved East was to help her former brother-in-law gain release from slavery and to partner up with the legendary abolitionist John Brown in the battle against pro-slavery militias and government-backed forces. Fatalities on both sides were high, including Brown's own two sons. Mary Ellen supplied Brown with guns and money. She also provided the destination for slaves to escape to – land she owned in Canada.

A supporter of John Brown and infiltrated the prison. Brown spurned the opportunity to be freed, preferring to be hung as a martyr to the cause he fought for. In 1859, John Brown was hung for treason – four years before President Abraham Lincoln outlawed slavery in the US, on January 1st 1863. Now free from the threat of re-enslavement, Mary Ellen Pleasant declared her black identity. Nevertheless, she was now being hunted, charged with treason for consorting with John Brown, as well as being in breach of the law for taking slaves from states that were not at war with the union. Despite this she remained free. Change was upon America and universal freedom (if not equality) swept through the land like a blizzard.

Before Rosa Parks

In 1868, a century before Rosa Parks refused to give up a seat for a white passenger, Mary Ellen orchestrated court battles against Omnibus Railroad Company and North Beach and Mission Railroad to test the right for black people to ride the San Francisco trolleys, setting a precedent in the California Supreme Court. She dropped the charges against Omnibus Railroad after they capitulated and agreed to allow black people to use their service. Mary also won her case against North Beach and Mission Railroad. Her precedent in the California Supreme Court was used to win a Civil Rights case as late as 1982. She was awarded $500 ($7,000).

To Mary Ellen the money was a drop in the ocean. She funded a paternity case on behalf of a poor white woman against a wealthy and popular Nevada senator, William Sharon. Pleasant lost the case and $63,000 ($1,240 million) in the process. An 1870 census listed her as having property worth $30,000 ($500,000). Her boarding house had servants in her employ catering to wealthy boarders.

In 1874 The Cleveland Gazette wrote an article about her, saying: "She has an income from eight houses in San Francisco, a ranch near San Mateo, and $100,000 ($1,700 million) in government bonds."

Having lived to see the end of slavery in the US, Mary Ellen turned her talents and riches to helping plaintiffs in human rights abuses. She endowed organisations such as the African Methodist Episcopal (AME), Black Masonic lodge, AME Zion churches and Black Baptist with financial support. Her approach to religion was pragmatic: "I am a Catholic, but one church was the same as another to me," she said. Much of what this lioness accumulated was spent on freeing slaves, setting up homes for destitute black women, and on civil rights cases. The San Francisco Examiner said of Mary Ellen: "Her deeds of charity are as numerous as the grey hairs on her proud old head."

Precursor to the civil rights struggle

Mary Ellen Pleasant was a 'walking razor': tall, lean and erect. She was often seen moving among the stalls of the old Sutter Street market in her black straw bonnet, gold hoop earrings, and spotless scarf fastened with a brooch. She was revered and feared by blacks and whites, men and women alike. The press accused her of every heinous act, including eating children. She was reputed to be the wickedest woman in San Francisco by white folk. But she was also known as 'Black City Hall', such was her political power and reputation in the metropolis.

Bradley & Rulofson, S. F., Cal.

Mary Ellen amassed a fortune worth $30 million ($600 million) much of which was shared with her secret partner, Tom Bell. On January 4th 1904 the irrepressible entrepreneur extraordinaire died aged 89. She became a legend, a ghost story shared among San Franciscans and written about in local newspapers for decades after her death. She was a one-off, a wonder woman and a truly great entrepreneur.

P. T. BARNUM (1810 – 1891)

"Let's get this show on the road"

Entertainment required

The British attack on America's wallet, via taxation legislation, caused the American Revolutionary War (1775-1783). As victorious post-war America settled down, the country continued to fill up with immigrants in search of opportunities and a better way of life.

As the cities began to prosper, their residents found themselves with disposable income and leisure time. The masses needed to be entertained as they sought to offset the drudgery and boredom of city work. The scene was set for the entrance of one of the most cunning entrepreneurs to have lived, a man who would make billions simply by amusing people.

His name was Phineas Taylor Barnum, and he was born in the small Connecticut community of Bethel, to Irena Taylor and Philo F. Barnum. The name Phineas Taylor was derived from his maternal grandfather, a member of one of the oldest settler families in New England. His father, Philo, was the son of Ephraim Barnum, a revolutionary war veteran. Philo worked in various types of businesses as a tailor, a farmer, a store manager and landlord of the local pub.

Young P. T. Barnum was a smart kid, the oldest of five siblings and a precocious mathematician. His entrepreneurial career kicked off very early, with the sale of his own homemade delicacies. He got a job in a 'buy or barter' grocery store where the general idea appeared to be to get one over on the other guy. He would later say: "I was born in an atmosphere of merriment" and "I believe in a cheerful Christianity...."

Barnum grew up in a community where it was customary for people to play tricks on each other and indulge in general tomfoolery. "I was always ready to concoct fun, or lay plans for moneymaking, but hard work was decidedly not in my line." At the age of 12 he touted lottery tickets, was good at it and knew it. Barnum lost his father just three years later. Poor, and now having to make his own way in life, he earned money around town drumming up extra business for proprietors and negotiating a cut of the sales.

The pleasure of amusement

As a young adult, Barnum travelled in pursuit of opportunity. In New York he invested in a grocery store and sold lottery tickets. In Danbury, Connecticut, Barnum cut out the middle-man and ran his own lottery.

In 1829, aged 19, Barnum wed Charity Hallett, a dedicated abolitionist and Universalist. The marriage would last 40 years and produce four children. Having a wife depend on him simply added to his need to succeed. He would often sniff out opportunities by reading the advertising pages of the newspapers first thing in the morning. Barnum came to one definite conclusion: a universal truth – everyone loves to be amused.

Between 1831 and 1834 Barnum edited his own paper in Danbury, the *Herald of Freedom*, which reflected his Universalist religious ideas and ideals. He ended up in prison for 60 days, convicted of libel after accusing a deacon of usury. The public loved the whole episode. On his release 60 days later, Barnum was met at the prison gates and given a fanfare release, a band, six-horse carriage and a parade through the town. At the age of 24 he moved back to the great metropolis of New York.

One morning in July 1835 Barnum's friend Coley Bartram informed him of an opportunity to buy an exhibit called The Wonderful Negress. He had spotted the advert in the Pennsylvania Inquirer, of July 15th 1835: "CURIOSITY. ...one of the greatest natural curiosities ever witnessed, viz., Joice Heth, a Negress aged 161 years, who formerly belonged to the father of Gen. Washington." Barnum sold his share of a grocery store that he owned and raised $500 ($11,000). He borrowed another $500 in order to pay $1000 for the sole rights to the 'exhibit' (negotiated down from $3,000).

THE GREATEST
Natural & National
CURIOSITY
IN THE WORLD.

JOICE HETH,

Nurse to Gen. GEORGE WASHINGTON, (the Father of our Country,)
WILL BE SEEN AT

Barnum's Hotel, Bridgeport,

On FRIDAY, and SATURDAY, the 11th, & 12th days
of December, DAY and EVENING.

JOICE, HETH is unquestionably the most astonishing and interesting curiosity in the World! She was the slave of Augustine Washington, (the father of Gen. Washington,) and was the first person who put clothes on the unconscious infant, who, in after days, led our heroic fathers on to glory, to victory, and freedom. To use her own language when speaking of the illustrious Father of her Country, "she raised him." JOICE HETH was born in the year 1674, and has, consequently, now arrived at the astonishing

AGE OF 161 YEARS.

The Wonderful Negress was Barnum's ticket to stardom. At 25 years old he'd found his calling in life. People would buy tickets to stare at the old paralysed black woman he now owned. She made him $1,500 ($33,000) a week. The great entrepreneur had a distinctive ability to manipulate crowds. When his attendance started to falter he placed an ad stating the Negress was a hoax and was simply a clockwork dummy! This drew a new crowd, and brought the old crowd back to check for themselves whether his exhibit *was* a fraud or not. All paid to take a closer look and paid Barnum for the privilege of doing so. He toured America with the show, but business was tough and money still in short supply.

The American Museum

In 1841, Barnum bought John Scudder's 'American Museum' on Broadway, New York City, (it would burn down on July 13 1865) and made it the most popular entertainment venue in the country. Barnum did not actually have any money to make the purchase, but he had a strategy. His friend asked him how he would pay for the business Barnum replied: "[with] Brass …for silver and gold I have none." Barnum mortgaged himself to the building's owner: instead of cash he offered fine references, an indomitable spirit of success, and a "valuable and sentimental" piece of land known as Ivy Island (bequeathed to him by his grandfather and described by Barnum as "worthless").

The American Museum featured Feejee the mermaid and the original bearded woman. Barnum exhibited 500,000 natural and artificial curiosities from every corner of the globe. One of his tricks was to put up a sign saying 'This way to the Egress'. 'Egress, another word for exit, is similar to the word "Negress" – his main draw. Many visitors inadvertently left the venue in search of the Negress, and had to pay to re-enter.

Barnum's nemesis Charles Peale had a great routine of a girl being hypnotised on stage, so Barnum put on a similar show of his own. His little girl could act as though she'd been hypnotised very convincingly. When she appeared to be under, Barnum would hold a glinting blade up to the crowd whilst announcing to the audience that to prove the stunt he would cut off one of the girl's fingers with the knife. On hearing this, the little girl would leap up and runoff the stage. The crowd would roar with laughter. Soon no one took Peale's hypnotism seriously and his hypnotising routine waned.

Barnum launched a new exhibit in 1842 – Charles Sherwood. The exhibit was better known to the world as General Tom Thumb. Barnum signed him up and included him in his newly founded circus. The relationship would last 40 years. Together they toured the capitals of Europe, entertaining kings, queens and the general public. In 1844 they entertained Queen Victoria and she was *very* amused. Barnum even tried to buy Shakespeare's birthplace and hire the Zulu leader who had recently routed the British in South Africa.

In 1850, Barnum signed Jenny Lind, the Diana Ross of her time. She did a 95-concert tour for the entrepreneur, making him an absolute fortune. He paid her $176,675.09 ($4.14 million). As much as $650 ($13,000) was paid at auction for a single admission ticket to one of her concerts. By then Barnum had already built a countryseat named Iranistan. One would expect the home of a showman to be very impressive. It was, and it did the trick. Jenny Lind told him; "Do you know, Mr. Barnum, that if you had not built Iranistan I should never have come to America for you? ... I said to myself a gentleman who has been so successful in his business as to be able to build and reside in such a palace cannot be a mere adventurer."

IRANISTAN: THE RESIDENCE OF HON. P. T. BARNUM IN 1848.

Ever the trickster

In 1866 P. T. Barnum played a grand hoax on George Hull, a competitor. Hull, an archaeologist and palaeontologist, took note of the rugged terrain of Fort Dodge, Iowa. The gypsum quarry there revealed some out of the ordinary features similar to the vascular system of the human anatomy. Years earlier eccentric preachers had been preaching that giant men once roamed the earth. Hull thought Joe Public would go for a story of "a local land once inhabited by giants." So, he got hold of a massive lump of gypsum and had it carved depicting a giant man who appeared to have died in a state of writhing agony. Hull shipped the carving to Newell, his cousin in New York, who followed Hull's instruction to bury it near his house.

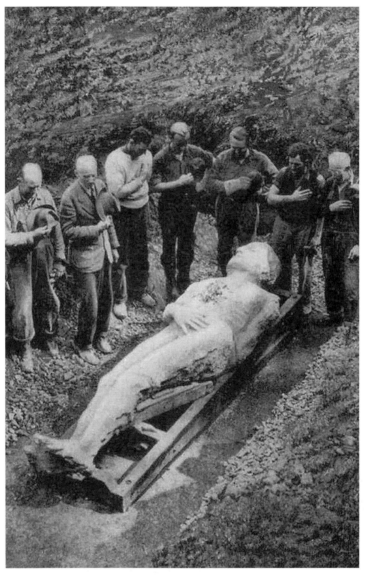

The following year Newell got some builders to start work on the dwelling. They needed to dig close to the house and eventually discovered the colossus. The public went bananas. Tents went up and the brothers started charging the naïve public to view the exhibit. The story went national and a Syracuse syndicate was sold a two-thirds stake in the venture. They 'exhumed' the giant, moving him to an exhibition hall where the public could get better access and the promoters could up the price to a dollar a head. At times there were more than 3,000 people attending. The giant was the biggest thing on exhibit in the US. Barnum was not prepared to be upstaged and offered $50,000 ($650,000) for it but was turned down.

Barnum carved his own giant, announcing that he had bought the original from the syndicate and they were now displaying a fake. The syndicate sued. In court the original hoaxer,

George Hull, admitted he had created the *original* fake, and promptly lost the case. The judge pointed out that he could not uphold a case of a *fake* fake!

P. T. Barnum marketed his show as the 'The Greatest Show on Earth'. In 1880 he merged with competitor James A. Bailey. During 1882 P. T. Barnum purchased Jumbo the elephant from London Zoo for $10,000 ($176,000). The elephant had been captured from Central Africa as a calf and grew to a hefty seven tons and eleven and a half feet tall. Jumbo became a popular and much-loved attraction, capturing the imagination of the public. It is from this famous elephant's name we get the term 'jumbo', meaning very large. The name became even more famous when Walt Disney used it for his cartoon character. The elephant died in 1881 after being struck by a train, and America went into mourning. Over 3,000 people attended the Jumbo's funeral.

No business like show business

Part of P. T. Barnum's contribution to popular culture came through his catchy language. He gave us terms such as 'grandstanding'; 'let's get this show on the road'; 'come rain or shine'; 'the greatest show on earth'; and 'throw your hat in the ring'. The last term was coined when a local politician actually threw his hat into Barnum's circus ring to declare his candidacy for political election.

Barnum's savvy not only provided him with a fortune – he also had a successful career as a politician, serving several terms as a Connecticut state legislator. In his shows he would cast blacked-up characters but use them to satirise stereotypes about black people. He is credited as casting the deciding vote in the senate for the abolition of slavery. Not only did he want slavery to end, he was also in a tiny minority that "wish[ed] to see [the vote] extended to every educated moral man within our State, without regard to color." Barnum wrote several books, including *The Humbugs [Hype] of the World* (1865), *Struggles and Triumphs* (1869), and *The Art of Money-Getting* (1880). He wanted to read his own obituary, because the press always said nice things about the dead. He was accommodated when a special issue of The New York Sun actually carried the headline "Great And Only Barnum – He Wanted To Read His Obituary – Here It Is."

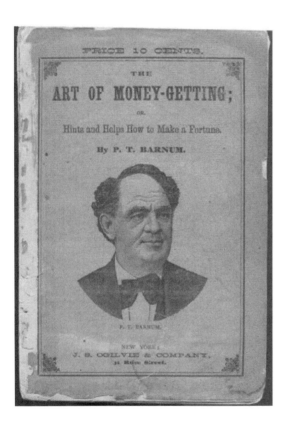

Barnum died at the height of his fame and popularity – in fact, shortly before his peaceful death on April 7th 1891, he asked what the box office receipts for the day were. By the time he died, Barnum was paying taxes on $1 million ($20 million) worth of property. The circus was valued at circa $400,000 (£9,600,000) and Barnum's net worth was $10 million ($200 million). He gave away the equivalent of millions to various charities. A statue was raised in his honour two years after his death at Seaside Park. Barnum had previously donated the land from his assets for the creation of the park in 1865. Today, Barnum's circus operates in association with Ringling Brothers.

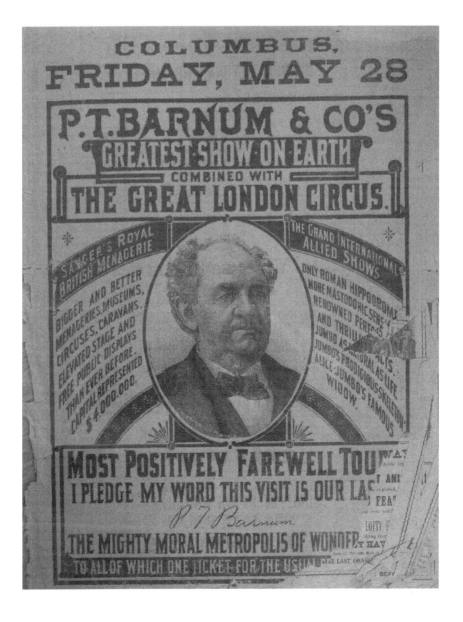

ANDREW CARNEGIE (1834 – 1919)

"The price which society pays for the law of competition…is great, but the advantages of this law are also greater still than its cost…we cannot evade it, no substitutes for it have been found and while the law may be sometimes hard for the individual, it is best for the race, because it ensures the survival of the fittest in every department"

Universal principals of success

Industrialisation put many Europeans out of traditional work, and famine and oppression accelerated the mass exodus from Europe to the New World. America meanwhile was hastily clearing land and building an infrastructure, whilst giving away land via the Homestead Act of 1862. Stories of great opportunities flowed into Europe as loved ones wrote home from the 'promised land' in the West.

Horatio Alger, Jr., a 19th Century American author, wrote over 130 so-called 'dime novels'. Many of his works were rags-to-riches stories, illustrating how down-and-out boys might be able to achieve wealth and success through hard work, courage, determination, and concern for others. The American Dream had been conceived.

Andrew Carnegie believed anyone, anywhere, anytime could become rich if they believed in and adhered to the principles of persistence, purpose, patience, belief, faith and desire. He used these principles throughout his own life to create one of the most profitable companies of all time. Furthermore, he would eventually give all of his personal wealth away to charity.

The story of this extraordinary man begins with William Carnegie, Andrew's father. William was a Swedenborgian chartist – a thinker. He was the last in a long line of entrepreneurial weavers from the Carnegie family in Dunfermline, Scotland. William had a reputation as a dreamer and employed several weavers in his workshop below the living quarters of the family home.

However, men like Matthew Boulton, Richard Arkwright and Eli Whitney were revolutionising manufacturing, changing the world forever – and weaving was one of the first industries to get the treatment. Change was occurring.

Carnegie's appreciation of culture and learning occurred very early in life. His father was part of a group of men who pooled books amongst themselves and enjoyed discussions about history and culture. Carnegie also had a maternal uncle, George Lauder, who took him on historic tours throughout Scotland with his cousin and life-long friend Dodd. He started school aged eight, around the time his brother Tom was born. At school he was seen as an intelligent model student.

Emigrating to America

In 1848, Carnegie's father joined the European exodus to America. By the time the Carnegie family arrived in America, Andrew had had only five years of formal education in a classroom of up to 180 children. After arriving in America, the family moved in with relatives in Allegheny (later to become part of Pittsburgh), a place of 22,000 inhabitants and only four police officers.

Andrew Carnegie began work at 14 years old as a bobbin boy, dipping the thread spindles in thick, stinking oil in a small, dark and dank room. It was a nightmare, and paid just $1.20 ($30) a week. Carnegie hid his suffering from his parents; his family needed his help and that was all that mattered. His supervisor discovered his superb handwriting and gave him a job as a clerk. But when his clerk chores were complete it was back to the dark, dank room for Carnegie.

Striving for excellence

A certain Mr. Brooks was running a business using a new communication system called the 'telegraph'. He arrived at the home of Tom Hogan, Carnegie's uncle, one evening for their usual game of checkers. Brooks asked Tom if he knew a really sharp young kid, ready to work as a messenger boy. Tom recommended his young nephew.

As a boy and a young man, Andrew Carnegie's modus operandi was to undertake each task he was given as though his very life depended on it. His reliability was legendary. It was because of this that he was presented with so many great opportunities during his youth, from businessmen looking for partners and protégés. Carnegie's father had major doubts about the weight of responsibility about to be placed on his little boy's small shoulders. His normally quiet and acquiescent wife stepped in to ensure her boy did not miss his cue. She knew his potential and knew he was ready.

Carnegie got the job and was now earning $2.50 ($48) per week. He memorised the names and faces of the men he delivered to, efficiently avoiding the need to travel all the way to their homes. Instead he delivered messages where he saw them, in the streets or in their usual haunts, thus getting the job done more efficiently. The older teenagers manned the telegraphs, which intrigued Carnegie. He wanted to learn more about them and weaselled his way into the operating room, pretending to be an apprentice. Carnegie learned to interpret messages by ear instead of reading from the dots on the paper. Only a few kids in the country could do it, and Carnegie could now be counted amongst that elite group. It made him a minor celebrity and earned him a promotion.

Aged 19, Carnegie changed jobs to work as a telegrapher and assistant to Thomas Scott, the superintendent of the Pennsylvania Railroad's Western Division. This represented a major increase in earnings: Carnegie's salary was now $35 ($740) per month. Carnegie didn't miss a step, bringing about changes, keeping the telegraph office open 24/7 and (a new method) burning railroad cars to clear tracks following accidents, keeping trains moving along the line.

Unfortunately, Carnegie's willingness to embrace of change was in stark contrast to his father. William continued flogging a dead horse, weaving and peddling weaved goods far and wide. He fell sick and died after being exposed to bad weather on the cheap seats during a ferry crossing. Carnegie was just 20 years old and now had to support the family single-handed.

Fast learner

Carnegie watched and observed how his boss handled train disasters, assisting on a couple of occasions. Once, during a train disaster, Carnegie couldn't get hold of the boss, so he cleaned up the whole mess on his own. His success in dealing with the crisis set off a chain reaction that would transform his life forever. Carnegie's boss could see that he was a one-off and rewarded him with the option to purchase ten shares in Adams Express.

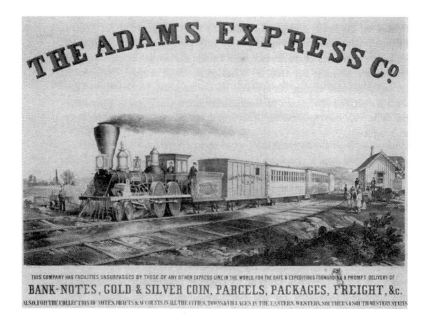

THE ADAMS EXPRESS Co.

THIS COMPANY HAS FACILITIES UNSURPASSED BY THOSE OF ANY OTHER EXPRESS LINE IN THE WORLD, FOR THE SAFE & EXPEDITIOUS FORWARDING & PROMPT DELIVERY OF

BANK-NOTES, GOLD & SILVER COIN, PARCELS, PACKAGES, FREIGHT, &c.

ALSO, FOR THE COLLECTION OF NOTES, DRAFTS & ACCOUNTS IN ALL THE CITIES, TOWNS & VILLAGES IN THE EASTERN, WESTERN, SOUTHERN & SOUTH WESTERN STATES

However, the shares weren't cheap. They were offered to him for $610 ($10,000) – a larger sum of money than Carnegie could afford. The boss loaned him the cash (repayable in six months). The family rushed around trying to raise it for him to pay back. He eventually borrowed the money from a man called George Smith, at 8 percent, using the stock certificates as security. Soon he received the first of his monthly dividend cheques for $10 ($163). This afforded him the money to pay the loan back. The penny dropped – one could make money without sweating. It was a wonderful discovery.

Carnegie's early opportunities all flowed from his boss, who couldn't do without him. As his boss rose through the ranks he brought his young protégé with him. In 1859 Tom Scott became Vice-President and promoted the young cub Carnegie to superintendent, on a salary of $1500 ($27,000) per year. As superintendent, Carnegie met and worked with influential players in the industry, who proved to be very useful to him later on in his career.

Land of opportunity

Carnegie began to grasp the nettle of entrepreneurship, investing in oil exploration land in 1861 (among the first oil fields in the USA). The sleeping cars gave him around $5000 ($100,000) a year, providing the money to pump into other investment opportunities. This is where the $11,000 ($200,000) he put into the Columbia Oil Company came from. In one year it brought in $17,868.67 ($316,000). During 1863 Andrew Carnegie's income had risen to $42,260.67 ($850,000), almost exclusively from investments.

America was building a new country and opportunities for a risk-taker were rife. At 30 years old Andrew Carnegie did not need to work for anyone ever again. Money even allowed him to (legally) buy himself a replacement after being drafted in the 1864 American Civil War. It cost him $850 ($9,000). The purchase of Storey Farm on Oil Creek in Pennsylvania in 1861 cost him (and his old school-friend associates) $40,000 ($430,000) and yielded over $1 million ($11 million) in cash dividends alone, in one year.

In 1862 Carnegie convinced John Piper (an engineer who worked for his old boss at the Pennsylvania Railroad) and Aaron Schiffler (Piper's partner) to form the Piper and Schiffler Company with him, taking 20 percent interest at a cost of $1250 ($20,000). The idea was to focus on building iron bridges for the railroads, which he believed would become a booming sector. He reorganised the company in 1865, renaming it the Keystone Bridge Company. The company was profitable before he became involved, but it began to boom afterwards.

A promise to oneself

When Carnegie turned 30 years old he wrote himself a letter promising to retire at 35 (Napoleon Hill would instruct those wanting to become millionaires to do this). He had a net worth at this time of $400,000 ($5,700,000). But, two years later, Carnegie was busy consolidating the more popular Pullman sleeping cars with his Woodruff Company. He had increased his ownership in Woodruff's sleeping cars since his boss sponsored him.

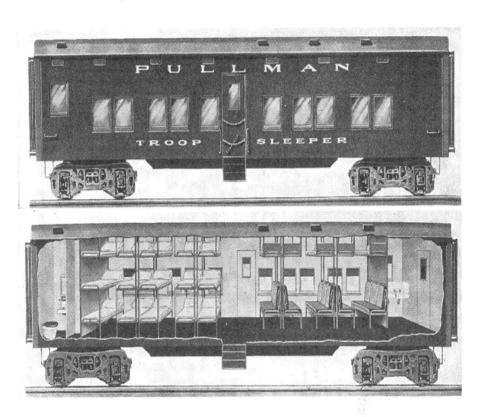

Carnegie met boorish George Pullman at the entrance to a hotel where interested parties were offering bids on providing sleeping cars to Union Pacific. Pullman did not want anything to do with Carnegie. He was an arrogant man and dealing with him was like pulling teeth. Nonetheless he understood the language of "dollars and common-cents." The railroad was big business; the country was big and getting bigger. Trains were the way to cross it. Union Pacific (creating what would become America's first transcontinental railroad) was holding a Dutch auction the following day at the hotel and both Carnegie and Pullman were up against each other. Carnegie described such encounters as 'lion in the path'. They ran into each other on the steps of the entrance to the hotel and Carnegie decided to overlook Pullman's boorishness and pitch him. When Carnegie had finished his soliloquy, he had a new partner in George Pullman, and had removed a powerful competitor, making him an ally and not an adversary. Their combined bid guaranteed them the win. Carnegie didn't consult his partners and had to sell it to them when he got back. This was easy, as all concerned would make a fortune.

In 1872 Carnegie visited the Bessemer steel plants in the birthplace of the Industrial Revolution, the city of Birmingham, in England. He also travelled further North to the home of the world's most famous steel-producing city – Sheffield. Here he witnessed Henry Bessemer's patented process for producing steel.

When he got back to the USA, Carnegie announced to his partners that iron was dead and that he was going into the steel industry. They thought he was crazy. Everything was made from iron: bridges, rails, nails, trains – the lot. The entrepreneur said he'd do it without them, but they all eventually followed their leader.

People power

Andrew Carnegie opened his first steel plant in 1875. The plant was named the Edgar Thomson Works, after the President of the Pennsylvania Railroad (and his former boss). The first order was for 2000 steel rails. Demand was strong, and entrepreneurial tigers such as the up-and-coming James J. Hill bought Carnegie's steel rails to build the Great Northern Railroad Company.

Carnegie had a formula for business: he would develop and invest in the production process, reducing the cost of manufacture, during the good times. This increased efficiency and competitiveness, so when financial panic hit he could withstand the reduced prices. During those times he could also acquire inefficient plants on the cheap. With geniuses like Captain William R. Jones and Charles Schwab working for him, plants would be made super-efficient. Andrew Carnegie's greatest power was to recognise genius and employ it. Jones and Schwab both became legends in their own right. Without them Andrew Carnegie couldn't have achieved what he did during his life.

Andrew Carnegie tried to avoid another 'lion in the path' by the name of Henry Clay Frick. Frick was stinking rich, self-made, abrupt and offhand. He controlled 80 percent of the coke business in Pennsylvania and the surrounding area – and coke was needed to make steel. This made him a danger to Carnegie's business.

Sun Tzu wrote in his book *The Art of War*, in 6 BC: "Keep your friends close and your enemies closer still." To this end Carnegie made Frick a partner on January 1st 1882. He also offered partnerships to all key workers and loaned them the money to buy a piece of the pie – much as Tom Scott had done with him as a young railroad employee.

In 1890 Carnegie's salary was $25 million ($444 million). The consolidated company's annual profits hit $40 million ($700 million). It was no walk in the park. In one incident in 1892 Frick's hired guns, the Pinkerton Company, backed by an 8000-strong state militia, clashed with striking workers. They fought each other in a 13-hour war, leaving 12 dead. Carnegie was out of the country at the time and rebuked Frick for his handling of the affair. It had a profound effect on Carnegie's reputation as the workingman's friend.

Humanist, abolitionist, Darwinist

Carnegie was a humanist, a staunch abolitionist and a sycophantic follower of British Darwinian sociologist Herbert Spencer (who coined the phrase 'survival of the fittest'). So offended was he by American imperialist moves to buy the Philippine islands for $20 million ($390 million) he offered the Filipino government the same amount of money to reject the deal.

Carnegie led America in superseding Britain's predominance as the world's foremost steel manufacturer in the ongoing trade wars. He was by now arguably the richest man in the world, challenged only by the rising star of John D. Rockefeller. In 1901 Andrew Carnegie signed one of the greatest business deals of all time. He sold out to J.P. Morgan for $480 million ($9 billion).

Andrew Carnegie spent the rest of his life (as he always intended) giving away all his money to charity. It was difficult, as his capital earned $15 million ($332 million) per year. He wrote many books on wealth, and believed that if people adhered to his principals they would inevitably become rich. But he believed it was a disgrace to die rich.

The Morgan offer was attractive because it allowed partners like the aggressively violent Henry Clay Frick to go their separate ways. Mark Twain described Andrew Carnegie as 'The Saint' but Frick did not share this view. Frick once chased Carnegie down a corridor over a disagreement, with a view to accosting his partner. Carnegie tried to bury the hatchet with Frick, especially when he heard Frick was close to death. Frick sent a message back replying: "I'll see you in hell where we are both going." Andrew Carnegie died on August 11th 1919; Frick followed him a few months later.

Carnegie's lasting legacy was The Carnegie Institute, which has played a part in many of the great scientific, social, educational and medical endeavours of our time.

Skibo Castle and Birthplace of the Late Andrew Carnegie Esq. L.L.D.

CARNEGIE MANSION, 5TH AVENUE, NEW YORK

MADAME C. J. WALKER (1867 – 1919)

"I want to say to every Negro woman present, don't sit down and wait for the opportunities to come. Get up and make them!"

Post-slavery

Life for the 19th Century black American was a complete contrast to that of all other immigrants. They were the only group in America that had not chosen to be there. For them the American dream was an American nightmare. For a black entrepreneur the barriers were almost insurmountable, and for a black female entrepreneur, even more so. Madam C. J. Walker was one of those born into the midst of that nightmare.

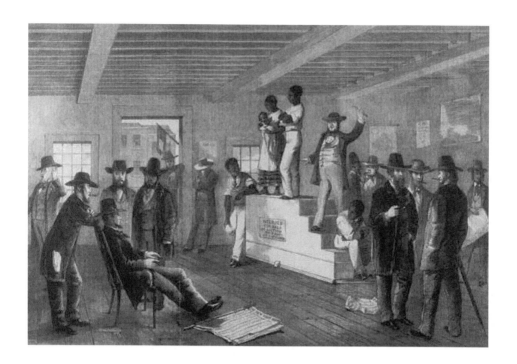

She was christened Sarah Breedlove and born on the plantation where General Ulysses Grant staged the famous 1863 Siege of Vicksburg during the American Civil War. Her parents could offer her nothing. They had lived all their lives as slaves. Sarah was born just as America was about to go through its greatest change, as slavery came to an end.

When Sarah was born she was condemned to a life of public indignity and drudgery. Many laws were created to prevent the upward mobility even of freed black slaves. After the American Civil War new state laws called the 'Black Code,' similar to the anti-Jewish Nuremberg Laws of 1935, were written to ensure black people could not compete with whites for opportunities and resources. These laws prohibited blacks from owning property or guns the great equaliser), and in some states even denied them the possession of knives and forks. Constitutional amendments and Federal laws had to be introduced to combat prejudicial and discriminatory state laws.

America's first female self-made millionaire

Against all the odds, Sarah would become the first female American self-made millionaire (according to *The Guinness Book of Records*). Today, her memory is treasured by America: her face appears on stamps and her former home is registered on the National Register of Historic Places. She had almost every disadvantage you could name: poor, single-mother, racism, sexism, orphaned and no education. She didn't start with nothing; she started with less than nothing!

By the age of seven, Sarah was an orphan with no formal education. She moved in with her sister and her difficult brother in-law. Desperate to get away, she married Moses McWilliams at the age of 14, in her own words "just to find a home."

Sarah's daughter Leila (known later as A'Lelia) was born four years later. By the time Sarah was 20 she was on her own again. Her husband disappeared suddenly without warning and without a trace.

Sarah and her small daughter escaped Mississippi in 1889. They fled to St Louis, New Orleans, where she toiled for eight years as a washerwoman. The black washerwomen picked up jobs rejected by white immigrants. It was both backbreaking and painstaking work. Breaking a button or scorching a shirt whilst ironing could cost you $12 ($200). Washerwomen could keep their children with them as they worked, and Sarah would do whatever it took to provide for her daughter. No matter what the job was, Sarah took great pride in her work. As far as she was concerned she was not just a washerwoman, she was a good washerwoman.

In St Louis the budding black middleclass developed support mechanisms for their less well-off brethren. This enabled A'Lelia to be taken in at an orphanage for black children for part of the week. They also saw to it that she was educated at a local school.

The restrictions and threats placed on black people forced them to herd together the good, the bad and the out of order. There were many fraternities, lodges and upwardly-mobile church groups. Groups such as The Invincible Sons and Daughters of Commerce (formed in 1896) were secretive and organised nationally. These groups defied the gravity of America which held them down to a sentence of life with hard labour. Suddenly there was space for dreams and aspirations.

Sarah fell in with the church and fraternities who believed education was the way out. She always saw to it that her daughter never missed a day of school. Sarah herself attended night classes, taking advantage of low-cost tutoring funded by the black middle classes. This young and industrious woman also worked for the church, collecting charitable donations to benefit those who couldn't fend for themselves, often showing great initiative.

Around this time Sarah remarried; single motherhood was not in vogue with the upwardly-mobile black middle classes. However, new husband John Davis did not make Sarah happy; she even began to lose her hair before eventually leaving him.

Sarah smartened up and started courting a gentleman called Charles Joseph Walker (C. J. Walker) who lived close by. He was a journalist with a talent for writing advertising copy. C. J. Walker was a smooth and dapper gentleman who could sell ice to Eskimos. His complexion was 'light', which made life easier in the heavily colour-conscious world of America. He was short on neither ambition nor self-praise; a man most satisfied with himself.

Extracting opportunity from disaster

Sarah's hair loss was becoming an increasing problem. After using every snake oil concoction she could find to restore her hair, without success, she contacted a hair treatment specialist called Annie Pope-Turnbo, who fixed Sarah's hair problem. Sarah was so impressed she teamed up with Turnbo to sell the product.

Sarah did well at first, going door-to-door in St. Louis. The two women had a lot in common. Both were in their mid-30s and had been orphaned early in life, and both were entrepreneurs. Sarah soon began creating shampoos and selling her own hair-care products. With a burning ambition to do her own thing, coupled with a need to get away from the chattering classes (she and C. J. Walker were 'living in sin') she left for Denver on July 19th 1905. Sarah had grown

confident, becoming familiar with sophistication and absorbing the values of the inspirational well-to-do blacks of St Louis.

This newly self-assured woman grasped the reins, renting an attic whilst working as a cook. Sarah set up a 'laboratory' in which she concocted her own hair-care formulas. Business was good but C. J. had a wait-and-see approach. He eventually made the trip up to Denver, buoyed by his consort's success, and drummed up even more business, using his huge talent for advertising and marketing. In the black community they had blanket coverage – church groups, excursions, door-to-door, posters – and they were in the black press every week. The couple were doing so well that they decided to marry in 1906.

A dispute arose between Turnbo and Walker over product rights. Sarah parted with Turnbo and re-launched under the brand name 'Madame C. J. Walker'. The product invited controversy. Some people argued the product was culturally destructive, even though black and white women had been curling and straightening their hair for ages. Sarah simply took the view that she was offering easier hair management treatment for anybody who cared to buy her product.

A booming business

By 1910 operations had to be moved from the Denver and Pittsburgh offices to new headquarters in Indianapolis. In Denver she founded the A'Lelia College, and offered people a piece of the action with a $25 ($400) correspondence course teaching her methods. In Indianapolis, she set up a laboratory and a beauty school. During September 1911, Madam C. J. Walker incorporated the Walker Manufacturing Company, with herself as the sole stockholder. Walker College of Hair Culture was also founded and she splashed out on investment property. This included the house next-door to the one she was renting. A couple of razor-sharp black lawyers were also brought on board full-time.

Sarah divorced C. J. in 1912, yet continued her ascent up the wealth ladder. Madam C. J. Walker (as she was now known) earned $10,989 ($250,000) a year. She reinvested everything earned. In 1914 she made the big move to New York, where she built a $90,000 ($1,400,000) Indiana limestone townhouse. Sarah had recruited self-employed agents up and down the country to sell her products and hair care system. They were predominantly black women, most of whom would otherwise be washing clothes for a living. Now they earned several times more without the crippling physical workload.

Madam C. J. Walker College of Beauty Culture graduating class, Chicago, 1934 (Madam C. J. Walker Collection, Indiana Historical Society)

The innovative entrepreneur even went so far as to recruit agents in the Caribbean and Africa. By 1916 the agents were organised into the 'National Beauty Culturists Benevolent Association' and 'The Madam C. J. Walker Hair Culturists Union of America'. Members paid 25 cents ($3) a month and their beneficiaries were entitled to a $50 ($650) payment at their death. She drove the local unions to engage in philanthropic and educational activity, running competitions with prizes for the winners.

Confident of the continued success of her business, Sarah built a mansion (Villa Lewaro) in 1918, designed by Vertner Woodson Tandy (the first registered black architect in the great metropolis of New York). The property was in one the county's most prestigious areas, very close to the world's richest entrepreneur John D. Rockefeller. It was furnished with a 24-carat gold-plated piano and phonograph, a $15,000 ($250,000) pipe organ, Hepplewhite furniture, Persian rugs, huge oil paintings and two Japanese prayer trees imported at a cost of over $10,000 ($165,000) each.

By 1920 Sarah owned one of America's largest hair-care companies, employing over 3000 people, in addition to 20,000 agents up and down the country. *The Guinness Book of Records* records Madame C. J. Walker as the first self-made female American millionaire (though many might argue the true title belongs to Mary Ellen Pleasant).

The campaign against lynching

Sarah was not driven by business alone but a sense of justice or injustice (what Andrew Carnegie and Napoleon Hill described as "purpose"). Madame C. J. Walker was a tireless campaigner against the lynching of black men by members of the white public in the streets of America. After the bloody East St. Louis Race Riot of 1917 she became dedicated to the campaign to make lynching a federal offence. She spent the equivalent of hundreds of thousands of dollars on the fight against the practice, which was *openly* supported by many members of the Senate, Congress and Cabinet as a means of keeping law and order amongst blacks.

The entrepreneur used her money and fame to support the instigation of anti-lynching legislation, hoping to make it a federal offence. This would allow the policing of an investigation to be removed from local forces, who were ineffective in prosecuting the perpetrators of lynchings and murders. At the point of writing, there has never been a recorded conviction against a white perpetrator for the lynching of a black man or woman. Nevertheless, the struggle provided Sarah with the drive, energy and purpose in the quest for wealth.

Workaholic

On top of her other commitments, Sarah was also heavily involved in developing and financing facilities for black people suffering under the US-supported South African apartheid regime. The doctors warned the relentless entrepreneurial soldier that if she didn't slow down she'd be in grave danger. She ignored the advice and continued her public speaking, campaigning and driving her business forward. Madam C. J. Walker died of chronic interstitial nephritis, kidney failure and hypertension on May 25th 1919, leaving an estate worth $600,000 ($13 million). Her choice of weapon in the fight for freedom for herself and her race was entrepreneurship. She had used her own ability to free herself, and then to free others, as far and wide as Africa and the Caribbean.

Global Trailblazers

MAYER ROTHSCHILD (1744 – 1812)

"There is but one power in Europe and that is Rothschild."

- French journalist

Jewish plight – disadvantage becomes advantage

The Jews are central to the growth of the Western banking industry. Perpetually ill-treated, this robust group became adept at withstanding the buffeting Europe had singled them out for. And Europe found the Jews a useful means of circumventing the biblical laws preventing participation in usury.

Jews were exempt from ecclesiastical law. In 1236 the Holy Roman Emperor declared Jews "servi nostri et servi camerae nostri." This supposed the Jews were now the Emperor's chattels and his slaves. Under German hunting laws it literally meant no one else but the King could hunt them. The move protected the Jews and encouraged them to settle in various European conurbations as a ready source of funding by way of commercial loans.

Banks have always had the means of creating money out of thin air like a magician producing a rabbit out of a top hat. Early bankers (goldsmiths) would print notes and receipts for the gold deposited by customers requiring safekeeping (they called the storage vessel a 'safe'). Goldsmiths then realised they could print or write receipts (known as notes) for gold they did not have. These un-backed notes (not worth the paper they were written on) would then be lent out and repaid in gold with interest.

Money from nothing

It was because of this phenomenon that Mayer Rothschild stated in 1838: "Permit me to issue and control the money of a nation, and I care not who makes its laws." The Rothschild dynasty would go on to finance many of those mentioned in this book such as Rhodes, Vanderbilt and Carnegie. The growth of industrialised manufacture and economies of scale meant growth for the banks.

Mayer Amschel Bauer (later changed to Rothschild, meaning 'red shield') was the fourth of eight children belonging to Jewish couple Amschel Moses Bauer and Schoenche Bauer. They lived in Frankfurt, where Rothschild's father had begun business as a goldsmith, moneychanger and a silk cloth dealer in 1750. Like all European Jews they were subjected to apartheid, but Frankfurt was an extreme case. The law required the Jews to live apart from the Christians in a single narrow lane called the Judengasse, translated as 'Jews' Alley.'"

The street was filthy, smelly and overcrowded. The 3,000 Jewish inhabitants were imprisoned and locked into this ghetto at night, and on Sundays and Christian holidays. They were banned from doing particular jobs, entering the public gardens, visiting coffee shops, or walking more than two abreast in the street.

Ability to focus

Mayer Rothschild may have started life as part of an impoverished sub-class and ghettoised group, but he overcame all hurdles to control much of Europe's wealth. Key to his success was his focus. He did not care if he was considered sub-human as long as the superior race paid their bills. As a result, his financial dynasty would influence the outcome of wars and history.

Rothschild's business education began when, as a child, he ran errands to other moneylenders and sorted the various coins for his father. He started formal education aged four, attending a Jewish school and studying the Jewish sacred books; the Torah and Talmud. When he was eleven, after graduating to a Jewish seminary, he lost both his mother and father to a smallpox epidemic that ravished the Judengasse.

That same year European nations sank into the colonial Seven Years War.

The orphan returned home from his studies near Nuremberg (a place where Nazis would go on trial 200 years later for the murder of 6 million Jews) to live with relatives. At 13, Rothschild was sent to Hanover to become an apprentice to Wolf Jakob Oppenheim, who owned a bank there. The Oppenheims served as moneylenders to royalty.

The Jews often had to flee countries and thus a natural network sprang up across the Western hemisphere and the Near East.

Rothschild observed how Jewish bankers utilised their diasporic connections abroad to carry out foreign trade transactions and to issue cash or bills of exchange.

Royal connections

By 18 Rothschild was an expert in the field of rare coins and medals. Collectors often bought medals as an investment. One of his major clients was a General von Estorff. After returning home to Frankfurt in 1763, Rothschild joined his brother Calmann's money-changing business, adding his own twist of trading rare coins, medals, curios, jewels, engravings, and antiques. The General introduced Rothschild to Crown Prince Wilhelm (grandson of George II of England and richest monarch in Europe) the future Prince of Hesse and heir to a massive fortune. Rothschild slowly built up the business relationship between himself and the Prince. By 1769 he had wangled himself the designation of 'Crown Agent'. The title did not allow him any special privileges however; he still had to suffer the indignity of the Judengasse.

In the following year Rothschild married Guttle Schnapper, the 16 year-old daughter of Wolf Salomon Schnapper, a bill broker, money changer and court agent to the Prince of Saxe-Meiningen. By now Rothschild was out on his own. His family motif was an eagle on a red shield, a variation on the City of Frankfurt coat of arms. He would later add five golden arrows protruding from the eagle's talons, representing his five sons.

Business continued to thrive and by 1784 Rothschild was Frankfurt's leading coin and medal dealer. When a large house became available in the ghetto he bought it. Behind the house, he built a counting house, fitted out with secret shelves in the walls.

In 1792, French troops occupied Frankfurt and the Prince, Wilhelm, had to make a choice; to join the grand coalition of England led by Wellington, or to join Napoleon. A backhander of £100,000 (£9 million) from England as a subsidy cleared his mind and he joined the coalition. Rothschild profited by managing these funds. His burgeoning business empire also included a transportation and forwarding agency. This helped him to win a contract with the Austrian army to supply it with wheat, uniforms, horses, and equipment.

Napoleon's troops attacked Frankfurt, accidentally setting the Judengasse on fire and destroying half of it, leaving 2,000 inhabitants homeless.

Brandstätte der Judengasse in Frankfurt am 16 Jul 1796

The newly displaced Jews were allowed to live in the Christian part of the city for six months. Although Rothschild's house had not been damaged the entrepreneur took advantage of the relief from the ghetto. The relaxed city laws allowed his family a more comfortable place to reside, and also provided more space for all of his wares. That same year, he made his three eldest sons partners in the business.

The European conquest

Rothschild sent his sons to all the major economies of Europe to create bases in their respective countries. Nathan Rothschild was the most gifted of his sons and would become famous as an international banker. He was in charge of importing goods from the manufacturing powerhouse, England, leader of the industrial revolution. It was there Rothschild established his first foreign branch. In the mid 1790s he had become a major importer of woven cotton cloth from England. Nathan would boast he increased the £25,000 (£2 million) his father gave him 25 times over.

By 1800 Rothschild had arrived. Emperor Franz II (the last Holy Roman Emperor) named him his Imperial Crown Agent, which gave the Rothschild family the right to bear arms.

A year later, Wilhelm appointed Rothschild Chief Court Agent.

Mayer Rothschild understood the power of wealth. He knew law-makers were beholden to their financiers and he sought to leverage his position as a wealthy benefactor to rich nobles. He loved his people, who were suffering the daily ignominy of the Judengasse, and he took personal responsibility for improving their plight. When Karl von Dalberg became ruler of Frankfurt, Rothschild granted him loans, then requested full citizenship rights for Frankfurt's Jews.

Von Dalberg offered Rothschild rights, but only as an individual, and stalled on widening the offer. The altruistic Rothschild turned him down flat. He did eventually gain major liberties for his people.

Napoleonic wars

At the end of 1806, Napoleon ordered an embargo of English goods, prohibiting all trade with England. Rothschild simply smuggled goods in, making a packet selling the high-priced contraband. By 1807 Rothschild was doing almost all of the international banking of the Landgrave. The strategy he used to increase volume was to accept smaller returns; in doing so he wrested and defended markets from competitors. Rothschild amassed enormous capital and his bank became one of the biggest in Frankfurt. However, Rothschild was far more than a banker; his periphery businesses included textiles, colonial goods, coins, antiquities, wines, indigo, tea, dried fruit, sugar and coffee.

During the American War of Independence, Rothschild brokered a deal between the British royal family and Prince Wilhelm of Germany. Wilhelm was to provide 16,800 Hessian soldiers to help Britain stop the revolution in America.

WASHINGTON, APPOINTED COMMANDER IN CHIEF.

The Continental Congress, June 15 1775, elected George Washington Commander in Chief of all the forces raised, or to be raised, for the defence of the Countries. He being then 43 years of age, and a member of that body, when President Hancock announced to Washington his appointment, he modestly and with great dignity signified his acceptance of the important trust.

By 1810, the House of Rothschild not only had a substantial stake in the Bank of the United States but was also quietly gaining enormous influence with the Bank of England. By 1811 Rothschild had become so powerful he was finally able to secure his altruistic aims for his kith and kin, the Jews of Frankfurt.

Now in poor health, Rothschild allowed his sons to run the business. He reorganised, making his sons full partners, but retaining a decisive vote for himself. He married his sons to other close family members and put a dictate in place to ensure this method of keeping the money in the family continued. From here on in he was able to relax and focus on his passion for studying English. In 1812 Mayer Rothschild, one of Europe's richest men, died in Frankfurt leaving a vast Europe-wide business empire to his five sons. The Rothschilds operated as the go-between for major banks in Frankfurt such as the Bethmann Brothers, and Rueppell & Harnier.

Mayer Rothschild had become the puppet-master of Europe, despite operating from a cramped and restricted ghetto in Frankfurt. His fortune would today exceed that of the Saudi royal family, and his dynasty and business have endured right up to the present day. In 2005, Mayer Rothschild was ranked 7th on the Forbes magazine list of 'The Twenty Most Influential Businessmen Of All Time'. The business magazine referred to him as a "founding father of international finance."The secretive Rothschild family wealth was worth over $6 billion, 38 years after Rothschild's death.

JAJA OF OPOBO (1821 – 1891)

"To hell [with the slavers]"

Africa's palm oil in the spotlight

The loss of her American colonies was a major blow to (now not so Great) Britain. However, the defeat of Napoleon at the battle of Waterloo in 1815 ensured Britain retained world superpower status and supremacy in Africa. This meant continued access to slaves (by 1730 Britain was the world's biggest slave trading nation) and palm oil. Both items were critically important and profitable trade commodities in the competition for predominance. In the late 18th Century *three-quarters* of Britain's foreign earnings came from slavery. At that time 16 ships per month left Liverpool for Africa, pursuing slaves and palm oil. Consequently, Britain populated America and the Caribbean with three million black Africans, five hundred thousand via Liverpool alone. The rate was eventually slowed by industrialisation, and insurrections led by notables such as Gabriel Prossor, Nat Turner and Bussa, until slavery was completely abolished.

Black slave Toussaint L'Ouverture successfully defeated Napoleon, after the emperor reinstated slavery in France's biggest Caribbean contributor (Saint Domingue/Haiti) to the national purse, in a military campaign. In the Caribbean alone compensation to former slave owners amounted to 40 percent of the British national budget.

However, there was an alternative African resource that would continue to make money for colonist: palm oil, for the lubrication of the unfolding industries. The demand for palm oil from the West African region was brisk, and accelerated as a result of the end of the enslavement of black men, women and children. Additionally, Europeans had woken up to the idea of soap, which also required palm oil. In 1810 Palm oil sales from West Africa to Britain reach 1,000 tons.

Household brands such as Palmolive would eventually emerge. To this day, palm oil is internationally traded, with investors exchanging billions of dollars each year.

Jaja of Opobo lived in a region known as the 'Slave Coast' during the height of European colonialism. Today this region would make up a large swathe of modern-day Nigeria. Jaja's rise from slave to King is worthy of a Shakespearian epic. Jubo Jubogha, who shortened his name to Jaja, would live to make the equivalent of £6 million a year in today's money and to establish a city-state from scratch.

Palm trees grew in abundance in Africa but were concentrated and harvested near the coast, close to the Niger, populated by the Igbo nation. Groups of Igbo operatives transported the oil to rivers and streams that led to the Niger Delta for sale to European import traders.

Jaja (Mbanaso Okwaraozurumbaa) was born in the village of Umuduruoha. After being sent to Nkwerre to be educated, he was kidnapped and sold as a slave. However, slavery on the African continent was a very different institution to the *chattel* slavery of blacks in Europe and North America. Captives would often be integrated into the owner's family, and slaves regularly occupied the upper echelons of society.

Oil franchise

The palm oil business in Africa was franchised by city-states called 'bonnys'. The chiefs controlled everything. They owned hundreds of trading-boats and numerous (non-chattel) slaves. A successful house could comprise thousands of members, both free and captive. If you had talent or ambition you could go far, slave or otherwise. Many of the delta town's chiefs were former slaves. Kalabri, Nembe and Orika towns all had chiefs who were former slaves or the decedents of slaves. The African region was a meritocracy.

Jaja was smart, with great emotional intelligence. He got on well with all the various nationalities, neatly slipping into their customs and ingratiating himself. He had good looks, charm and integrity, and abstained from anything that interfered with his mind stating: "drink make man fool." Both the locals and the Europeans valued him. He moved up a rung from oarsman to trader.

The whole business of palm oil worked on the system of trust. A captain of a trading vessel (or the manager of the enterprise) trusted goods to the local trader, who was usually a chief or their nominee. In return, the chiefs would deliver the required value in exchange goods like humans and/or palm oil.

As industrialisation grew and slavery ended, palm oil became West Africa's main export. Jaja, ambitious and driven, did well in the growing oil market. He had already generated enough cash to purchase his own freedom during his early 20s, and after being promoted to management he continued to thrive. When the incumbent Chief died Jaja was eventually offered the leadership of the Anna Pepple House in 1862. Many saw the post as a poisoned chalice because of the burgeoning debt accrued by the King: the equivalent of £15,000 (£1 million). Jaja took it and didn't look back. By 1864 he had added 15 houses to the original five that made up the Anna Pepple group. He gave incentives to younger men, providing debt write-offs, generous loans and trading concessions for increased productivity and performance.

From entrepreneur to King

Jaja's success and rise to power upset the status quo among competitors. Civil war erupted on September 12th 1869. Jaja's opposing army was made up of Christians, and he was fiercely anti-Christian, considering the religion's followers to be hypocrites and usurpers. Nevertheless, in a magnanimous gesture, and with great chivalry, he obliged his opponents (who refused to fight on the Sunday) by deferring his attack until Monday. The casualties caused by this 36-hour war were devastating. Jaja's sister was one of the dead.

Jaja decided diplomacy was a better strategy than war. He retained the support of the other chiefs by offering to cut them in on all revenues levied on European trading. He then shrewdly negotiated with the Andoni clan to legitimise a move into their territory. He knew that if he could build a settlement, his control of the traffic to and from the abundant palm oil markets would be absolute. He called the island he settled on 'Opobo,' in reverence to the chief who had taken him in as a slave and promoted and freed him during his youth.

The main town was built in two months and Jaja was declared a sovereign monarch.

A police force (the Owuogbo) and an army (the Perio-Ogbo) were instituted to maintain law and order as well as to protect the fledgling kingdom from external aggression. War games were constantly enacted for military readiness. The destabilising religion of Christianity was monitored and kept in check.

Managing Britain

'King' Jaja was constantly harried by rival chiefs, but consistently outmanoeuvred them. He now had a near-monopoly on the palm oil trade. He clashed with the British over broken agreements and resisted them militarily. His hold on the palm-oil business and local economy was such that he was able to secure the power to tax British traders (ratified by a treaty signed with the British government). Jaja had the right to arrest and hold European detainees until fines were paid for European trading ships going beyond the trade boundary as defined by him.

The European firms established in Opobo were under serious financial pressure. Competition was forcing down retail prices and eroding margins. The firms' representatives sheepishly told King Jaja they were no longer prepared to pay the current prices for palm oil. The King organised deals to ship large quantities of his oil direct to Liverpool instead. The European traders formed a cartel to increase the pressure on the entrepreneur-King, but Jaja outsmarted them by singling out one of the European traders and giving him the complete regional trade. It took about three months to recoup his money and profits from shipping direct, but the trick had worked: the European trader dropped out of the cartel and it was dismantled.

Jaja later befriended two other European traders who were having a hard time trading against the bigger boys. He arranged for them and his own team to develop a system for ocean-bound ships to navigate closer inland along the river-ways. Notification signals were positioned along the banks. This allowed the smaller traders to forage further inland. Ships started to arrive at Opobo in ever-increasing numbers. Demand went through the roof. Jaja's status as King was recognised in a signed agreement with the British government in 1873, a reward for helping the British war effort against his competitors the Ashanti, in Ghana. That year he established a schooling system and employed a private secretary, D.C. William, and a teacher, Mr. Gooding, both from Sierra Leone.

Deeply suspicious of the destabilising menace of white supremacy (with a great concern for its impact on local trade) he recruited blacks from both the continent and the diaspora (including the US), to address the teaching of English and secular studies.

The King of Opobo could now concentrate on trade and British intrigue. His main market for palm oil was Liverpool, England. In 1884, King Jaja did a deal with the British, his kingdom becoming a protectorate. He did not trust the British and asked them to specify what they interpreted a 'protectorate' to mean. Jaja, like most people at the time, was unaware that European states were busily agreeing the carving up of Africa and its resources among themselves, as part of the infamous 'scramble for Africa' organised at the 1885 Berlin Conference.

Too good to compete with

During 1885, King Jaja's school had an attendance of 60 boys and girls who received free education at a standard equal to that of English schools. He sponsored the students to travel to England for further education, but banned them from missionary schools. To help the children keep in touch with their culture, he made them visit home every school holiday.

The traders, unable to compete on level ground, persuaded the British vice consul, Henry Hamilton (Sir Harry) Johnston to remove the obstacle. In 1887 the King was invited into a business meeting with British traders, who promptly kidnapped him. He was then arrested by the British government. No resistance was offered by Jaja and his entourage, as the King's sons were in London at the time, as part of a delegation dealing with a territorial dispute, being handled at 10 Downing Street. King Jaja was sentenced to five years; his only crime was being an unassailable opponent, and competing with the British for control of a scarce resource – oil.

By 1895, the entrepreneur William Lever was manufacturing 40,000 tons of soap a year at his factory just outside Liverpool, using West African palm oil. Britain's gunboat diplomacy ensured a steady and cheap flow of palm oil from West Africa to Britain from then on.

Exiled to the Caribbean

Jaja was exiled to Accra, Ghana and then to Fort Charlotte, at St. Vincent in the Caribbean, on June 9th 1888, where the black populous greeted him as a *cause célèbre*.

There he caught pneumonia and was moved on February 28th 1890 to Barbados. After being released by the British from exile he boarded HMS Comus on May 11th 1890 for the trip to Tenerife, homeward bound to Opobo. At 6am on July 7th 1891 he died at the Camacho Hotel, Santa Cruz, Tenerife. He arrived home on August 12th 1891. Rituals were performed for 32 days and then the kingdom began a year of mourning.

Even in captivity the British recognised Jaja as a King, allowing him to receive £800 (£15,000) a quarter. This allowed him to maintain his servants and household. However, it was well short of the £300,000 (£6 million) a year he was used to. Jaja was born a captive and died a King, but he lived as an entrepreneur.

JAMES J. HILL (1838 – 1916)

"Work, hard work, intelligent work, and then more work."

Hazards of migration

Travelling across the American continent was at one time fraught with danger. On February 18th 1851, whilst on the trail from the East to California, Oatman, an Apostate Mormon, and his family were attacked by a group of Native Americans. The Natives murdered nine of the eleven travellers, sparing two very young girls in order to enslave them.

One of the girls remained in captivity for five years before she was rescued and the other died of starvation. Canadian entrepreneur James J. Hill was destined to be the person who would remove the dangers and perils of transport across the continent of America.

Hill was born in Eramosa Township, Ontario, with a rusty spoon in his mouth. His father died when he was 14 and the boy had no choice but to work in order to provide for his family. He did eventually receive a free education, courtesy of Rockwood Academy, and displayed skill in algebra and geometry. Hill set his heart on a career in medicine, but a hunting accident deprived him of the sight in his left eye at the age of nine. Adversity may have ended one dream but it sparked another.

Marco Polo pioneering

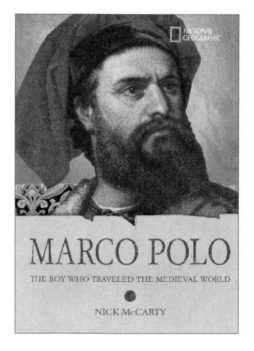

Unable to pursue a career in medicine, Hill developed a burning desire to travel and become a trader in the Orient, like his hero Marco Polo. At the age of 18 he crossed the border into the USA, arriving into St. Paul on a steamboat on July 21st 1856. His intention was to link up with the trappers, who were known to congregate in the town, and travel with them, but they'd left two days earlier. Hill knew he would have to wait until the following season to begin his adventure.

Having previously worked as a clerk, Hill settled down and secured a job at a freight-forwarding company. His job consisted of the gruelling task of carrying cargo on his back for $2 ($36 in today's money) per day, but it did afford him the opportunity to learn about the steamboat business – something that would later prove invaluable to Hill's' entrepreneurial success

The business of war

When the American Civil War broke out, the adventurous young man tried to enlist, but demand for one-eyed soldiers was low. Not to be deflected, however, Hill founded the First Minnesota Volunteers, supplying goods to support the war effort. Hill's particular skill was his understanding of how to move products to buyers cheaply and efficiently. It wasn't long before he was making a tidy profit.

In 1864, James J. Hill met a waitress – Mary Theresa Mehegan – who was working at the Merchants Hotel in St. Paul, where he often took his meals. She was the daughter of Irish immigrants who had settled in the frontier area. The couple married, and produced ten children over the next 18 years.

A more mature and experienced James J. Hill emerged from the war. He was now in his late twenties and still in the freight business, working for the St. Paul & Pacific Railroad. The sub-zero winter months froze the rivers, stopping the steamers from operating. Hill began bidding for supply contracts himself. He obtained a few, including a deal to provide wood fuel to an Army fort. The budding entrepreneur convinced the railroad to switch from wood to coal winning the contract that went with it. James J. Hill and Chauncey W. Griggs created a partnership, forming Hill, Griggs & Company. Griggs was a wholesale grocer. The pair collaborated and achieved a profitable monopoly supplying fuel, undertaking freight forwarding and warehousing. Hill also teamed up with Norman Kittson, formerly of the Hudson Bay Company, to form the Red River Transportation Company. The transport business started to contribute significantly to Hill's growing fortunes. This included buying bankrupt businesses, building them up and selling them off at a profit, as well as directorships on the boards of several banks.

The financial panic of 1873

The natives and plagues of grasshoppers contributed to the decline of the St. Paul & Pacific business. Hill wanted to grab the opportunity to buy the ailing business and extend the line to Fort Garry. The Grant Administration Panic of 1873 produced an opening to seize ownership of railroad companies on their way out of business.

In 1872 he merged his transport interest with associate Norman Kittson's steamboat business. By 1874 their turnover had increased 500 percent. In addition, Hill had almost monopolised the anthracite coal business by 1877, a business he entered just after the war. He, Kittson, George Stephen (president of the Bank of Montreal) and Donald Smith of the Hudson's Bay Company raised the $280,000 ($3,900,000) needed to buy St. Paul & Pacific. Hill put everything he owned on the line, including his home. If the business went belly-up so would he. But he knew what rails meant to the aspirations of millions of immigrants and the business community on the continent.

Hill was a highly-strung character. To him everything was personal, and he took competition to the point of neuroses. This made him a natural megalomaniac. But he had the ability to quickly absorb the nuances of a new business. Hill was brilliant and able to carry the hearts and minds of men with him**'Animal spirits' fuelling entrepreneurial dreams**

Hill dreamt of a transcontinental line spanning the width of the landmass, linking the East and West coasts. He was willing to fight with government-subsidised transcontinental lines to achieve it. The public and powers-that-be thought he was crazy and his ideas became known as 'Hill's Folly'. It may have been folly to observers, but his company doubled in value within two years, as he linked various conurbations by rail. Hill completed the building of Manitoba's 'grand progress' on time and received two million acres in land from the government. The territory was then ethnically cleansed of its previous owners, the Sioux and the Chippewa.

"Give me snuff, whiskey and Swedes, and I will build a railroad to hell."

— James J. Hill

CHIPPI WAS
LAKE MILLE LACS

James J. Hill now owned fertile land producing bumper harvests, increasing migration to the region. This meant more money in Hill's pocket. Masses of Scandinavians wanting to experience the American dream immigrated to Minnesota (about 600,000 Swedes emigrated to the United States, Chinese, Scandinavian and Irish immigrants laid 73,000 mile of railroad tracks in the USA).

Today they make up 27 percent of the population. Hill sold them homesteads for up to $5 ($90) an acre from the Minnesota Land Grant. Settlers were incentivised by travel discounts granted if they settled along his routes. This sowed the seeds of future freight traffic.

By 1883 his railroad stock was valued at $14 million ($231 million). A couple of years later it was up to $25 million ($475 million).

Frontiersman

In 1887 Hill, a Canadian, completed one of the US's greatest engineering feats: building a railroad from East coast to West coast. Hill was still unsatisfied. For it to be truly transcontinental he needed it to be fully connected. The truculent entrepreneur threatened to nail obstructive Washington officials to the walls by their ears; he built around towns that wouldn't cooperate, leaving them with inconvenient distances to travel to their own town's station; he fought in court to stop rival railways blowing up his rails and dumping rubble on his intended routes; he personally battled temperatures of 40 degrees Celsius as well as sub-zero with the great engineer John F. Stevens. All to find the lost Maria's Pass which, on December 11th 1889, he did.

James J. Hill was at the foot of the Rockies in January 1893 when the announcement was made that the transcontinental undertaking had been truly completed. Hill was the first entrepreneur to build a crossing from East to West without a dime from the government. In fact, Hill's opinion of politicians was aptly summarised thus: "The wealth of the country, its capital, its credit, must be saved from the predatory poor as well as the predatory rich, but above all from the predatory politician."

Hill's was the only transcontinental engineering project that did not end up bankrupt. The 8000 men employed to complete this world-famous feat of engineering were even banned from celebrating, in case their hangovers caused delays to the work that needed to be done.

Trading with the Orient

By now, as he once said himself, Hill had more money than he could spend in his lifetime. He consolidated the railroad companies, renaming the entity the Great Northern Railroad. Hill helped develop the lumber business in the East to create freight traffic for his railroad service. In bad times he downsized, closing non-profitable stations, and reduced wages to survive. One-way East-bound lumber traffic wasn't going to be enough to withstand difficult times, so Hill sent employees out to Japan and China looking for goods to be shipped from West to East, thus achieving his dream of trading like Marco Polo. James Hill's agents were productive in finding products to ship to the Orient. Hill was aided by European nations, as well as the US, entering into war with China. By the end of May 1900 Britain, Italy and the US had warships anchored off the Chinese coast at Taku, the nearest port to Peking (Beijing). The sovereign nation of China had by now been divided into six spheres of influence by European powers. This ensured that markets were kept open for Western entrepreneurs like Hill. Naturally the entrepreneur took full advantage of international political machinations.

Addicted to work

In 1905 Hill got into a fight with rival E. H. Harriman over an Oregon route. Fist fights, night raids, court battles, and even dynamite were used to blow up railroad tracks to impede progress. Nevertheless, Hill won through and his rival called him up and threatened to batter him as soon as he was released from his hospital bed!

Hill was getting a bit long in the tooth for this wild, frontier-style brand of entrepreneurship and handed over the reins to his son Louis in 1907. Nevertheless, he still came into work every day and admitted: "It is hard for me to see things out of joint and keep my hands off."

In his later years Hill undertook scientific research to help farmers produce improved yields. The business he built kept producing stacks of money for him. His home cost $931,275.01 ($16,500,000) to build. But not once did he draw a salary. Ex-Senator John J. Wilson described the achievements of James J. Hill, stating in 1909 that "He has captured more territory with a coupling pin and made it habitable for man than did Julius Caesar with the sword."

In 1912 James J. Hill was named Minnesota's 'Greatest Living Citizen'. In May 1916 he fell ill with painful blood-poisoning. After slipping into a coma on May29th, he died. His net worth at the time of his death was $53 million ($1 billion). Just before he died, Hill was asked by a newspaper reporter to reveal the secret of his success. He responded with characteristic bluntness, "Work, hard

work, intelligent work, and then more work."

CECIL RHODES (1853 – 1901)

"We must find new lands from which we can easily obtain raw materials and at the same time exploit the cheap slave labour that is available from the natives"

A 'superior' race

One of the consequences of modern colonialism was the creation of ideologies based on its justification. The celebrated 19th Century commentator John Ruskin, a Freemason, attended Oxford and became a lecturer there (an independent college was also named in his honour). He successfully conveyed to the students of Oxford the divine right and destiny of the British middle and upper classes to rule the world delivering improvement to all. Many entrepreneurs, in pursuit of success, found a sense of purpose in this new philosophy and responded to what they believed was a call from providence.

Cecil John Rhodes was the fifth of nine children. His father was a middle-class clergyman and gave Cecil a grammar school education. As a child, Rhodes was diagnosed with a tubercular lung condition. On doctors' advice he was shipped off to recently conquered South Africa, where the climate was more congenial. His brother Herbert was already there, farming in the coastal region of Natal.

Discovery of diamonds and gold

Rhodes minded the shop and tended the crops. He needed a reliable income to fund his great dream of attending Oxford University. He had a stint at growing cotton and set up a fruit farm. The first crop of cotton failed and then when crop prices hit the floor Rhodes's chances of making enough for university evaporated. Adversity gave him no choice but to head to Kimberley, where diamonds had been discovered a few years previously. Rhodes' brother Herbert had struck out in the diamond region, but by March 1871 he was ready to take another stab at it.

Eighteen year-old Rhodes was given a job supervising and speculating for his brother. The young man discovered he possessed leadership qualities when he was given charge of teams of African labourers in the cotton fields. His talents in leadership were self-evident, but Rhodes's health was still a problem and just when things were going well it gave out again.

Around the same time, in 1872, the Rhodes brothers went North, prospecting for gold. They had already achieved modest success prospecting for diamonds. Within two months they were discovering £100 (£6,500) worth of diamonds a week. Despite bad health and being submerged in an exotic land, mining for gold and diamonds, Rhodes was still desparate to make enough money to attend Oxford. That year he made £10,000 (£500,000) and left the diamond fields in the hands of his partner, Charles Dunhill Rudd. He sailed for England in 1873. For Rhodes, illness was not going to be a barrier to his dream.

Oxford education

Rhodes bought land in Hampstead and paid for admission to Oriel College, Oxford. He unfortunately managed only one term during 1873, before returning for his second term in 1876.

John Ruskin's inaugural lectures at Oxford stirred Rhodes's spirit. Ruskin eulogised the cause of British imperialism. Nothing could stop Rhodes from returning to Africa and fulfilling the Ruskin cause.

Kimberley had become the second most populous city in the southern region of Africa, with more than 50 thousand hardened men looking to dig a fortune out of the earth, in Kimberley's diamond fields. The scene was described by a contemporary: "I have seen strong men tremble while they looked into this great human ant-hill, the giddy heights, the noise, the bustle, the elbowing, are sufficient to bewilder anyone."

The pickings for most prospectors early on were slim but Rhodes saw another angle. Like the American entrepreneur Sam Brannan, Rhodes would service the dreams of others. Seeing the great potential of the throng, he decided to import ice cream, and then containers of water, which he sold to the parched black labourers, hired to do the digging. Digging rapidly progressed below the water table. So, Rhodes dragged a massive great water pump through the African bush and into the town. This allowed work to continue uninterrupted during the rainy season by removing water from flooded mines. Just as it arrived there was a massive flood. Rhodes would charge exorbitant fees for its usage.

Rhodes was shrewd, and the pump allowed him to create a lucrative 'water monopoly'. He sabotaged other pumps, ensuring his water monopoly remained intact. Those who couldn't pay gave him a slice of their mining claims. Rhodes took a long-term view of the region, buying up numerous additional diamond concessions. He afterwards set about amalgamating the major mining interests of Kimberley into one solid entity, its sum being greater than its parts.

The young student was engaged in world-changing projects and making a fortune. Even when studying at Oxford, Rhodes was still working on his business. He and his partner, Rudd, invested in a very large claim known as Vooruitzicht farm owned by the famous Johannes Nicolaas de Beer and his brother, Diederik Arnoldus de Beer.

The de Beer brothers wanted to mass-produce diamonds and sell them to a mass market. Rhodes thought differently; he saw that rarity would exaggerate the value of diamonds in the market, so he set about making sure that the market was never flooded. That way, they would retain their value over time.

Diamond cartel

In April 1880 the De Beers Mining Company was established, under Rhodes's control.

All the small claims willing to participate were brought together. Ernest Oppenheimer, who had benefited from changes in the colonial and political machinations of German ambitions, integrated his powerful Namibian Anglo American company (Anglo because of J. P. Morgan's influence). Amalgamation made regulation possible. So now Rhodes was able to create a global illusion – that a stone found on the ground is worth a fortune. This illusion is still maintained even today, 'enforced' by the company he founded.

Rhodes was now the big cheese (and being financed by the Rothschild dynasty). He held the position of company secretary, and was the company's largest shareholder with £200,000 (£4 million) worth of shares. Despite his wheeling and dealing Rhodes still managed to obtain his much-coveted Oxford University degree in 1881. He also won a seat in the colony's parliament for the newly established parliamentary seat of Barkly West, near Kimberley.

In 1884 Rhodes's vision of the British Empire led to his appointment as Resident Deputy Commissioner in the Northern territory of Bechuanaland (modern Botswana). Rhodes wanted to see the Northern lands connected to the Southern Cape Colony. The British had

Mashonaland (Northern Zimbabwe) and neighbouring Matabeleland (South-East Zimbabwe) in their control. Rhodes now dreamed of building a Cape-to-Cairo railroad travelling the length of a British empire carved out in Africa.

He created Consolidated Goldfields in 1887. By 1888, the De Beers company had a monopoly over Kimberley diamond production. He secured mining and commercial rights from the Matabele King Lobengula, whose realm lay to the north of Bechuanaland. The following year Rhodes formed the British South Africa Company and obtained a Royal Charter from the British Government to occupy Mashonaland. In 1890, Cecil Rhodes took office as Prime Minister of the Cape. He used the post as a means of establishing a British outpost at Fort Salisbury (flattering the British Prime Minister of the day) deep in Mashonaland. Rhodes was anxious to control all aspects of black labour. He supported the Master Servants Amendments Bill, which made flogging black servants a legal right of a white master.

Destructive edge

The general transportation of dynamite in the form of nitroglycerin was now feasible. Increasingly larger quantities of the explosive were imported into South Africa. Paul Kruger began local production, founding The Dynamite Company in 1896. Rhodes, fuelled with unfettered ambition, instigated laws to suit the miners and industry owners. He introduced the Glen Grey Act to expel the country's black people from their native lands – similar to US policy on the Native Americans. This allowed the white settlers who accompanied the British South Africa Company to Mashonaland to claim the land and become farmers. A native revolt ensued, the repercussions of which are still felt today with the expropriations as a backdrop to the controversy between Britain and Robert Mugabe.

The British South Africa Company's police had acquired the world's first automatic portable machinegun – the Maxim. For the natives it was no contest. The Maxim balanced the British numerical disadvantage and then some. The resistance was crushed; the blacks slaughtered

However, the political fall-out from the Jameson Raid, which was an attempt to overthrow the Boer Republic in South Africa, forced Rhodes to resign his premiership of the Cape Colony. The raiders (who were trying to trigger an Anglo-Saxon uprising) were sentenced to death – later commuted to life imprisonment. Rhodes bailed them out with a payment to the Transvaal treasury for £25,000 (£2 million) per head.Rhodes had a weak and troublesome heart for much of his life. It eventually caught up with him when he passed away, aged just 49, at his beachside cottage in Muizenberg near Cape Town at 6pm, March 26th 1901. Britain was in the middle of the Second Boer War at the time. He was worth £3,345,000 (£100 million) at the time of this death. Rhodes' companies survive and thrive today as world leaders in the mining sector.

Rhodes left a will that created one of the most successful educational endowments of all time: The *Rhodes Scholarships*. But just as in life, he was in death: the scholarships were for whites only (they have since been modified). Cecil Rhodes was one of the main architects of the apartheid system. He had a global vision of bringing about a worldwide Anglo-Saxon empire. His will, written in 1877 and called *Confessions of Faith* included the following clause: "To and for the establishment, promotion and development of a Secret Society, the true aim and object whereof shall be for the extension of British rule throughout the world."

ARISTOTLE ONASSIS 1906 -1975

"I have no friends and no enemies - only competitors."

The influence of family

Children who are rebellious, vociferous and fearless have the making of great entrepreneurs. Aristotle Onassis was such a child: he had all the makings of a person who would become one of the world's first billionaire celebrities. He was born in the picturesque city of Smyrna, modern day Izmir. As a young man his father, Socrates, was a charmer, and head of his family despite having a number of elder bothers who all did well. Socrates was an entrepreneur, involved in banking and import/export, specialising in tobacco; his brothers were involved in politics. Onassis's mother died when he was six years old. He and his brother Artimede were brought up by their stepmother (who later had three daughters) and grandmother, Gethsemane.

At school Onassis was a complete no-hoper. He was an angry kid, always in trouble. Although very astute, the young Onassis made the bottom of the class his own domain.

Turkey's invasion of Greece

The Onassis family got caught up in the mix of murder and mayhem between Greeks and Turks that followed the founding of the modern Turkish state after the Balkan Wars, World War I, and the Greco-Turkish War (1919-1922). Several members of the family ended up in concentration camps after the Turkish invasion in 1922, and a few didn't make it back out. It was during this period that Onassis's favourite uncle was hung.

Onassis managed to get out of the country, and then came back to help his family. He started hustling, selling alcohol and little luxuries to the Turkish soldiers. He was able to get on side, manipulating the guards and officials in charge, freeing his father and 17 other family members. They all then escaped to Greece. The war in Izmir, the dawning of the Oil Age and World War II would provide the next sequence of great change that gave rise to the unleashing of the entrepreneurial gifts of Aristotle Onassis.

Unrelenting, tireless ambition

Whilst attending his school's graduation ceremony, a friend of Onassis's tried to console him about his very disappointing results by saying: "Don't worry, you'll get yours next year." Onassis reacting sharply saying: "Idiot! Do you think I'm going to hang around here? The world's a small place. I don't need a diploma. One day you'll be amazed by what I can do." His grandmother Gethsemane had drummed into her young grandson the idea that "men have to construct their [own] destiny."

Against his father's wishes, Onassis left Greece for Argentina, arriving in 1923 with $450 in his pocket. He was too young to work, but falsified his age, adding six years in order to secure a job. The young and aggressively ambitious Onassis worked as a dishwasher and general dogsbody. After a few months he secured another job at a telephone company working as an apprentice electrician. He later landed a role as a telephone operator, moving to the night shift giving him a less strenuous workload. Onassis now discovered how little sleep he needed, getting by on just a few hours with no ill-effects. His energy levels were monumental.

Onassis spent a lot of time scouring the financial papers for investment opportunities and made $700 ($6,500) as a result of various investments. With that he got himself some glad-rags ready for business. When the sun rose he was a dapper don, partying and doing deals. At night it was back to the 11pm-7am shift as an ordinary Joe.

Now established in Argentina, Onassis made a move into the tobacco import business, with his father as his supplier. Onassis left his samples with small-time nickel and dime dealers but no big deals emerged out of the pipeline. He decided to aim a little higher, spending 15 days outside the office building of the chairman of a major Argentine tobacco company. Onassis was emotionally intelligent and knew it would only be a matter of time before the boss would become intrigued as to why he was hanging around. He was right, and got invited upstairs for a chat. The deal done in that office that afternoon made Onassis $500 ($5,000). Decades later, Onassis would say he *still* had that $500.

Onassis decided to expand into manufacturing his own cigarettes. His major target was the woman smoker. In 1925, the year he obtained Argentine citizenship, he began importing opium and manufacturing fake 'BIS' cigarettes. In Argentina BIS cigarettes were the premier brand. When BIS caught wind of Onassis' high jinks they nailed him to the wall in court, but he continued importing, exporting and manufacturing. By 1929, with the help of cousins Kosta and Niko Konialidis, he had had established the business as a force to be reckoned with. By 1932 The Sunday Times had cause to estimate his net worth to be £600,000 (£7,500,000).

But his father was still unimpressed. Their relationship had always been strained and one of Onassis's greatest incentives was to be recognised as a success by his father.

A shipping magnate in the making

When Onassis caught wind of Greece's intention to introduce a thousand-fold increase on import duties, he headed back to Greece. On his agenda was to use the trip back home to patch things up with his father as well as patch things up between Greece and Argentina and restore the crumbling trade relations. The minister dealing with the matter would initially hardly look up from admiring his manicured finger nails, and was completely contemptuous of Onassis, dismissing the young entrepreneur out of hand. Onassis began to paint a picture of where such policies eventually lead, not only winning over the minister but, by the time the meeting was finished, securing an appointment as the Greek consulate in Argentina! He then went on to address the issues between himself and his father and won him over too. It was a trip that would change his future.

Onassis' work at the consulate required him to assist with resolving shipping and seaport issues. This brought him into contact with the shipping industry. The measures he implemented helped shippers maximise profitability. Izmir, his birthplace, was essentially a shipping port (and remains so to this day). Shipping was a familiar part of Onassis' life one way or another, and as a result he moved into shipping. The 1929 stock market crash left ships on the market for two cents on the dollar. Often in business one man's bad luck is another's good fortune and Onassis picked up six ships in 1932 for $20,000 ($250,000) each. He borrowed $120,000 ($1,500,000) to finance the deal. He named the first two ships that went to sea in honour of his parents, 'Onassis Socrates' and 'Onassis Penelope'. The business grew and so too did the deals.

Onassis would often construct mind-boggling deals. He would perform continuous role-play rehearsals, mimicking whomever his opposite number was going to be, going over the imagined scenario scene after scene. This process was designed to throw up all the obstacles he'd face during negotiations and flush out the answers beforehand. Along with his excellent listening skills, the process helped him to convince the other party he understood their problems and needs sympathetically.

The Hindenburg

In 1937 Aristotle Onassis had reason to visit the US. His new ship was under construction in a Swedish shipyard and negotiations relating to his foray into shipping were still being hammered out. On a planned visit to the US to complete negotiations on a business deal Onassis decided to travel using the revolutionary new transport vehicle the airship. He booked a seat on the airship 'Hindenburg' to Lakehurst, New Jersey. On May 6th 1937, at 6.30pm local time, the German Zeppelin LZ 129 Hindenburg caught fire while approaching its mooring mast at Lakehurst Naval Air Station.

The flames started at the tail end and within just over half a minute, the ship was completely engulfed, tail to head. Of the 97 people on board, 35 were killed. Onassis had cancelled his trip at last minute to deal with a problem relating to his new ship in Sweden.

His new ship, the 'Ariston', cost Onassis $800,000 ($9 million). Obtaining the finance and building a ship was a mammoth task, but only half the job. The adventurous entrepreneur needed cargo. During 1937 Jean Paul Getty had won control over the massive Tidewater company, which would become Aristotle Onassis' first customer for his new boat. This got the business well on the way. The following year, Onassis gave birth to the new oil-tanker industry – just as World War II was about to ensue.

The premium of war

It turned out that war was good for business. Aristotle Onassis rented three ships to the US Navy for $250,000 ($300,000) a year until 1945. After World War II ended, Onassis began buying up ships at fire-sale prices when other ship owners were running for cover. He planned to launch two ships which would become the world's first oil super-tankers. When completed he named them *Aristo* and *Aristofanous*.

Both were capable of carrying more oil than any other transport vessel in history. When the end of the war arrived his oil tankers went to work, making him a fortune transporting oil. His shipping business in general was also booming. Routes were being reopened as war-torn countries needing materials and counties desperate to supply them opened for business.

In 1946 Onassis married Athina Mary Livanos, daughter of shipping magnate Stavros Livanos.

It was in this same year he did a deal with the US Navy buying 13 ships from them. Each ship was worth a reported $1,500,000 ($12 million) but Onassis picked them up at $500,000 ($4 million) a-piece. He fronted $125,000 ($1 million) the balance being paid over the next seven years at 3 percent. The ships' earnings would pay the loan, leaving the surplus and the ships for him. The deal almost got him jailed in 1954. The US government tried him, found him guilty and fined him $7 million ($42 million).

OPM – Other People's Money

By 1947 Onassis continued his leap forward. He borrowed $40 million ($300 million) in a mega deal with the Metropolitan Insurance Company to build new super-tankers. He secured the loan using the credibility of his customer. Essentially Onassis offered his 'AAA' clients contracted shipment as security for the lender, so he could build the ships he needed. As he said: "Why worry about the state of the house?" Whether the roof leaked or was made of gold was irrelevant if the tenant accepted liability and his name was John D. Rockefeller. The period of the loan would coincide with the length of the shipping contract.

Onassis worked on the principle of 'Other People's Money,' as coined by fellow shipping magnate Daniel Ludwig. This manner of financing became common practice as a result of Onassis. He systematically utilised every facet of a deal to create a self-financing venture, always using the OPM principle. This was the beginning of the Onassis legend. His fortune would now move from tens of millions of dollars to hundreds of millions.

Onassis was not a mere businessman, he was a free-styling entrepreneur who just loved making money. He simply wanted to enjoy himself and said: "If women didn't exist, all the money in the world would have no meaning." In 1947, he had an affair with the famous Eva *Don't Cry for Me Argentina* Peron.

He eventually divorced his wife in 1960 and ended up marrying John F. Kennedy's widow Jackie, an episode he described as "an act of conspicuous consumption."

Onassis began thinking about moving his headquarters to the playground of Monte Carlo. He mentioned it over lunch with his adviser, a French banker. The banker showed him how, by obtaining control of a company called SBM (who had tenure of pretty much the entire 350-acre district of Monte Carlo and its choice businesses), Onassis could own the town instead of rent it. Ari and Prince Rainier worked in cahoots with each other. In 1953 he became known as 'The Man Who Bought the Bank at Monte Carlo'. The feat made headlines around the world. An envious Howard Hughes called it "the perfect set-up."

Saudi Arabian oil

During this time Onassis was bribing the Saudis to allow him to gatecrash the oil party. He lured the Oil Minister with $1 million, and recruited Hitler's former Finance Minister, Dr. Halmar Schacht, to handle the transactions. The 'Jeddah Agreement' in January 1954 provided a joint-venture arrangement between Onassis and the Saudi government called SAMCO (Saudi Arabian Maritime Company). It guaranteed SAMCO the shipping of 10 percent of Saudi oil, training for young Saudis in the maritime industry, and non-renewal on existing shipping contracts due to run out in ten years, after which time Onassis would take over the shipping of virtually all Saudi oil. The Saudis would by then be quenching 45 percent of the world's thirst for oil.

The Jeddah Agreement made Aristotle Onassis one of the world's most powerful men. The USSR and US were embroiled in the cold war and oil supply had major strategic implications. Industrial and military offences could not be executed without Saudi oil. And now Onassis, a solitary entrepreneur, was in a position to affect the global geo-political landscape. The US wasn't going to let it happen. Onassis had upset too many people. Vice-President Nixon was reported as saying: "If it turns out we have to kill the bastard just don't do it on American soil." Eventually King Saud caved in to political pressure from the USSR and the USA. Onassis simply shrugged it off as one of those things and got on with living the good life.

Onassis did all kind of deals. They didn't have to be sexy. He even made money in illegal whaling, working with a Norwegian Nazi collaborator. In 1957 he founded Olympic Airways,

derived from the defunct government-owned airline. With it he negotiated several large concessions including a $3,500,000 ($19 million) government loan and an income tax rate of 2.5 percent. In 1963 he bought the Greek island of Skorpios as his private hideaway. However, his life had a fair share of tragedy. His cherished son and heir apparent died that year whilst piloting a plane. It would be a wound that never healed. Onassis died in France, of bronchial pneumonia, aged 69 in 1975. His death was headline news around the world.

DHIRUBHAI AMBANI 1932 – 2002

"Pursue your goals even in the face of difficulties, and convert adversities into opportunities"

The power of business

A popular gag in India is: "Which is the most powerful political party in India? Answer: The *Reliance* party." This joke exists because of the outstanding success and influence of Indian entrepreneur Dhirubhai Ambani, founder of the Reliance Group.

India's destiny changed when it gained independence in 1947, after an intense struggle for liberation from its coloniser Great Britain. With its huge population, free market and global ambitions its opportunities for economic development were, and still are, gargantuan.

Dhirajlal Hirachand Ambani was born on December 28th 1932 to Jamunaben and Hirachand Govardhandas Ambani. His father was a poorly paid schoolteacher in Chorwad, a village in Gujarat, India. The family were from a merchant community. Nicknamed Dhirubhai, the young man showed no particular promise at school or college. As he grew, Ambani developed a sense of adventure and a love of high jinks. He left India at the tender age of 16, arriving in Aden (in modern Yemen). Previously, Aden had been plagued with pirates, disrupting Britain's lucrative shipping of goods back and forth from India. But when the Brits waded into the natural port in 1939 to take control of the area, piracy came to an end and normal service resumed.

Ambani got a job pumping gas for Besse & Co Ltd, the sole retailer of Shell products in the area. The young adventurer was working with some friends at the harbour's edge when he had an idea for a bet. Ambani liked long odds and bet his mates he could dive off a ship and swim across the shark-infested bay. He succeeded in doing so, and won a load of ice cream for his trouble.

The hustle

His foray into commodities was less theatrical. It was discovered by the Yemeni administration after they noticed there were fewer and fewer riyals (the Yemeni coin) in circulation. The coin was made of solid silver and the shortage was traced to a port in Aden. It turned out that Dhirubhai Ambani had created a market for the riyal and put out an unrestricted buy order. He melted down the coins he bought into ingots and sold them to London-based bullion dealers. The caper lasted three months.

After arriving back home in India, aged 26, he prepared to unleash his ambitions on his poor and unsuspecting country. The family (Ambani would have four children with his wife his Kokilaben) and second cousin Chambaklal Damani set up Reliance Commercial Corp from his one-room home. The name was a tribute to a mentor and friend, Pravinbhai Thakker, a successful trader in Aden, whose company was named 'Reliance'. Ambani started selling a range of products, including spices and fabrics. Chambaklal based himself in Yemen, taking advantage of all the contacts they established there. Aden, Yemen's capital, was a place frequented by many Indians looking to work and a desire to expand their horizons. In India Ambani literally got on his bike, just as Godric of Norfolk had metaphorically done in England 800 years before, and went from village to village selling yarn and spices.

Unashamed visionary

In 1958 the Indian government were hamstrung by a foreign exchange crisis. A change relaxing the laws on fabrics gave Ambani the green light to push on into the fabrics business. As things progressed he moved the team into their first office, a 350sq. ft. room above the hustling

bustling streets of Bombay. It contained a telephone, three chairs and a desk. During staff meetings personnel had to stand due to lack of chairs. None of this impacted upon the ambitions of Ambani. He simply kept plugging away and the business grew steadily in size and strength.

He was lampooned by the local community when he purchased some abandoned marshland. They thought he was crazy. But Ambani had a vision to transform the area by building a major textile plant.

Ambani pursued his dream to reality. He opened his first textile mill in Naroda, near Ahmedabad, in 1966 and carved out a major export market to Russia, the Balkans, Poland, Zambia, Kenya, Uganda and Saudi Arabia. He also continued to upgrade the mill he had built, introducing modern technology. The high risk-taker kept driving forward with continued expansion, thumbing his nose at opportunities to consolidate.

Entrepreneurs and investors were nervous at the time about Indira Gandhi's pro-nationalisation speeches. But Ambani instinctively understood ordinary people and knew most Indians worshipped and paid homage to Lakshmi, the goddess of wealth of and fortune.

His emotional intelligence told him that Indians would not accept extreme socialist policies. And any party who wanted to have a realistic prospect of governing would be brought to heel eventually by India's natural entrepreneurial character.

Ambani's cousin and partner Chambaklal was a different animal. Whilst Ambani was going for broke, Chambaklal was trying to put the brakes on. He thought risk-loving Ambani was looking at the future through rose-tinted glasses. Ambani recognised the steady increase in Indian's income would continue and went out on a limb anticipating a yarn price rise. He wanted to stockpile inventory so as to benefit from its greater sale value in the future. Risk adverse Chambaklal was having none of it and the two-parted company. The yarn prices rose, and Indira later embraced big business, vindicating Ambani.

By 1968, Ambani no longer lived in a one-room apartment, having moved into Bombay's first high-rise luxurious residential building. The 740-acre factory site was now home to the $6 million ($27 million) industrial plant that Ambani had envisioned for the former marshland. It had taken him eight years to achieve his goal. Staff now numbered950, growing along with his Vimal brand. In 1975, the World Bank sent a delegation to India to inspect Ambani's textile mill, declaring it on par with the best in the world.

People's man

Dhirubhai Ambani tapped into the ordinary men and women's consciousness and aspirations that he understood so well. He knew that if the public thought they could get ahead by investing in the stock market they would do it. He was ready for them and they were ready for him. He floated Reliance in 1977, marshalling 58,000 mainly small investors.

He had to fight with the merchant banks who tried to throw a wet blanket on the public offering. Nevertheless, it was a landmark success. Ambani struck a chord with the Indian public just as Maggie Thatcher and the 1986 British Gas 'Tell Sid' campaign did in Britain. The high-risk player raised further capital as one of the first Indians to use convertible debentures (one of many firsts). He personally opened over one hundred franchised retail outlets.

Reliance had a large number of shares on the market. In 1982 he was the target of a bear raid. Ambani got his now extensive connections in the brokerage market to back him, buying the stock in order to support the share price. But the bears sold shares they did not yet possess and Ambani's group demanded the securities settled. The Bombay Stock Exchange closed for three days and the bear cartel was thwarted. Dhirubhai Ambani was now a mover and shaker. He was a big dog and bears never tried raiding his lair again.

Ambani cultivated an amazing relationship with small Indian investors. He brought big business into the life of poor ordinary Indians, and he always paid generous dividends to shareholders. In 1985, Ambani held the company's annual meeting in a major football stadium with 12,000 in attendance. He was on a crusade.

Accusations of attempted murder

However, Ambani encountered a series of set-backs. In 1986, he suffered a debilitating stroke, which left his right side paralysed. Soon after this attack on his body, an attack was launched on his character. He was accused of 'smuggling in a plant' when spare parts imported were estimated as double Reliance's capacity. *The Express* publication also took issue with his cosy relationship with Indira Gandhi's government. He was continually surrounded by controversy emanating from accusations of sharp practices. This was not really surprising, given the names he chose for some of the companies he registered in offshore tax havens: Crocodile Investments, Iota Investments and Fiasco Investments to name but a few! His sense of humour was legendary. There were Reliance shares bought at 20p in the pound all in the name of Shah. An investigation found no evidence of wrongdoing.

The year before Ambani's stroke, Reliance went head-to-head with arch-rival Bombay Dyeing, headed by Nusli Wadia. Ambani eventually won, but anti-Ambani articles began appearing in *The Indian Express*. Rumour had it that Wadia organised a dirty tricks campaign. Ambani's own newspaper retaliated by accusing Wadia of illegally holding two passports and cast aspersions on him as a relative of his grandfather Mohammed Ali Jinnah (founding father of India's nemesis Pakistan). Ambani's general manager was arrested for conspiracy to murder Wadia. The case was unproven.

A pioneer to the end

In 1987 another Indian first was achieved when Ambani entered the US bond market, and the move into oil refineries was achieved by completing the Hazira complex that year same. By 1988 he owned over 25 percent of India's refining capacity. He continued his love affair with small investors, floating the refinery business in 1988. He'd been back to the market 34 times in all, raising $1.6 billion and picking up two million investors along the way.

Dhirubhai Ambani continued trailblazing fearlessly, trying exotic fund-raising methods and sorties into unrelated markets, leading *Business Week* magazine to rate Reliance in their top 50 companies of the developing world in 1993. A worldwide poll voted Ambani Indian Businessman of the Century in 1999. *Business Baron* magazine voted Reliance one of the best-run companies in the world. *Asia Week* magazine voted Ambani amongst the 50 most powerful men in Asia in 2000, 1998 and 1996.

The kid who simply thought big and acted, who starting out hustling silver on the docks, had created a conglomerate, trading in a range of markets from fabrics to oil to telecommunications, resulting in India's largest private concern. India received no less than 5 percent of its government revenues from Ambani's Reliance Group. The company had 85,000 workers on the payroll. By 1995 it had 2,600,000 investors: one in eight of India's stock-holding community. Ambani's drive delivered not only his dreams but offered other poor people the dream of getting rich.

Dhirubhai Ambani suffered another severe stroke and this time it killed him. He died on July 6th 2002. His company's profits for that year were over $600 million. His own nation recognised him as their greatest-ever entrepreneur. Had he lived to today he'd be the world's richest man, the accolade briefly bestowed upon his son and successor Mukesh Ambani. During one of Ambani's last public speeches he said to the kids listening: "Be daring. Think big. You can be the best. If you believe in this you will be the best."

IVAR KREUGER 1880 – 1932

"We've chosen some new high priests and called them accountants. They too have a holy day, the 31st of December, on which we are supposed to confess…. Yet you have got to tell the public something, and so long as it's satisfied and continues to have faith in you, it's really not important what you confess"

One day, opportunity came knocking at the door of a young man, an opportunity he grabbed with both hands. He was an immigrant, down on his luck and forced to eat from garbage cans. He heard the knock, opened the door and was met by a chap enquiring as to the whereabouts of an architect who was working on some drawings for him.

The caller wanted to discuss the completion of drawings for a small home he planned on building, but the architect he wanted to speak to had since moved out. The young man who answered the door had earlier found some old drawings in a drawer and, rather than directing the visiting client to his former roommate, he instead announced that he was the replacement architect and that he would be taking over the job of finishing the plans. He did. He got paid, and no longer needed to visit garbage cans for meals. This is the legend of Ivar Kreuger and it has been said that, from this point forward, he realised that in order to live the quality of life he desired it would be necessary for him to break rules and disobey the law.

Kreuger's emergence as one of the world's most powerful men was sudden and no mean feat. His contemporaries were characters like Jack Morgan of J. P. Morgan bank (a financier with super powers), as well as Adolf Hitler and Joseph Stalin. Krueger's face would become a constant daily feature in the global press during the 1920s. The entrepreneur's counsel was sought by presidents, prime ministers, kings and queens. Not only was he an architect of grand buildings; he would also become an architect of history. He gave the commercial world new ways of packaging opportunities and investment offerings, such as the B-share (basically ownership with virtually no voting rights); he created the convertible debenture, pioneered the practice of off-balance-sheet financing; and he introduced revolutionary construction and engineering practices to Europe.

Whilst shopping in a department store Kreuger became enamoured by a beautiful and charismatic 15 year-old shop assistant and promised to make her a star. He owned a film studio and felt that she had star quality. Nearly one hundred years later, the American film industry would rank her as one of the greatest female acting stars in history. Her name was Greta Garbo.

As a child Ivar Krueger loved school. By the age of six he was recognised as having a photographic memory. He was so clever that they moved him not one but two years ahead of his peers. This would become quite normal throughout his academic life. His classmates knew him as 'The Sneak.' They recalled how he devised an ingenious method to cheat on tests, using his well-honed forgery skills. He once climbed through the headmaster's office window and stole exam questions, then sold the answers to fellow students. He was enterprising in his own very unique way. Ivar was the eldest son of banker, industrialist and Russian consul Ernst Kreuger.

As a child, Ivar would share with his brother Torsten stories and secrets about the great adventures he planned. The adventures included amassing great wealth and becoming a 'big man.' Kreuger loved adventures; when he was 15 he had an affair with his mother's friend. She was twice his age. During a visit to the New York Stock Exchange, 20 year-old Kreuger spoke of how he would one day have his own company and how it would be listed on the famous exchange. Torsten would be by his side throughout Ivar's great adventures, right up until Ivar's sudden and curious death. He would witness his older brother make a number of independent fortunes, all featuring great innovation in their respective fields. Not only a great innovator, Ivar would single-handedly save great nations from bankruptcy and become a European messiah.

Europe at war

As for all great entrepreneurs, the context in which Kreuger's achievements took place was key to his success. Economic and imperial competition, along with nationalism and the fear of war, dominated late 19th and early 20th Century Europe.

What naturally followed was the forming of military alliances among the various nations, along with an arms race. An expansion in industrial capability resulted in an increase in manufactured goods, forcing the leading nations, like Great Britain, Germany and France, into an aggressive competition for foreign markets.

Their battlefields would be places like Africa, the Indian subcontinent and the Middle East. The crumbling Ottoman Empire offered alluring opportunities to the Austria-Hungary axis, and their withdrawal from the Balkans attracted the Russians. Soon after the Oriental Railway (Balkans to Constantinople) had been constructed in 1888, German bankers received permission from Turkish leaders to begin constructing a new extended railway system, deep into Ottoman territory in the Middle East.

By 1903, other European nations realised that Germany was planning to construct a railway providing a transport link from Germany to the Persian Gulf.

This would give Germany open access to African colonies, trade with India and oil from Persia. The major powers were converting their navies from coal to oil, and the implications of a monopoly of this new fuel were clear. The potential it offered Germany's growing industrial might and naval power was seismic, since the Suez Canal and the British grip on shipping could be circumvented by this rail link. The British, French and Russian entente needed to check German ambitions. They feared the Baghdad Railway would permit German domination of the European economy and thus the European political arena. Relentless ambition and growing tension would eventually lead to the outbreak of World War I.

The environment before and after World War I was well suited to entrepreneurs, who could take advantage of the instability and volatile economic geography of the period.

Precocious talent

Young Kreuger was cunning, completely fearless, and rebellious, with a natural sense of curiosity. He was born in Kalmar, an ancient city in Sweden, where his family owned two ailing matchstick factories.

He sailed through university, graduating aged 20 from one of Europe's best technical universities, with two master's degrees: one in mechanical engineering; the other in civil engineering. He was refused permission to marry a Norwegian girl, because he did not measure up to her family's financial requirements. This would only intensify his already stellar ambition. Kreuger decided to leave Scandinavia for New York, USA, to seek his fortune and return triumphantly after proving his worth.

World travel, global vision

In 1900 20 year-old Kreuger (who looked far younger on account of his inability to grow a beard or moustache) travelled steerage from Sweden, on board a ship bound for New York City. During this first trip he struggled to find work on construction sites and decided to try Chicago instead. America, New York in particular, impressed Kreuger. The young man became absorbed by its vibrant self-confidence. In a later trip he would write home saying: "The people are hard but they give one a chance. At home everyone talks about his love affairs, but here people discuss their prospects. That suits me. I can breathe here." Whatever one wanted, America had it.

The future entrepreneur struggled to find employment. He got the odd job before going to Colorado to work in the mines, where he fared no better. It was during this period that Kreuger took an unforgettable trip visiting the Big Easy. There he got hooked on a habit that would stay with him for the rest of his life – jazz music.

Young Kreuger received a medal from the city for saving a girl from drowning. He was at ease in the eclectic city, with its diverse cultures. He had a ball before travelling on to Vera Cruz, Mexico, then to Havana, Cuba, to help build a bridge. There was a sudden outbreak of yellow fever on the Cuban site, in which every site-worker died, apart from Kreuger and one other.

Kreuger would make numerous trips between Sweden and America. He was in New York in 1903. It was then that he began working for building construction company M. N. Pott & Co, before moving on to Germany to work on an iron skeleton building, advanced for its time.

The next move was to the East, via Africa. His initial stab at entrepreneurship began with a start-up restaurant in Johannesburg, which did reasonably well. Southern Africa was booming, thanks to entrepreneurs like Cecil Rhodes, with whom Kreuger had a natural affinity. It was during this visit that long-term friend and business partner Anders Jordahl found Kreuger crying on his bed, with a letter clutched in his hand. Kreuger had just learned of the sudden death of the woman he had been refused permission to marry. He had gone out into the world to seek his fortune in order to become worthy of her hand in marriage and now she was gone. After a brief depression, the event seemed to inject him with a greater drive to succeed. He still had a lot to prove.

It was at first hand that the young globetrotter observed the brave new world emerging into the new epoch of modernity. In 1904 Kreuger continued East through the Transvaal and along Africa's East coast. The small fortune he made in Johannesburg, speculating on diamond and gold shares, was soon to be exhausted by his itinerary. This included pushing on to the great mediaeval city of Dar es Salaam and continuing to India.

In 1905 Kreuger studied language, history, literature and law in Paris, France. In Denver, USA, he studied minefields and mining (a business greatly influenced by fellow Swede and entrepreneur Alfred Nobel). He returned to New York as chief engineer for various companies. He worked on the construction of Humbolt Station, the Metropolitan Life Tower, the Plaza Hotel, the St. Regis Hotel, Hotel Carlton and the famous triangular Flatiron Building, which was one of the tallest in Manhattan at the time. Before getting back to Sweden in 1907, he described himself as "bursting with ideas" and proclaimed that he had served his "apprenticeship" and was fed up with "making money for second-rate people". He started his own construction business, Kreuger& Toll, in 1908.

Kreuger introduced Albert Kahn's new method of construction, learned in America, of using reinforced concrete instead of wood in the walls, roofs and support structures. This meant that a building could have larger open spaces. It allowed companies like the car manufacturer Ford to reorganise their factories, resulting in increased productivity. The market demand was tremendous. Kreuger revolutionised Scandinavian building methods overnight and extended the business to Russia and Finland. He announced his arrival when he built the Stockholm City Hall and the Olympic Stadium for the 1912 Olympic Games in Stockholm. His contractual negotiations with potential clients were also radical. Most builders wanted to protect themselves from overrunning their deadlines. Kreuger proposed that if he were late in completing a build he would pay a calculated daily penalty. However, if he were early he would receive a calculated daily bonus. Kreuger would then unleash his creative cunning, tripling the shifts, and bribing local police and neighbours to overlook noise and light pollution at night. He always finished early without undermining the quality of the build. Kreuger &Toll became one of Europe's leading companies. Kreuger was uncontainable as an engineer. But it soon became clear that he was much more than that – he was already a millionaire when he took on his next challenge – the matchstick industry.

The business of matchsticks

When Sweden changed its laws, allowing banks to invest in industrial companies, it furnished Swedish industry with a flood of new capital. One of Sweden's top banks approached Torsten Kreuger with a view to unifying the Swedish match industry. Sweden invented the safety matchstick, making the product much more user friendly. But barriers to entry were low and many factories were popping up and causing margins to erode. Torsten told his brother Ivar to stay away from the bank's overtures, but Ivar decided to take the bank up on its idea of unifying the Swedish match industry. Ivar was a megalomaniac and an aficionado of commercial history. The achievements of men like Robert Harley of the South Sea Company and John Law of the Mississippi Company were not lost on him. He was a well-known admirer of John D. Rockefeller and his Standard Trust monopoly. Kreuger saw an opportunity to emulate his heroes and enter the history books, via the matchstick industry.

Kreuger provided shares in Kreuger & Toll as collateral for loans from the Swedish banks. He used the money to acquire, modernise and consolidate matchstick manufacturing factories throughout Sweden and those the family owned abroad. Indeed, Kreuger would apply the ruthless technique of 'join us, or be buried by us' employed by John D. Rockefeller (whose nephew Percy Rockefeller would become one of Kreuger's key financiers). In 1917 The Jönköping & Vulcan Company held eight factories and was bigger than Kreuger's company. By the end of that year Kreuger owned it. The consolidated business became known as 'Swedish Match'.

That year Kreuger was in Russia. During the revolution there the Bolsheviks robbed him of land, property and other assets, including Kreuger & Toll (Russia). They'd be back 'cap in hand.'

But it didn't slow him down. Krueger gobbled up ten acres of land in the centre of Berlin, whilst a young capricious politician called Adolf Hitler looked on with interest. Germany was in turmoil over the communist threat, and Kreuger seized the opportunity to make a fortune in currency dealing, betting against the German mark. He dumped substandard matches in both Russia and Germany on account of the difficulties associated with getting money out of the countries. From 1914 to 1916 profits more than tripled and hefty dividends (12 percent) were paid. From the 1919 Kreuger& Toll's reported profits were $3 million, up 5 percent. The dividend was increased to 25 percent. Kreuger &Toll was one of the most profitable companies in the world. Profitability at Swedish Match soared by 50 percent between 1918 and 1919 and the dividend leapt to 18 percent. The Swedish banks and shareholders were very happy. It had begun. Kreuger came up with an intriguing scheme: in exchange for loans granted to state governments he would require the borrowing government to grant him a monopoly on the manufacture of matchsticks within the borders of that country. Owning monopolies allowed Kreuger to raise prices without fear of loss of market share. Europe was suffering from the problems of World War I. Beset by crippling unemployment and debilitating inflation, Europe, like early 18th Century France, needed a saviour. Back then France had John Law. Early 20th Century Europe would have Ivar Kreuger.

The great economist John Maynard Keynes would later describe Kreuger as "a saviour in a world not quite ready for him".

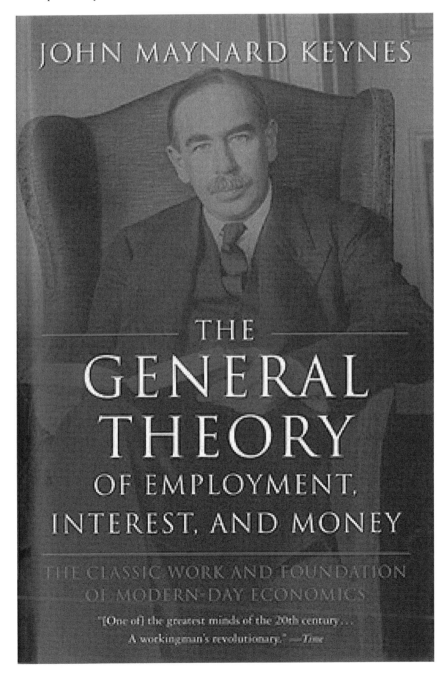

The power of the US dollar

It became increasingly difficult for Kreuger to raise cash in Sweden as the auditors and authorities became suspicious of his business practices. Earlier attempts to broker a match-manufacturing deal in the US faltered. Nevertheless, this new scheme (loans for monopolies) would make any previous attempts to break into the US market pale into insignificance.

The Americans, who prosecuted World War I on foreign soil, had no need of rebuilding and therefore had hard cash readily available for attractive foreign investment opportunities. Kreuger travelled to America – but this time it was in first-class. He worked the passengers, wooing, charming and intriguing them. When they eventually discovered the enchanting mystery passenger was Ivar Kreuger, the news of his imminent arrival reached American shores before he did.

Steerage passengers could never dream that years ago this celebrity entrepreneur travelled as they did.

When Kreuger presented deals to an assembly of bankers and investors he would have them mesmerised. His photographic memory meant he never required written notes during presentations and speeches. His detailing of facts, dates, balance-sheet entries and the like, from among the hundreds of companies he owned, would often be checked by doubters – only to find him invariably correct. If his unbelievable memory for minute details was not enough, he would also reel off the names of the various individual flowers that were visible. Kreuger did deals with American banks and loaned American money to European governments via his new and innovative financial instrument, "the participating debenture." Americans could make a secure investment in his companies and financial instruments, receiving a set rate of return, payable at a set time in the future. They could be converted into shares so that investors were able to participate in the upside increased value of the issuing company.

Kreuger was able to attract investors by offering American citizens the opportunity to make secure investments, with great flexibility and generous payouts, in monopoly businesses abroad. Such opportunities were not available locally. But there was a special twist. Borrowers (governments) were attracted by the income offered by the monopoly business operating in their country: the borrowing government would be paid a portion of the profits generated by the new monopolising company. In many cases the expected dividend for the government would match the interest payment due on the loan! It was a symbiotic scheme, and the greatest business ever embarked upon (and yet to be equalled) by a private individual operating without government backing.

America had emerged from the 1921 recession and gone fill tilt into the Roaring 20s. US citizens were experiencing a stock market frenzy, with credit being extended to anyone with a pulse and wanting to buy shares. The timing was perfect.

Kreuger's first loan deal was to bankroll the Polish economy. The banking syndicates that formed in order to fund Kreuger's deals doubled their money within three years, hailing Kreuger as 'The Match King.' He loaned the modern-day equivalent of trillions of dollars to countries such as Greece, Lithuania, Bolivia, Estonia, Guatemala, Turkey and Ecuador. In 1927 Kreuger gave France a $75 million ($870 million) low-interest loan so that they could pay off existing loans and interest due to J. P. Morgan. Jack Morgan wasn't happy about the disruption to his business of financing Western governments.

The French economy eventually recovered and Kreuger got another medal. In 1928, Yugoslavia and Hungary also benefited from a Kreuger loan. His funds financed European building works for irrigation, soil improvement, telecommunication infrastructure, repatriation programmes and industrial plants. In 1929 Kreuger loaned $28 million ($320 million) to Romania. In return, he received a monopoly on match production. This was at a time when cigarette sales were exploding. Thanks to American cinema and the antics of PR agents such as Edward Bernays, the ten years leading up to 1929 saw US cigarette sales double. When the dust settled Krueger emerged as the world's largest matchstick manufacturer, controlling two-thirds of the entire world's production. His payments to shareholders and other investors were mouth-watering. Kreuger paid far in excess of what competing American companies were willing to offer to American investors. Often, he paid out more than he had promised, in less time than he had indicated. He had the market hooked.

Kreuger gobbled-up a staggering wealth of assets, including factories, forests the size of Belgium, and the best gold and iron mines in the world (he owned 50 percent of the world's top iron mines). He acquired majority shares in market leaders such as the telephone company Ericsson. Companies were also built from the ground up. He founded the pulp manufacturer SCA, developed the lucrative mining company Boliden, and held major interests in ball-bearing manufacture and the like. His vertical integration saw him not only acquiring forests and harvesting wood for matchsticks, but also owning chemical factories for the match heads and so on.

He succeeded in transforming a struggling family-owned matchstick business from a provincial Swedish city into a global force and eventually into a commercial leviathan, a Microsoft of the matchstick industry, if you will. He was now arguably the richest man in the world, with a business that stretched from Norway through the Near East down through Syria and all the way round to Japan and the Far East.

The Kreuger debenture was now a virtual currency in its own right, used by governments to carryout transactions. The entrepreneur had given up engineering building constructions and was now engineering global domination. Rather than building property, he rebuilt economies, inheriting the title' Prince of Global Finance'.

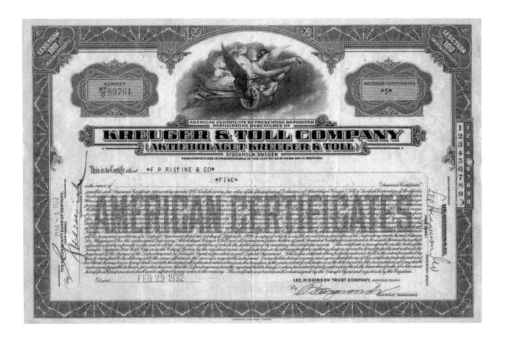

Kreuger did business with both Nazis and Communists. He offered strident Germany hundreds of millions of dollars. He battled with giants: Jack Morgan, Mussolini, Hitler and Joseph Stalin. If you measure a man by the greatness of his enemies, Kreuger was colossal. He was a frequent visitor to the White House during the Hoover administration. On October 18th 1929 (days before the Wall Street Crash) he appeared on the front cover of *Time* magazine and was hailed as the "saviour of Europe" and "saviour to the world." In his book *Match King*, author Frank Partnoy highlights "The international media compared him to the Medicis and Fuggers, history's other great funders of governments."

By 1930 Kreuger's wealth would have been calculated in the tens of billions today. The Kreuger Trust business continued to expand, giving him nearly 30 percent of the world cellulose market. A hush-hush deal was done with Hitler in return for a monopoly on

Germany's matchstick business. By 1931, $387 million ($56 billion) had been loaned to national economies by Kreuger. Many despised his 'pan-European' vision as the harbinger of a single European market. Revolutionaries hated his stabilisation programmes and super-capitalists like Jack Morgan rebuked him for reducing margins and destabilising the global banking industry.

Crash and burn

Part of Kreuger's enticement was the hefty great dividends and profits he offered to investors. The money he raised also had the heavy cost of interest attached to it. It was an expensive operation floated by the heady and liquid American investment market of the era. Often the money coming in from the new investors would cover payments due to older investors. It wasn't a Ponzi scheme but it had all its hallmarks. Kreuger was simply hustling in order to make ends meet.

His fall from grace was sealed by the 1929 Wall Street Crash. His stock proved comparatively resilient early on. His sprawling business finally unravelled in 1932, when the low point of the great bear market eventually hit. The result was bankruptcy for Krueger's empire, but he wasn't alone. Thousands of investors lost their shirts during the period; many committed suicide.

Kreuger went progressively from his normal ice cool urbane disposition to being a frantic neurotic wreck. He often required sedation and was caught speaking to himself in unguarded moments by his housekeeper. He would scream to himself about not being able to remember, not being able to think. He was reported as answering phones that weren't ringing and answering doors that weren't being knocked.

He took desperate measures, hiring agents to buy in his company's stock to help support the share price, but the brokers read the scheme and wouldn't play ball. A deal with IT&T offered reprieve. When the agreement was reached Kreuger deposited 600,000 shares of his Ericsson holding with IT&T, but the deal came with an American audit inspection from Price, Waterhouse and Company. Why would Kreuger risk having to reveal the holes in his accounts, chancing a complete loss of credibility if things went awry? He had no choice– he was hemmed in, buying time, looking for a miracle. The deal was being driven by Kreuger's nemesis Jack Morgan and the J. P. Morgan bank.

The audit would eventually reveal major discrepancies and misrepresentations. IT&T wanted their money back and were entitled to it. Jack Morgan's vantage point at last enabled him to put the squeeze on his enemy.

During a visit to a sick and dispirited Ivar Kreuger in Paris, his close cohorts rummaging around his apartment, desperately looking for titles to any assets, discovered valuable Italian treasury bills in Kreuger's safe. They thought the bills would allow them to plug their financial gaps and that they were saved. Sigurd Hennig, Kreuger's schoolmate, who had been his book-keeper over the decades, asked the 64 million dollar question: "Ivar, are these Italian bills genuine?" Kreuger paused before answering. He had a peculiar technique of pausing for effect, for long excruciating moments, during presentations. This time it wasn't for effect. The moment he had hoped would not arrive was upon him. He was now forced to play his ace card – which had the potential to become the joker in a gargantuan game of poker. He never suggested the Italian bills be used. He was so mentally incapacitated at the time of their discovery that he knew very little about what his colleagues were going to do with them. What he eventually learned was they were to be put up as collateral. He had no choice but to go along with it. But they were fakes. Kreuger had had them printed and personally forged signatures after his negotiations for an Italian loan for a monopoly deal, with Mussolini and other relevant ministers, broke down.

He had recalled their signatures from memory. When this came to light, his reputation was shot to pieces. The one-time financial saviour of Europe was now viewed as a common thief.

Kreuger's financial catastrophe continued to intensify. He was due to appear in front of his bankers, assembled in a Parisian hotel. It was a crisis meeting – judgement day. They needed to know if there was a solution to the Kreuger crisis. He was due to leave his apartment for the venue of the meeting with secretary Miss Karen Bokman–one of his most trusted employees– and his close friend from engineering school, Krister Littorin. Kreuger told them he had something he needed to attend to, and instructed them to go on ahead as he would be late. Before his secretary left he handed her a letter in a manner that attached special importance to the object being entrusted. She and Littorin then made their way to the venue of the meeting. There they found men anxiously pacing the floor of the hotel conference room. Ivar was very late. They hung about for hours before Littorin, along with Bokman, went back to Kreuger's apartment and found him asleep. They called his name in an attempt to rouse him but he did not stir.

The room was dark despite it being mid-afternoon. Kreuger laid still. Walking further into the room, Littorin realised his friend was not sleeping – he was in fact dead. A gun lay close to the body and a red spot was visible on his shirt over his heart. Next to the wound lay a leather locket containing a gold coin.

The New York Times.

LATE CITY EDITION * 2 CENTS   NEW YORK, MONDAY, MARCH 14, 1932

THE MATCH KING IS DEAD

Ivar Kreuger, "The Match King"

Ivar Kreuger was discovered today by his personal assistant, a bullet through his heart and a gun by his hand. The financier and popular hero, whose empire was built on his international match monopoly, had shot himself in his Paris hotel.

WIELDING POWER IN SECRET

For long reputed to be one of the richest men alive, the actual controller of one of the world's biggest industrial organizations, the financier to whom Governments themselves resorted when bankruptcy stared them in the face, for whose goodwill they would risk their very existence—Kreuger wielded his enormous power in secret.

The complete competitor, he was familiar with all the capitals of the world, but was known personally only to a few people in each—those who mattered. He visited them regularly. Erring from one to the other unannounced, almost furtively.

"Silence, silence," was his motto. When he was not abroad he was at Stockholm, the headquarters of the famous Swedish Match Company which he had formed, working for the furtherance of that enormous trust, or of the equally powerful financing corporation of Kreuger and Toll, which specialised in share association.

Then, in a closely guarded room, he brought to fruition some of the greatest schemes of international finance the modern world had seen.

Always he worked; always he was silent. For even the smallest relaxation on the destinations of social intercourse he had no time. The inclination might well have been there, for his low intrigues were in pressing the empire, towhis 'units which were uppermost in all his personal relations.

ENDS LIFE IN PARIS

Letters Tell of His Plan to Die Because of Poor Health and Reverses.

ASSOCIATES AWAITED HIM

Body Is Found Fully Clothed on Bed With Pistol Wound Under Heart.

HIS STOCKS SOLD HERE

A FAMOUS MATCH MAGNATE

EFFECT IN SWEDEN

FROM OUR OWN CORRESPONDENT

PARIS, March 13

M. Ivar Kreuger, the Swedish financier, managing director of the Swedish Match Company, Kreuger and Toll, Limited, and numerous other concerns, shot himself through the heart on Saturday morning in a flat of which he was the tenant in the Avenue Victor Emmanuel III.

M. Kreuger had recently spent three months in the United States and returned to Europe in this Ile de France, which ...

PANIC HITS LEADING BANKS

Following Ivar Kreuger's suicide, the world's leading bankers nervously await news on some forged Italian bonds.

SWEDEN AUTHORIZES PRIVATE MORATORIA

ACTS TO AID KREUGER FIRMS

Stockholm Stock Exchange to Be Closed Tomorrow and Possibly Longer.

Though his fiancée later said he had appeared quite happy the previous night, and although no shots were heard, no bullet was found, and the gun eventually disappeared, the official cause of death was suicide, The Kreuger diaries were immediately and officially burned, no autopsy was ever allowed, and his body was rushed off to the crematorium and tuned to ash, just like his diaries. He left three letters: the first for his sister (the contents of which have never been revealed), the second for a business colleague and the third for a friend, which read: "I have made such a mess of things that I believe this to be the most satisfactory solution for everybody concerned." He left instructions regarding various possessions and business issues that he required tidying up, including cash that was to be distributed to various people. When Miss Bokman opened the envelope that Kreuger had handed to her before the bankers' meeting it was stacked with Swedish bills. She never revealed until much later on that Kreuger had in fact written a letter that amounted to a suicide note some months earlier. He had clearly had a change of heart, and told her to ignore it and the instructions he outlined within it. The genius that saved much of Europe from bankruptcy could find no way of saving Ivar from ignominy.

Japan's Technology Revolution

TOKUJI HAYAKAWA 1892 – 1980

"Imitation gives rise to competition, raises the level of technology, and leads to progress in society"

Japan looks to the West

Tokuji Hayakawa would live to the ripe old age of 86, becoming a multi-billionaire, and the founder and major shareholder of a global corporation he moulded from a small workshop in the back streets of Japanese cities. The corporation would develop a household brand name that is today recognised around the world, in both developed and developing nations. And right up to the end he would remember Inoue, the blind woman who recognised his adversity and put him on the road to greatness.

On March 31st, 1854, Commodore Matthew Perry and the 'Black Ships' of the United States Navy forced the opening of Japan to Western trade with the Convention of Kanagawa. After the Boshin War of 1867-1868 (which led to the resignation of the Shogunate and a government system centred on the Emperor) a central figure, Fukuzawa Yukichi, wrote an article called 'Leaving Asia'. It encouraged Japan to change and modernise through Westernisation.

Japan thereafter adopted numerous Western institutions, including a modern government, legal system and military set-up. The reforms would help transform Japan into a world power, expanding its sphere of influence through victories in the First Sino-Japanese War (1894-1895 against China) and Russo-Japanese War (1904-1905). The latter war was highly significant because it was the first time that an Asian country had defeated a European imperial power in modern times.

A new resilient breed of tiger would emerge from Asia. One such was Tokuji Hayakawa who, from the start of his career as a nine year-old apprentice, would display a consistent and unbroken track record of manufacturing great quality products.

Living in squalor

Hayakawa learned how to adapt to change from early on. He was born into poverty in central Tokyo. As a toddler he and his five young siblings suffered a tragedy when they lost their mother, as well as her income as a seamstress. Within two years of their being given up to foster parents, Hayakawa's foster mother died and his foster father remarried. Despite a serious lack of funds, the family continued to grow, exacerbating their financial predicament even further.

Sharp founder, Tokuji Hayakawa, during his apprenticeship at the decorative metal ornament workshop (13 years old; front row, far right)

Hayakawa was in a bad way, underfed and overworked in his job gluing matchboxes together. The boy would never see his parents again after his father died in March 1899. A year into infant school (he had only one year of formal education) he was already producing more than he consumed. At the age of nine he moved out of the family home to work as a live-in apprentice in a metal workshop. In September 1901, a blind female called Inoue, who lived close by in a tenement, took pity on young Hayakawa, and arranged an apprenticeship for him at a metal workshop run by Yoshimatsu Sakata. Hayakawa became a highly skilled metalworker and developed a flair for innovation. He caused a sensation when he invented a Western-style snap buckle belt called the 'Tokubijo,' which he patented.

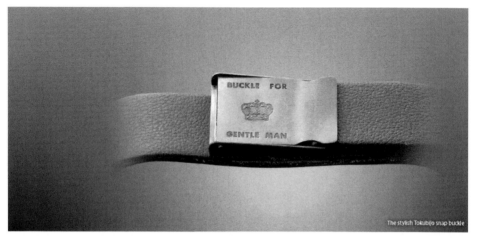
The stylish Tokubijo snap buckle

His master sold nearly 5000 units of the buckle in a very short space of time. Hayakawa clearly recognised that he had something special to offer and requested permission to leave and do his own thing in the world of entrepreneurship. The master granted Hayakawa's wish to leave and pursue his own career. It was 1911, and Hayakawa was still a teenager.

Now aged 19 and filled with optimism Tokuji Hayakawa and two partners rented a house in central Tokyo, within which he organised his new metal workshop venture. The three young entrepreneurs were always up early, to begin work at 4am and finish at 10pm. The team kept bashing out new products with an innovative bent, setting the pace for the other workshops to follow. The young entrepreneur patented a new flow faucet, umbrella ferrules and of course belts. It was all lovely stuff and the market voted with its wallet. By 1914 it was time to move on to even larger premises, with electricity rather than manpower to run the machines.

Within a year Hayakawa had another innovative hit on his hands, creating a self-sharpening mechanical pencil made from metal, with the graphite driven forward and sharpening itself. He called it the Ever-Sharp. In reality he had merely ripped off and improved an existing product designed in the West. This was what he was good at: improving other people's designs and manufacturing them more cost-effectively.

Sales grew slowly during 1916 but then suddenly took off. News had got out that the pencils were being exported in their thousands to Europe and America. When the local market caught wind of the product's popularity abroad the Japanese decided they wanted it too. The company put its full weight behind the manufacture of the mechanical pencil with enormous success.

The Great Kanto Earthquake

Hayakawa became the first Japanese entrepreneur to introduce an assembly line in a modern factory setting. Three years after moving, however, disaster struck. A couple of minutes after 12pm on September 1st 1923, the Great Kanto Earthquake hit. It was 7.9-8.4 on the Richter scale. 105,385 people lost their lives and over 37,000 were reported missing, believed dead.

The world's greatest modern earthquake killed many of Hayakawa's 200 workers and completely destroyed his factory. Worst still, it killed Hayakawa's wife and two children. Tokuji Hayakawa's whole world was destroyed in less than four minutes. Everything but his debts had been wiped out. He had to part with all his patents to meet financial commitments to his creditors and then it was back to square one.

Hayakawa was back in business in the relative safety of Osaka by December. The workforce comprised the entrepreneur and just three employees. Reverting to his bread and butter occupation of producing mechanical pencils ensured a good start.

However, the next big thing was radio. As Hayakawa was going about his daily business he happened across an American-made radio playing in a local shop. He immediately recognised the future.

Radios had never before been manufactured in Japan. National broadcasting was scheduled to begin in June 1925 and Hayakawa didn't have the first idea how to build a radio. Nevertheless, by February he had built his first 'crystal' radio, subsequently founding Hayakawa Electrical Industries.

He later took advantage of the popularity of his mechanical pencil's name, dropping 'Ever' and keeping 'Sharp' to create a new brand. Sharp radio sales hit 10,000 units in no time, purely through domestic demand.

Disaster strikes for a second time

Throughout the 1930s and early 1940s, Sharp went from strength to strength.

Sharp Dyne Type 31 with a newly developed horn speaker. (1930)

Hayakawa expanded into the Far East, reaching a distribution deal with Hong Kong and opening offices in Shanghai on the back of Japanese imperialist ambitions.

In 1936, Hayakawa introduced an intermittent conveyor belt system, which gave him the ability to produce one radio in less than in 56 seconds. Radios from the West were pulled apart, studied and improved. Sharp's product range started to expand fast.

All of this ground to a halt in the aftermath of Japan's decision to bomb Pearl Harbour. On August 6th 1945, the US avenged itself by dropping an atomic bomb on the city of Hiroshima, and finished the job three days later with an atomic bomb for Nagasaki. Japan fell to its knees.

Hayakawa now faced his toughest challenge since the Great Kanto Earthquake destroyed his pencil manufacturing business. His first action was to scale down the business in order to focus on his core competency of manufacturing radios. The company limped through the following depression.

In 1949 Tokuji Hayakawa floated Sharp on the Osaka Stock Exchange. Things began to pick up, but Japan's new master, America, imposed tight fiscal measures to curb runaway inflation. The measures included increased taxes, the termination of all subsidies and the cessation of loan issuance, coupled with active debt recovery. Electrical manufacturers went out of business by the dozen. Only 18 out of 80 survived.

The revival began with US procurement required to prosecute the war in Korea, which drove up sales. As late as 1950, Hayakawa was still 4,650,000 yen in debt and his stock was struggling on the stock exchange. Nevertheless, he emerged triumphant, just as he did after the Kanto disaster. The entrepreneur fought the earthquake with radios; he would now fight nuclear devastation with TVs.

The era of television

Sharp's share price had doubled by 1951 and Hayakawa unveiled Japan's first working prototype television the following year. Just like Henry Ford before him, his ambition was to get the price of his product down to such an extent that everyone could afford it.

Hayakawa's strategy paid off. By 1955 he controlled 25 percent of the television market in Japan. When sales began to slide in 1965, Hayakawa sent a team of 47 salesmen out to knock on doors. Sharp's TV sales recovered and kept rising.

TV production line of that time (1953)

When RCA head David Sarnoff visited the Sharp plant, he was taken aback by the grand facilities of Hayakawa's business, such as a kindergarten catering to over a hundred children, and a workshop exclusively dedicated to blind workers.

The Sharp brand

The company took its place on the world stage, changing its name to Sharp Corporation after conquering the American market. Sharp now sold everything from washing machines to calculators. By 1979 they were involved in every electrical consumer market, improving on and adding value to other people's designs and inventions. The Sharp name as a premier brand was reinforced when Manchester United Football Club and Sharp signed a shirt sponsorship deal in 1982. Manchester United won everything during this period, increasing Sharp's global profile.

When he died, Hayakawa donated his personal assets to the City of Osaka for use in building the City of Osaka Hayakawa Welfare Hall for the physically impaired.

Children greeting Mr. Strauss (center) on a visit to Ikutoku-en (1968)

KONOSUKE MATSUSHITA 1894 – 1989

"No matter how deep a study you make, what you really have to rely on is your own intuition and when it comes down to it, you really don't know what's going to happen until you do it"

A childhood turned upside-down

Konosuke Matsushita was a survivor. He was small in stature but would have great ambitions, arising out of a sense of purpose; a paradigm of his country, Japan. He was born the youngest of eight children fathered by Masakusu Matsushita, a well-off entrepreneur who in 1889 was elected to the village council as a revered member of the community.

Life for this rural family was relaxed, laid-back and easy-going. That was until 1899, when Matsushita Sr. lost everything he had on the stock market, speculating on rice.

The family traded their large house, compound and fields for inner-city ghetto squalor. Poverty soon took its toll. By 1900 Matsushita's sister Fusae had become extremely ill. Next, his brother Hachiro died from an infectious disease. Within a year his eldest brother Isaburo passed away after catching the flu, aged 24. Matsushita was now the eldest surviving son. Entrepreneurial Matsushita Sr. tried to stem the tide of poverty by opening a business fixing and selling shoes in 1901. It soon failed.

Things went from bad to worse when Matsushita's sister Fusae passed away from her illness. By 1906 his sister Hana was also dead, aged 18. The following month his sister Chiyo died aged 21. The poverty-stricken parents had to watch as their children were taken away one by one, despite the availability of doctors and medicine. But there simply was no money. Something had to be done to bring in extra cash. Enter ten year-old Matsushita. The boy was sent to live and work in the big city, Osaka. He initially found a job working for a charcoal heater dealer before settling down at a bicycle retailer. Though he worked as a skivvy, there were many opportunities to learn. Bikes were new to Japan and Matsushita was close to the action in the bicycle shop.

In 1910 he got a job at the Osaka Electric Light Company. The job required him to wheel a cart about for the technicians as they wired houses for electricity. Within three months the forceful and industrious Matsushita was promoted with a big pay rise and management responsibilities. But death and tragedy continued to dog Matsushita. His father died at the relatively young age of 51, a few months after Chiyo. Three years after he joined the electrical company, his mother died aged 57.

Peculiar need to struggle

Konosuke Matsushita spent a number of years working at Osaka Electric Light. Despite his personal losses he rose through the ranks. However, he grew despondent. Work was too relaxed and the mystery malady that would plague him all his life made its first appearance. Matsushita began throwing up blood and was sure he was about to die. He would not take time to rest, as rest meant being poor. Poverty meant no money for medicine, or food for himself and his new wife. Matsushita always had to fill his time with some challenging stressful activity. Instead of using downtime to rest he started designing a new socket for the company on his sick bed. When it was finished he presented it to his new boss with great excitement and expectation. The boss thought it was rubbish.

Now Matsushita had a *real* quest – to prove his boss wrong. On June 15th 1917 he left the company to begin manufacturing his own sockets. Destiny was now firmly in his own hands. He started out with 100 yen of savings – about five months' salary – and four assistants, including his wife and 14 year-old brother-in-law. The business premises were Matsushita's two-room tenement. The whole house was given over to industrial manufacturing. Only a small area was reserved for the married couple to sleep in.

It took four months to produce the first sample for demonstration purposes. It wasn't going to be an easy market to crack. As far as retailers were concerned the socket was a one-hit wonder. It was logistically impractical for retailers to take a product from a one-product company.

Matsushita lost two assistants through lack of capital in the first five months. The fate of his father began to haunt him, but he stuck to his guns. A few more products were created and a few more retailers visited. The entrepreneur's persistence eventually paid off, in the form of a wholesaler who got wind of what Matsushita was up to and told him to forget sockets as he had a better idea. He was aware of a manufacturer who needed to source asbestos bases for a newly upgraded electrical fan. Matsushita, with the help of the wholesaler, got a deal with the Kawakita Electric outfit to produce one hundred units; if he got it done quickly there would be more that came from. He did and there was.

Rising sun

The margins were 50 percent net and during 1918 Matsushita was able to move home twice, ending up in a two-storey house with three rooms on the first floor.

These were dedicated to factory production of the Kawakita Electric's electrical fan component. Matsushita founded the Matsushita Electric Appliance Factory and the product range grew, initially adding single and two-way sockets. Matsushita got involved with every facet of the business, from sweeping the floor to design and testing. A wholesaler named Yoshida then approached him, requesting exclusivity rights to market the young entrepreneur's two-way sockets. It was granted in exchange for a 3000 yen loan.

Things were going well when his old companion Tragedy returned for a visit. In 1919 his sister Ai died aged 28, and a couple of years later his eldest sister Iwa passed away. This left Matsushita as the sole survivor of a family of two parents and eight children.

By 1920 Matsushita was in a position to send his brother-in-law to Tokyo, opening up a new office with a plan to expand into new markets. Matsushita expanded both his family and his business. A new factory was built in 1921, shortly after his daughter Sachiko was born.

New products were being introduced fortnightly. They were copies of other people's products, only better and cheaper. With the new philosophy of free trade replacing the old one of traditionalism Japan was soon dominating the supply of electrical goods, winning the trade war

in spite of losing the military one. Matsushita's strategy (like Tokuji Hayakawa) was to bring in someone else's product, study it, better it and then sell it into an existing and proven market.

He launched a new, bullet-shaped bicycle lamp but, despite his faith in the product, retailers were reluctant to stock it. Matsushita was forced to offer up the lamps on a sale-or-return basis to convince the retailers to offer it to their customers. It did the trick and they then sold like hot cakes. The design had great integrity. Matsushita had woven his magic and knew that once it got into the hands of the consumers they would love it.

Expanding the business

Not only would Matsushita identify an existing product, make it better and cheaper and supply it more efficiently; he would also follow it up with an improved value-for-money offering – the upgrade. The whole thing worked a treat and he won the confidence of the consumer time and time again.

Matsushita bagged a contract with Yamamoto Trading Company, offering them exclusive nationwide distribution rights. The deal was in exchange for an order of 10,000 bicycle lamp units per month. It would be the bread and butter of the company for a long time. Matsushita later bought back these rights, at considerable cost, when he objected to Yamamoto refusing to pass on price reductions generated by reduced manufacturing cost.

In getting rid of Yamamoto, Matsushita ditched a back-seat driver and grabbed the wheel himself. This led to the creation of a national sales distribution team in 1925. The workforce expanded from 50 in 1922 to 300 in 1928. A major new office and factory plant was custom-built. But Matsushita's success was offset by the tragic death of his son: family death number eleven.

Good times = bad health; bad times = good health

Business was doing well but Matsushita was plagued by the return of his mystery illness. Then the 1929 world depression hit. Just like his contemporary, Tokuji Hayakawa, Matsushita was determined to succeed in the face of widespread adversity. He saw it as his duty to his loyal workforce.

The corporate culture Konosuke Matsushita cultivated was one of a family business. The company would not countenance any lay-offs. During this time Matsushita was asked to fight an election as an official in the Nishinda district of Osaka, despite being bed-ridden and insolvent. It looked as if he was going to join the rest of his family but he summoned his immense mental strength to fight on both financial and political fronts, which automatically heralded a return to perfect health almost overnight! .

Everyone kept their jobs but they all were now deputised as sales agents. The company's corporate culture was so dynamic that fitters and designers hit the streets as salesmen with a vengeance. This slowed the factory's build-up of inventory and sales increased. The upturn in sales was a reflection of how grateful the workers were to their boss.

Matsushita's product expansion included radio parts, electrical heaters and irons. He bought Hashimoto Electric, an ailing manufacturer, in 1929. He brought in his design team, ironed out the glitches and hadn't quite gone to market when they won the national radio design competition. Matsushita was shocked when the result came in. He then simply dropped the product into his national distribution machine, racking up the sales.

By 1938 Matsushita was selling nearly 250,000 radios a year, the export division was firmly in place and new offices were opened in the expanding Japanese Empire.

The jewel in the Japanese crown was its partial conquest of China.

Universal principals of success

It was around this time that Matsushita started producing a gargantuan amount of writing, resulting in his new ideology and mantra: *Service to People, Fairness and Honesty, Teamwork for the Common Cause, Untiring Effort for Improvement, Courtesy and Humility, Accord with Natural Laws and Gratitude for Blessings*. The latter two precepts were added after a brief flirtation with religion. The mantra was taught to Matsushita's growing workforce.

The entrepreneur stayed hot on the trail of the Imperial Army, opening a factory in China in 1938 and in Korea in 1941. The following year, Matsushita led his own commercial army into Peking and Taiwan.

The once poverty-stricken boy was now one of Japan's greatest commercial generals and its largest radio and dry-cell battery manufacturer. At the behest of the Japanese government, Matsushita became a major ship builder. His company was capitalised on par with the world's largest. He also owned a lumber company in the Philippines and his total empire employed 26,000 people.

The atomic bomb and economic fallout

The atomic bombs of 1945 affected Matsushita just as much as they affected Tokuji Hayakawa and all the other big Japanese entrepreneurs of the era. The collapse of Japan's economy, coupled with American control of the country, resulted in Matsushita being thrown out of his own company.

The reason for this was the company's status, which Matsushita and his family had designated as a 'Zaibatsu' (a sort of trust). The status was viewed as a threat to American post-war power in Japan and the authorities wasted little time purging the Zaibatsus.

Matsushita's subsidiaries were converted into stand-alone companies and parcelled off; his personal assets were frozen. The factories and companies abroad were confiscated by their respective nations and by 1947 his workforce had shrunk from 27,000 to 8,000. The entrepreneur was flummoxed.

Matsushita's reprieve came in the form of a staff rebellion, demanding the return of their patriarch. The entrepreneur had won the loyalty and support of his staff through years of treating them as family and now *they* would be the ones to give *him* a helping hand.

The company was not in a good way when its founder returned to take the reins. Matsushita Electric's competitors were going bankrupt by the dozen. In 1948, the entrepreneur literally had to beg the bank for a massive loan. His assets were still frozen and he was unable to sell anything he owned in order to raise funds or provide collateral. Broke for the first time since expanding into the two-storey house in 1918, the 56 year-old entrepreneur went cap in hand to friends. He finally shook off his American persecutors in 1956, when Korea and the Soviet communist threat became more pressing issues for the US than Japanese imperialism. Matsushita was back in business. Both America and the upper echelons of Japanese society were capitalist and the formula for manufacturing great goods at low prices in order to make a stomping great profit was the American way. And that was Matsushita's way – as well as Japan's.

The birth of Panasonic

In 1951, Matsushita began travelling to America and later to Europe in search of advanced technology. Matsushita Electric selected Phillips as its Western partner. The Dutch company often lost patience with Matsushita and abruptly disengaged with the Japanese company. Phillips was, however, impressed with Matsushita's calm perseverance. As a result, an equitable deal was eventually struck. In 1953 the new research laboratory led to cheap sophisticated electrical consumer products being launched. They chose to market in America under the name 'Panasonic'.

Exports increased by 600 percent from 1954 to 1958. Matsushita announced in 1956 a plan to quadruple current sales, more than double his employees, and treble turnover. It was called the Five Year Plan. Everyone thought the boss was off his head. He did it in four years.

All manner of dignitaries toured his famous factories, including US Attorney General Robert Kennedy, Indian Prime Minister Indira Gandhi, and Yugoslavian President Tito. Countries from around the world showered honours on the entrepreneur. The Dutch government gave him a major award, and *Time* magazine featured Matsushita on their front page in 1962. Though he warned against Japan's excessive growth he was one of its instigators.

A massive wage hike took place at Matsushita's behest in 1971, similar to Ford's in 1914. His employees would now pull in wages comparable with the highest-paid workers in the Western world's electrical sector. By 1974 he was the world's largest TV manufacturer.

Sixty Matsushita factories could be found around the world. The business consisted of 100,000 workers worldwide (50,000 in China alone), with almost 20,000 retail shops. His book, *Developing A Road to Peace and Happiness through Prosperity* sold four million copies.

In 1989, the year of his death, Konosuke Matsushita's company successfully purchased MCA Universal Studios for $6.1 million ($9 million), giving him a controlling interest. On April 27th he succumbed to a chronic lung disorder and died of pneumonia, aged 94. He left over $300 million ($400 million) to the Matsushita Institute of Government and Management, an institution designed to ensure Japan's dominant role in commerce in the 21st Century.

Konosuke became a billionaire twice during his lifetime. In revenue growth terms he outperformed J. C. Penney, Ray Kroc, Soichiro Honda, Henry Ford and Bill Gates. And his global brand – Panasonic – helped to instigate the 'Japanese Miracle Economy'.

The American Dream (20th Century onwards)

ASA CANDLER (1851 – 1929)

"Every human life is made to fit some place, and there is a place for every life"

Successful exploitation of a mass market

Coca-Cola is arguably the world's most recognised brand. Order a Coke in any country, any culture and any language and the vendor will understand exactly what you want. But how did the product become so ubiquitous?

To answer that question we must travel back to late 19th Century America. The country was experiencing exponential levels of immigration, combined with a vastly improved infrastructure, thanks to entrepreneurs such as Cornelius Vanderbilt and James J. Hill. Slavery had been brought to an end by the close of the American Civil War, thus releasing millions of new black *citizens* into society not as a product, but as consumers. This almighty melting pot was to produce one of the greatest single consumer markets of any historical period. All it needed was an entrepreneur like Asa Candler to exploit this change and America's new found stability.

Born in Carroll County, Georgia, in 1851, Asa Candler was the eighth of eleven children. His affluent father could afford this number of children, as he was making lots of money as a merchant and planter. As a boy Candler lived and worked within the precepts of the Baptist church and later the Methodist church. His family were fervent followers, attending church assiduously. During Candler's teenage years the country was in turmoil, tearing itself apart in a civil war, causing Candler to be in and out of school. The war brought with it financial pressures. Resources wouldn't stretch to sending both Candler and his brother Warren to college. Candler graciously gave way to Warren, who would go on to become a bishop. It was a good call.

Candler's dream to go to medical school was scuttled by the limits on available cash, so the entrepreneur-in-the-making decided to do it on the cheap. He trained as a chemist, or more accurately a 'prescriptionist'. People always got sick and doctors always cost money. Someone switched-on, with a bit of medical training, could make good money selling cures and treatments, without needing to be a qualified doctor. Consequently the lateral thinking Candler became an apprentice to doctors Best and Kirkpatrick, learning the business on the job. His earnings as an apprentice were so bad he upped and left, and travelled to Atlanta, where he didn't even have a place to stay, much less a job to go to. He canvassed the area looking for a role in a drugstore. Eventually Mr. George Howard (who would later become Candler's father-in-law) hired him.

Candler learned what he could about the drugstore business, but the entrepreneurial itch would not subside. Aged 25, after his fateful decision to go into business for himself, he opened his own chemist and marketed remedies for all sorts of ailments, even patenting some. He manufactured what he called 'blood balm' and perfume. Candler then went into partnership with a man called Marcellus Hallman, but bought him out in under a year. In 1883 the young entrepreneur survived a fire that destroyed much of his inventory. Despite this, over the next eight years he built his store into the biggest pharmacy business in Atlanta. The business was a huge success, but Candler was about to discover that he was destined for even bigger things.

The birth of Coca-Cola

In the spring of 1887, Candler, who suffered from frequent headaches, was advised to try a concoction invented by an old man called John S. Pemberton.

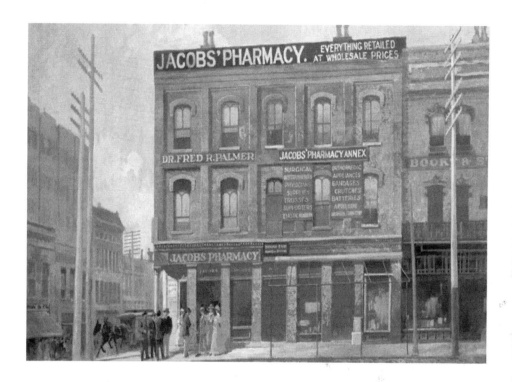

Dr. Pemberton was an inventor of medicines but also a morphine addict. The drink he was selling was a palliative for headaches and other ailments. It started life as French coca wine. However, the temperance movement of the late 1800s put a dampener on sales so the alcohol was replaced by sugar. In May 1886 Pemberton put lime, cinnamon, coca leaves, and the seeds of a Brazilian shrub in a three-legged brass kettle in his back yard and brewed a concoction, inadvertently mixing it with carbonated water. Pemberton called the drink 'Coca-Cola'. It sold well but not well enough to resolve Pemberton's financial problems. He was still broke and in a very poor state of health. He tried advertising, but the ad cost him $76.96 ($1340) and only produced revenue of $50 ($900). He needed money quickly and so put his Coca-Cola invention up for sale.

John Pemberton

COCA-COLA
SYRUP ❊ AND ❊ EXTRACT.

For Soda Water and other Carbonated Beverages.

This "INTELLECTUAL BEVERAGE" and TEMPERANCE DRINK contains the valuable TONIC and NERVE STIM-ULANT properties of the Coca plant and Cola (or Kola) nuts, and makes not only a delicious, exhilarating, refreshing and invigorating Beverage, (dispensed from the soda water fountain or in other carbonated bever-ages), but a valuable Brain Tonic, and a cure for all nervous affections — SICK HEAD-ACHE, NEURALGIA, HYSTERIA, MELANCHOLY, &c.

The peculiar flavor of COCA-COLA delights every palate; it is dispensed from the soda fountain in same manner as any of the fruit syrups.

J. S. Pemberton,
⊷ Chemist, ⊶
Sole Proprietor, Atlanta, Ga.

Pemberton walked into Candler's chemist store with a kettle from the back of his horse and buggy. The eager young entrepreneur had a taste of the concoction. Candler (already rich but still hungry) grabbed a percentage of the Coca-Cola invention in 1888 for $500 ($900). The price included a slip of paper detailing the formula.

A portion of the rights to the Coca-Cola drink had also been sold to Messrs G. S. Lowndes and Willis Venable, so Candler spent the next three years pursuing total ownership of the drink. In 1891 the entrepreneur spent $2300 ($41,000) buying out his two business partners. Candler reported how he raised the cash, "[selling] the entire stock of drugs, paints, oils, glass, and fancy articles, amounting in value to approximately fifty thousand dollars" ($900,000). Annual sales of Coca-Cola soon reached 9000 gallons.

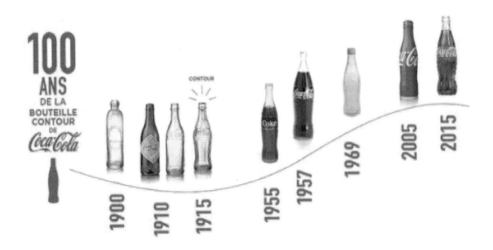

Candler had the foresight to see what this drink could do when others had walked away from it. Also, Candler was a teetotaller and was glad to have the opportunity to market a non-alcoholic drink. However, there were accusations that he was selling dope in the form of cocaine in a drink. Cocaine is an alkaloid, used as an analgesic in pharmacology, present in the coca leaf, which was heavily used in the early formula of Coca-Cola. Candler tweaked the product, fizzing it up, and by the time he'd finished it was virtually identical to the drink we consume today.

The Coca-Cola Company was incorporated in 1892. Candler knew protection of the formula with its secret ingredients was crucial to its future success so in 1893 he patented his new and improved formula. He spent huge sums of money advertising the soft drink. Nothing like it had ever been done before. The Coca-Cola contour bottle was invented in 1915, by Swedish immigrant Alexander Samuelson, who later patented the design. It came about after a bottler wrote to Coca-Cola suggesting the bottle should be recognisable in the dark. He also contended that if any bottle lay broken in the street it should be recognisable as a coke bottle. Marketing was key to Coca-Cola's success. Coca-Cola was being consumed in every state and territory in the United States as early as 1895. Candler cashed in some of his chips in 1900, liquidating part of his shareholding in favour of The Trust Company of Georgia. Nevertheless, he continued to hold a significant amount of the stock.

The road maps of the world are dotted with happy places to pause. And ice-cold Coca-Cola is there to make a pause *the pause that refreshes*. Familiar red coolers everywhere signal you to refresh yourself and be off to a fresh start.

An unstoppable entrepreneur

Asa Candler continued innovating. He began the construction of his own personal skyscraper in downtown Atlanta in 1904. It was the tallest and grandest building in the city.

He used the ground floor lobby for his next little venture – The Central Bank and Trust Company. He ran the bank for 16 years before it merged with the C&S Bank in 1922. During this time he went on to become a successful property developer.

In 1916 Coca-Cola Inc. was ranked 212th among America's largest industrials. That same year Candler became Mayor of Atlanta. Still a major shareholder, he eventually sold the rump of his holding to Ernest Woodruff and a group of investors for $25 million ($219 million). This was around the time of the new prohibition laws. He also gave his children a significant number of Coca-Cola shares.

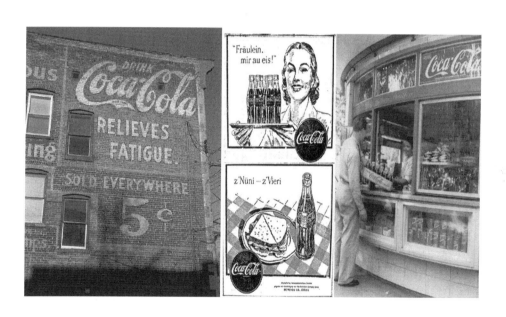

He died in 1929, having earlier suffered a stroke. Asa Candler achieved his life's mission, having built up four independent fortunes in pharmaceuticals, beverages, banking and property. By contrast, Coca-Cola's inventor, Dr. John Pemberton, died in 1888 without realising he had created the world's greatest ever drink.

JOHN D. ROCKEFELLER 1839 – 1937

"The way to make money is to buy when blood is running in the streets"

During the late 19th Century Karl Marx would have observed great entrepreneurs fulfilling his predictions about the means of production being in the hands of an exploitative few.

In witnessing the antics of John D. Rockefeller in particular he would have felt completely vindicated. John D. Rockefeller started with $3 ($52) and finished the richest man in the world; arguably the richest entrepreneur ever, based on share of GDP.

John Davidson Rockefeller was the eldest of six children born to William and Eliza. John's parents were a couple of opposites: his mother Eliza was a straight-laced, no-nonsense woman; William was trouble personified. In 1850 three of William's closest friends went to prison for horse-stealing and later the old men of his time would say, of William, "He was too smart to be caught."

After being accused and charged with rape Bill fled, moving the family to Owego, New York, close to the Pennsylvania border. 'Devil Bill,' as he was known, was soon on the run again, moving to Cleveland, Ohio after being accused of burglary, arson and counterfeiting.

Early learning

The Rockefellers were said to have lived in squalor. One neighbour is reported to have said: "I do not remember ever have to seen more pitiable neglected children … their clothes were old tattered and they looked hungry and dirty." [sic] Despite this John D. Rockefeller was an entrepreneur right out of the traps. His sister Lucy watched the boy's progress and observed: "When it's raining porridge, you'll always find John's bowl right side up."

In 1851 Rockefeller, aged 12, saved over $50 ($1,000) working for neighbours and turkey farming for his mother. The hand that rocked John D. Rockefeller's cradle would rock the world as she guided him into business. She cajoled the boy to lend money out to local farmers at 7 percent interest, payable in one year. Rockefeller's father kept the child-entrepreneur quick-witted, stating: "I cheat my boys every chance I get ... I want to make them sharp."

Rockefeller dropped out of school at his father's behest. He was an average student, though able to do complex mathematical problems without pen and paper (a talent he would make use of throughout his life). He went on to study single and double-entry book-keeping, penmanship, commercial history, mercantile customs, banking and exchange, attending Folsom's Commercial in the spring of 1855 for ten weeks. His father taught the youngster how to draw up contracts and the like.

In time, Rockefeller found work as an assistant book-keeper with Hewitt & Tuttle, commission merchants and freight forwarders on September 26th, 1855. It changed his life.

As an old man Rockefeller would often look back and speak about the day he started at the company saying: "I often tremble when I ask myself the question – what if I had not got the job?" He earned $30 per week ($530) but was no jobsworth. His approach to work was serious, meticulous and incorruptible. His performances made people sit up take notice, resulting in greater and greater responsibilities being placed on the broad but youthful shoulders.

Time to make a move

In 1858 Rockefeller wanted to do, as he put it, "something big," like trading on his own. Hewitt & Tuttle were becoming unsteady. So, on March 18th 1859, with $800 ($15,000) saved and $1,000 borrowed from Dad (at 10 percent), he and partner Maurice B. Clark (an adventurer from Wiltshire, England, and classmate at Folsom College) thought they would try their hand at being entrepreneurs. Rockefeller was 18 and Clark 28. They put up equal shares of capital to form Clark & Rockefeller. They were now commission agents selling grain, hay, meats and miscellaneous goods. John D. Rockefeller was able to secure transport discounts transporting the goods they sold on commission. They raked it in. Turnover was $450,000 ($10 million) producing profits of $4,400 ($83,000). By 1861 profits were up at $17,000 ($304,000).

The Civil War presented many business opportunities. Rockefeller did what any smart, gun-shy, rich kid would – he paid someone to take his place dodging Confederate bullets. Although in favour of abolition, Rockefeller was more interested in fighting in the war for market share than the war for someone else's freedom, and supplied both sides.

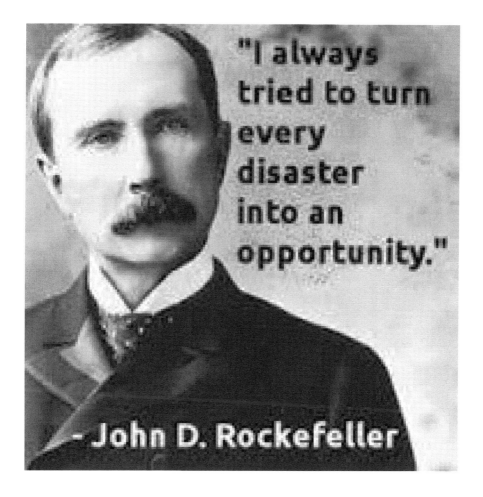

"I always tried to turn every disaster into an opportunity."

- John D. Rockefeller

The move into oil

An English chemist (again from Wiltshire, and friend of Clark's) named Samuel Andrews got into the oil refinery business around the time of the Civil War.

SAMUEL G. ANDREWS *1863
COUNTY CLERK 1835–1837. POSTMASTER 1841–1844
MAYOR 1840 AND 1856. REP. CONGRESS 1857–1859

The war caused demand to rocket and Samuel needed a partner. He was a mechanical genius and is credited by historians with creating one of the earliest oil-refining processes. Andrews put a deal to Rockefeller and his partner.

After much persuasion from his partner Rockefeller eventually relented and entered the oil business. He did not need the deal as commissions for brokering grain and produce were sky-high due to the inflationary effects of the war.

Although cashflow was tight, Rockefeller refused to advance monies on future harvests just because prices and demand were good. He borrowed heavily to get deals done, but never speculated or gambled and always paid back on time. He made the astute shift from the brokerage business to oil after weighing up the future development of the USA. The railroads had been granted over 158 million acres of land that needed settling. The geographic position of Cleveland, Rockefeller's home state, could not compete with the new railroads and the fertile grain-producing regions being settled. Cleveland was, however, well placed to distribute oil.

Rockefeller eventually bought out Clark and his brother (who also owned a portion of the business) for $72,500 ($700,000) in 1865. Clark didn't have the stomach for highly geared expansion, but Rockefeller knew how to improve the oil company. His secret was attention to detail. He would assiduously squeeze every penny out of efficiencies.

Everything he could bring in-house he did. He expanded vertically, starting with his own transportation fleet. By manufacturing oil barrels he regained 60 percent of the outlay. He was directly involved with the reduction of solder used in manufacturing the barrels and responsible for reducing it from 40 drops to 38. It actually needed 39 in the end. Nothing escaped his attention. He even dried wood to lighten it for transport via the railroads and reduce the cost of freight. In 1866 he bought a refinery called Standard Works and began exporting oil.

Rockefeller owed a great deal of his success to Henry Flagler, a talented entrepreneur who, although struggling at the time he hooked up with Rockefeller, went on to build much of modern Florida.

He had a lot in common with Rockefeller. Neither man swore; both were teetotal; and both had experience in the grain and distillery industries. The two met in Cleveland, when Rockefeller was still selling grain as a commission agent.

The Standard Oil trust

It was Flagler who introduced John D. Rockefeller to the idea of a Standard Oil trust. The men set up a partnership that included Andrews, the refinery specialist, and Rockefeller's brother William, who was a great success in his own right. They assembled a team and incorporated the organisation as the Standard Oil Company in 1869. The company held about 10 percent of the oil business at the time of its formation and John D. Rockefeller was its lynchpin.

Rockefeller presided over the oil industry like a colossus, controlling it, strengthening it, and removing weaknesses such as the wild price fluctuations caused by smaller players. In one period of six weeks in 1872, Standard Oil absorbed 22 of its 26 Cleveland competitors. The unwritten rule of the oil industry was simple: if you weren't going to join the trust you were to be destroyed by it. Rockefeller huddled all the players together to conserve profits as penguins huddle to conserve heat.

Vertical expansion continued throughout 1874, and Rockefeller intensified his efficiency drive. Plans were drawn up for pipelines to improve transportation. Companies began forming just to be taken over and get the Rockefeller 'improvement treatment'. Other entrepreneurs were given a simple choice: join the pack or be hunted and eaten alive by it. It was survival of the fittest. Rockefeller would show them the books to make the point – they could join and get rich or be made bankrupt and have their business bought for a song. Either way their market share would be absorbed. When he was shipping grain he had played the railroads off against each other, securing discounts. Now he levied a tax against competitors via the railroad companies who needed Standard Oil's business to survive.

Yet, for all his ruthlessness Rockefeller was an emotionally intelligent person. He never sat at the head of the table during board meetings, instinctively understanding that this could trigger envious reactions.

Monopoly

By 1879, 40 year-old Rockefeller was rated among the top 20 richest men in America. He held 90 percent of the US refining business and declared that: "The Standard Oil Company will someday refine all the oil and make all the barrels." Seventy percent of his production went abroad in exports (run by his brother William), bringing in major revenue for the USA.

By 1890 his distribution network could reach virtually every American household. This 'Schumpeterian' company reduced the price of kerosene by 99 percent during its lifetime, even though it owned a monopoly.

Unstoppable wealth

Rockefeller made money faster than he could count it, and nothing seemed capable of stopping him. But all work and no play made the entrepreneur positively ill. At age 52 he broke down, losing his hair, and his eyebrows – but he didn't lose a penny of his fortune.

In fact, his independent investments went through the roof.

Six years later Rockefeller retired, amidst brewing trouble. In the years 1910 and 1911, there was a minor economic depression known as the Panic of 1910-1911, which was followed by the enforcement of the Sherman Anti-Trust Act. The government enforced new anti-trust laws to break up Standard Oil into 37 smaller companies. Rockefeller didn't lose a single share in the break-up. Some argue the break-up released value and increased his net wealth still further.

ORGANIZED UNDER THE MANUFACTURING LAWS OF OHIO

No. ____   ____ Shares

STANDARD OIL COMPANY.

CAPITAL STOCK
$3,500,000.
ALL PAID.

35,000 SHARES.
$100 EACH.

This is to Certify that H. M. Hanna & Geo W Chapin
is entitled to _____ Shares of One Hundred Dollars each
in the Capital Stock of the **Standard Oil Company**, transferable on the
Books of the Company in person or by Attorney only on the surrender of this
Certificate and due payment of all liabilities on the part of the holder to the
Company, subject to the provisions of Law and the By-Laws of the Company
This Certificate is valid only when signed by the President and Secretary.
Cleveland, O. May 1st 1873

_____ Sec't   _____ Pres't

Competing with Carnegie

In 1901, Rockefeller sold his iron ore business to J. P. Morgan for $80 million ($1.5 billion) with an estimated profit of at least $50 million ($1 billion). Andrew Carnegie had recently sold out to Morgan for $480 million ($9 billion), and wrote: "[The] US is no longer a free capitalist country, as Rockefeller and I own it."

The Men Who Built America

Andrew Carnegie   John D. Rockefeller   J.P. Morgan

Like Carnegie, Rockefeller had a strong sense of altruism. In fact, the two entrepreneurs competed with each other to see who could give away the most money! Rockefeller always gave children a dime when he encountered them. He even gave dimes to millionaires and presidents as a playful gesture.

John D. Rockefeller died on May 3rd 1937, nearly 100 years old. His estate was valued at only $26,410,837 ($280 million) compared to his wealth at its peak of almost $1.4 billion ($20 billion). He had given it all away. One of the finest results of Rockefeller's great financial giveaway was the eradication of hookworm and yellow fever in the US. Another was his $4.8 billion endowment of the University of Chicago (formerly a small Baptist college), which Rockefeller referred to as "the best investment I ever made."

HENRY FORD 1863 – 1947

"determined never again to put myself under [another's] orders."

The Irish Potato Famine

Between 1846 and 1851 more one million Irish people left their homeland for the New World. Among them was a 21 year-old named William Ford, along with members of his family. They were victims of the Irish Potato Famine, in which an estimated 500,000 people died during a five-year period.

Population Fall in Ireland 1841-1851

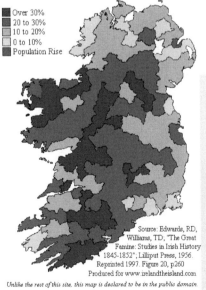

Over 30%
20 to 30%
10 to 20%
0 to 10%
Population Rise

Source: Edwards, RD,
Williams, TD; "The Great
Famine: Studies in Irish History
1845-1852"; Lilliput Press, 1956.
Reprinted 1997. Figure 20, p260
Produced for www.irelandtheisland.com

Unlike the rest of this site, this map is declared to be in the public domain.

The family was originally from England but had been evicted from their land in Somerset. William Ford found great opportunity in America. He overcame his adversity and began doing rather well in the farming business, but he never could have imagined that his son would one day found the second largest company in the world and kick-start the greatest transport revolution of all time.

Young Henry Ford's world was the idyllic countryside of Dearborne, Michigan. He lived in a rural paradise, where he learned to read perched on his mother's lap. His father taught him the names of the flowers and the birds, as well as an appreciation of nature in general. It was everything a child could ask for. Ford attended the local school, but he was neither a bookworm nor enthusiastic about farming. He preferred taking things apart and putting them back together again.

Curious mind

Steam power had seized Ford's curiosity. Working on the farm was tough and Ford was fascinated by the idea that machines and steam could make light work of various tasks. Thus, began a series of experiments.

One day in 1873 the ten year-old boy lit a fire under a large pot with its lid tied down, then waited. It blew up, showering him with boiling hot water. Unperturbed he continued his investigation of steam power with larger and more controlled experiment. He avoided scalding himself this time, but instead burned down the school fence.

Ford's attention soon turned to watches; he was fascinated by their mechanisms, and by pulling them apart and putting them back together again. He utilised and adapted abandoned tools, which he described as 'treasures'. After his clock-tampering went out on the grapevine, his little bedroom bench was soon brimming with watches and clocks from around the neighbourhood awaiting repair.

Ford's father gave him permission to expand his watch-repair business into a workshed on the farm. It was around this time young Ford lost his mother. "The house was now a watch without a mainspring," he would say.

In July 1875, 12 year-old Ford had a life-changing experience. He was out with his father on their horse-drawn wagon when a steam engine stopped to allow them to pass. Ford bolted out of the wagon and into the cockpit of the portable engine. The engine driver could see the boy was in his element, so he answered all his questions and allowed him to drive the engine and blow its whistle.

A determined nature

When Henry Ford was 16 he went to Detroit, working for various mechanical engineering firms. His father didn't approve, but nor did he stand in his son's way. Despite his reservations, William Ford helped Henry find work in Detroit. Three years later, Ford was back on the farm baling hay, but also operating a steam traction engine for a neighbouring farmer and repairing similar engines for others. Ford's father 'bribed' him with 40 acres of timberland to give up mechanics. Ford then spent two years cutting down trees in woods on his land and working a neighbour's a steam engine. The machines made short work of labour-intensive chores.

In 1888 Ford married Clara Bryant. His well-to-do father gave him an 80-acre farm to get them started. However, Ford was not satisfied with rustic life. He wanted away to the big city and machines. An electrical engineering job at the Edison Illuminating Company provided the escape. By 1892, Ford was in charge of the maintenance of steam engines in the Edison Lighting Power Plant.

Building cars

Ford read an article in the *World of Science* about the German engineer Nicholas Otto, builder of the internal combustion engine. He began to experiment. During June 1896, under a blanket of secrecy, Ford and some friends created the 'Quadricycle'. He sold it for $200 ($4,000).

Ford's second car was completed in 1898. He took wealthy Detroit lumber merchant William H. Murphy on a 60-mile demonstration ride. Murphy was impressed enough to buy the vehicle and become an investor.

With financial backing from Murphy, Ford ended his eight-year tenure with Edison. Not even Edison's promise of $1,900 ($38,000) a year to stay could keep him from pursuing his vision of producing his own car. He was appointed chief engineer of a new start-up called the Detroit Automobile Company. The very first vehicle they produced was a commercial van, in 1900. It went down well. Unfortunately, Ford was in over his head, managing the production of more than one type of car at the same time. The business failed.

Birth of Ford cars

Ford started making a name for himself by building racing cars with the backing of some former investors in the Detroit Automobile Company. The idea was that racing cars would create a reputation and improve business profile and prospects, which it did. They founded the Henry Ford Company on November 30th 1901. Ford was installed as chief engineer, owning 6 percent of the company. On June 15th 1903, Ford's main partner, coal dealer Alexander Malcolmson, suggested a change of name to 'Ford Motor Company'. Ford and Malcolmson now held around half the stock. It was that year that Ford undertook his vision of producing "a car for the great multitude."

In October 1908 Ford began manufacturing the Model T. It retailed for $950 ($15,000). The following year he announced he would produce the Model T exclusively and in only one colour. Ford sold 15,500,000 Model Ts in America alone and was able to get the cost of producing the car down to $99 ($700) by 1914. He had achieved one of the greatest entrepreneurial feats of all time: the delivery of a motorcar, affordable to the mass market.

So how did he do it? Henry Ford once observed a conveyor belt in a meat factory. It gave him the idea of bringing interchangeable car parts to the workers (rather than the other way round), saving time and money, inspiring the creation of the first assembly line in modern industrial manufacturing. The workers' tasks narrowed and they became dab hands at doing the menial repetitive jobs asked of them.

Ford then brought in Fredrick Taylor (of 'scientific management' fame) with his infamous stopwatch, to study workers' physical movement, in order to improve their speed on any given task. It was now possible to manufacture a whole car in 93 minutes, enabling the factory to churn out 1,000 units per day.

Ford even economised on fuel costs by sweeping the debris off the floor and feeding it into the furnace.

Henry Ford expanded to Britain in 1908 and by 1913 was the largest car manufacturer there. He went on to sell cars as far and wide as China.

The entrepreneur's passion for cars was evident. In 1911, Ford was interviewed by Napoleon Hill, who was searching for the secrets of success on behalf of Andrew Carnegie. The entrepreneur was reticent until Napoleon mentioned cars. Ford then lit up and took him on a factory tour (in a car), and sold him a brand new $680 ($10,500) Model T, which Hill drove home. Ford was besotted with his business.

Advanced people skills

Far from removing the need to reply on people, Ford's revolutionary system depended on a competent, loyal workforce. The conveyor belt development came from employees Clarence Avery, Peter E. Martin, Charles E. Sorensen, and C.H. Wills. In 1939, *Time* magazine reported that Ford was paying his close associates Martin and Sorensen $171,465 ($2,400,000) and $166,071 ($2,300,000) respectively.

Ford's company employed thousands of people, and in 1914 he gave his workers a wage hike, announcing wages of twice what was considered a good day's pay: $5 ($71) per day.

'GOLD RUSH' IS STARTED BY FORD'S $5 OFFER

Thousands of Men Seek Employment in Detroit Factory.

Will Distribute $10,000,000 in Semi-Monthly Bonuses.

No Employe to Receive Less Than Five Dollars a Day.

(TIMES-STAR SPECIAL DISPATCH.)
DETROIT, Mich., January 7.—
Henry Ford in an interview to-

Ford called it 'wage motive' and it made national headlines. Staff turnover – and therefore the cost of training replacement staff – was reduced. Productivity was increased. With the price of a car so low and their salaries significantly increased, many of Ford's workers became customers, putting their money back into the company.

But it wasn't all good news for employees of the Ford Company. Their boss – who by now had gained full ownership of the business – set up a department to prescribe how he wanted his employees to behave in their private lives, offering profit share bonuses for the compliant. The nefarious department was ultimately closed, and its records burned.

Nevertheless, Ford was generally a fair and progressive employer. In October 1926 he announced: "We have decided upon and at once put into effect through all the branches of our industries the five-day week...according to merit, [employees] will receive the same pay equivalent as for a full six-day week."

A complex character

By 1921 Henry Ford's company enjoyed a 55 percent share of the worldwide car manufacturing market and a major share of the tractor market. Ford owned rubber plantations in South America, a fleet of ships, a railroad, coal and iron-ore mines and thousands of acres of timberland, employing 100,000 workers. In 1927 he earned over $25 million ($230 million), second only to his contemporary John D. Rockefeller. That year, American citizens voted Ford the Greatest Man in the World, and then nominated him as the third Greatest Man in History. Ford lost out on the latter title, owing to competition from Napoleon Bonaparte and Jesus Christ. Money was not Ford's primary driver. That was simply a passion for what he loved since he was a child: mechanics.

Despite the level of his popularity amongst his peers, Henry Ford's character was full of contradictions. He was the only employer in the 1920s and '30s to offer wide-ranging employment opportunities to black people, including senior positions of authority where they were put in charge of white co-workers, a rare practice in apartheid America. By the same token, many people believed Ford to be fiercely anti-Semitic. He financed the translation of the anti-Semitic document *The Protocols of the Elders of Zion* into English, and was given the Grand Cross of the German Eagle medal by Adolf Hitler, who kept a picture of Ford on his wall and sang his praises in *Mein Kampf.*

Henry Ford died in 1947 aged 83. His personal character was hard to decipher, but to this day he is regarded as one of the world's greatest entrepreneurs.

ELIZABETH ARDEN 1878 – 1966

"Isn't it amazing what a woman can do with a little bit of ambition?"

Looking good

The influx of immigrants into America, along with industrialisation, created a new culture of city life. Women were about to discover that the better they looked, the more choices they had. Elizabeth Arden would help.

She was a farmer's daughter who created a world of glamour. Christened Florence Nightingale Graham, she lived in Ontario, Canada. Florence's maternal forebears were well off. Her father William was an entrepreneur of modest origins, operating as a market gardener, and was viewed by his in-laws as unworthy of Florence's mother, Susan. The young couple decided to elope to Canada from their native Britain to get married.

Florence was the third of four siblings. The family lived in the countryside where young Florence enjoyed her responsibility of looking after the horses. She accompanied her father to market, where she observed his pushy sales technique. As a child Florence learned that good looks sell products. She charmed the money out of the pockets of passers-by, perched strategically by her father. But the enemy of the age – tuberculosis – interrupted her young life, seizing her mother. Florence was merely an infant of six years old when Susan passed away. Tuberculosis targeted the poor and the weak. The hard work on the farm, lack of cash and the stress on the body whilst carrying four children in a rural environment took its toll.

Florence's father had tried different things to make money, such as rearing racehorses, but nothing worked out. It was exactly what Florence's grandparents in England had feared. As a teenager, Florence attempted to emulate her namesake by entering the nursing profession. She soon packed it in to become a dental assistant, a stenographer and then a clerk. For her being poor was not an option. She had plans and ambitions.

Escaping from small town life

Florence often created potions that she believed would improve women's looks. She tried experimenting in her father's kitchen, often forcing the rest of the family to retreat from the house to avoid being stifled by the stench of obnoxious gases. She ached to get ahead and knew she had to get close to where the money was, and that meant moving to New York. At the age of 24, Florence took the plunge and left for the big city. Her dad feared the worst for his poor little girl, alone and unmarried in the wild gangster-ridden city of New York, but he was powerless to stop her.

Florence got a job working for E.R. Squibb Pharmaceutical Company as a book-keeper, but ended up spending much of her time studying in their lab. Her big break came in the form of a post as a beautician at Eleanor Adair's parlour. She battered Adair into submission for a chance to become a treatment attendant, and clients loved the nice girl from Canada. Florence was now exactly where she wanted to be.

Strategic alliance

It wasn't long before Florence came to the attention of Elizabeth Hubbard, a woman cut from the same cloth with entrepreneurial ambitions. The two women recognised that by forming an alliance they could *both* make progress. Hubbard had the products and Florence had the touch. They opened a beauty parlour on Fifth Avenue, the centre of the boroughs of Manhattan and the Bronx, in 1909.

The alliance between the two feisty women was to be short-lived. After a series of fiery arguments, the two entrepreneurs parted company – but Florence managed to gain the upper hand. She used her attractiveness to charm the landlord into letting the property to her and not Hubbard, funded by $6,000 ($100,000) that she raised from her brother and an admirer.

Florence used the money to remodel the premises in bright pink. The colour became her signature; gone was the name 'parlour' and in came 'salon'. Florence was big on imagery and marketing, and 'salon' was chic. Florence altered her name and the name of the business to Elizabeth Arden. 'Arden' came from Tennyson's biographical poem, *Enoch Arden*. Florence also added 'Mrs' to her new name, aware that Western society regarded single women in business as suspicious. Elizabeth Arden's target was white women; her unapologetic, unadulterated, quest was for money, and selling beauty was the means.

The Suffragette movement

Florence's management techniques were straight from the school of Genghis Khan. It was all about the message. Products had classical-sounding names, evoking tales of mythological beauty and promising fresh-scented youth. Arden appealed to women approaching their sell-by dates. She gave new hope to plain Janes and those on the wane, all of whom were convinced they could transform themselves if they bought a jar of Florence's balm. Things moved ahead swiftly and went so well that within six months Florence's investors had their money back.

The key to the allure of the Elizabeth Arden brand was the movie business. Florence's secret vice – watching the disreputable nickelodeons – was about to pay dividends. Entrepreneurs like MGM movie mogul Louis Mayer were bringing glamour to the masses in the form of movie stars such as Oscar-nominee Lillian Gish, star of *Birth of a Nation*.

It was actresses like this who set the standard for ordinary women to aspire to. The Elizabeth Arden company capitalised on the opportunity, becoming the first cosmetics brand to advertise in cinemas.

Women were on the rise and Florence had every intention of her company rising with them. In 1912, she signed up as a member of the Suffragette movement, taking part in the big march on Washington on 6th May of that year.

Florence never underestimated the power of publicity. She travelled the whole country with her ballet troupe, who wore the seven colours of her new range of lipsticks. Up until then women had a very narrow choice: one colour which came in three shades (light, medium or dark). The white American female was actually under pressure to remain plain in some respects. The fire-and-brimstone brigade portrayed make-up as the devil's work. Arden was planning to free women from the tyranny of mediocrity and get rich doing it. As her advertisements said: "Every woman has a right to be beautiful."

After an inspirational trip to France, Florence introduced modern eye make-up to North America, along with the concept of the makeover. Upon her return from later trips to Paris in 1914 and 1915, she linked up with chemist Fabian Swanson, to produce a "face cream that was light and fluffy like whipped cream"; it was called 'Venetian Cream Amoretta'. She asked him to throw in a lotion in to go with it and with that a successful collaboration was born. Arden would come up with the most fanciful ideas for a product and her recruit, Swanson, mixed them. What Arden also mixed was the fact that the product was made in New York, but had an Italian name and was marketed as a famous French formula. However, her marketing message was as smooth as her cream.

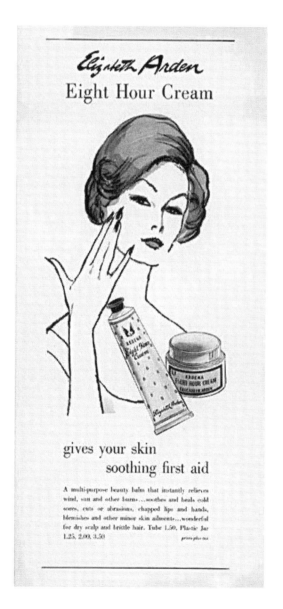

Mrs. Elizabeth Arden married banker Mr. Thomas J. Lewis that year. They had met previously when she applied for a loan and he turned her down. The poor unwary man was in for a lot more than he bargained for. A new branch was opened in Washington DC and she expanded the Fifth Avenue salon to seven storeys. Elizabeth had to get her banker husband involved to handle the books after being trounced by the taxman for neglecting her accounts. But the taxman is only a problem when you're making money and Florence was certainly doing that. She now had a thousand workers in salons worldwide, as she competed with the like of Helena Rubenstein and Dorothy Gray. Arden was the first European-American woman to build a brand using her name. She once claimed, "There are only three American names that are known in every corner of the globe: Singer sewing machines, Coca Cola and Elizabeth Arden."

Florence was driven by her aversion to poverty, and a desperate desire to avoid the humiliation of dying broke due to some poverty-related illness. During 1920 the Elizabeth Arden range made its debut in Paris. This was quickly followed by salons in Berlin, Cannes, Rome, Rio de Janeiro, Buenos Aires and Toronto. In 1929 Florence turned down an offer of $15 million ($135 million) for the business. She breezed through the Great Depression of 1929 (women still wanted to look good, even in bad times). A few years later she turned down a $25 million ($300 million) offer.

Her rural retreat, bought in 1931, became a racehorse business, in emulation of her father's dreams. Racehorses cost her money at first but she had a Kentucky Derby winner in 1947. Earnings topped out at $600,000 ($5,500,000) in 1943. It's not surprising that the horses did well, as the treatment they received was unprecedented: before and after training, they were given massages with expensive Elizabeth Arden creams and oils.

Hell to live with but generous

Elizabeth Arden's strength of character made her hard to live with. She personally hired and fired, and she hated criticism. A couple of typical quotes summed her up: "I don't want them [staff] to love me, I want them to fear me" and "Standards should be set by me and not imposed on me."

No one was safe. In 1934, hubby got the boot. By 1938, Florence was the top-earning woman in the country. She spread her wings in 1941, marrying a Russian prince, and in 1943 expanded into clothing. Clothing went well, but the Prince got the elbow after less than 13 months. Four years later she made the cover of *Time* magazine.

Elizabeth Arden suffered a fatal heart attack in 1966. Surprisingly, in fact quite astonishingly, she left a substantial amount of her $40 million ($183 million) fortune to be divided among her staff – the very people whom she'd ruled with an iron fist. She had over one hundred salons spread across the globe.

FROM **FARM** TO **FIFTH** AVENUE

How I Became a
Stylist to the
Rich & Famous at
the World's Most
Exclusive Salon

Lyonel Nelson with Stephen J. Anderson

RAY KROC 1902 – 1984

"If any of my competitors were drowning, I'd stick a hose in their mouth"

Motorcars, banking and oil were about to be joined on the Fortune 500 List by burgers, courtesy of Ray Kroc, the man responsible for the worldwide phenomenon of McDonald's.

City life changed the speed in which business was conducted, intensified competition and submerged all that dwelled in the city into one great rat race. Opportunities and jobs abounded, but that was part of the problem.

When pressure intensifies, most people run for the cover of a monthly pay cheque. Great entrepreneurs are different: they run from the cloak of cover into danger. Some are naturally well adjusted to it; others simply give up and settle for what they're given.

Observe Ray Arthur Kroc, who was born in the metropolis of Chicago. The epitome of persistence, he learned how to take advantage of the pressure of limited time. From very early on he realised he enjoyed competing at work as much as playing baseball. He was the child of Czech immigrant parents, cultured people who believed in education. Kroc's brother became a university professor, but Kroc had other ideas about how to get on in life. In his mid-teens he opened a music shop with three friends, throwing in $100 ($1,500) each. He may have had a talent for the piano, but he still had much to learn about business. The venture failed shortly after being founded.

Working all hours

Although only 14, he decided to give school a miss and conned his way into the US Army. Whilst training, Kroc met and befriended a guy called Walt Disney.

Kroc and the troops saw Walt as an oddball. When they all went out chasing girls Disney preferred to stay at the base and draw pictures. Just as they were about to be shipped off, World War I ended. Kroc was at a loose end figuring out what to do next. He tried sales and then music, as a pianist in an orchestra, eventually settling down to work as a salesman for Lily Tulip, a paper cup company. He'd previously sold coffee beans door-to-door, and now he was cold-calling companies selling paper cups. Kroc thought the market for a throwaway product like a cup would be huge.

Kroc's secret for successful selling was to squeeze every ounce of productivity out of every waking moment. He worked very late and would get to sleep immediately using a relaxation technique, relaxing each part of his body, working from his head down to his toes. The imperative was to wake up fresh and ready for the day ahead. So, from 7am to 5pm he would pound the streets of Chicago selling paper cups. From 6pm to 2am he slogged away working as a live pianist at a local radio station. Then it was to bed for four hours sleep.

Visit to the MacDonald brothers

In 1937, Kroc began a partnership with Earl Prince, a Lily Tulip client who had developed a multi-mixer for making milkshakes.

Prince wanted Kroc in the business to drive sales. It meant an immediate pay-cut and a loss of security, but it also meant control of his destiny. In 1948, Kroc hit record sales of 8,000 units.

In December that year, a couple of brothers called McDonald opened a restaurant in San Bernardino, California. The brothers had eight multi-mixers, which meant they were selling a lot of milkshakes. Kroc knew something was going on down there and in 1952 he took an opportunity to check them out. After spotting the McDonald's restaurant he pulled his car over to observe the activity from a distance. What he witnessed was military order.

It was lunchtime and the queues grew. He walked in and took this place in the line. The food was great and served promptly. Kroc set up a meeting that very night and got the story of the McDonald brothers. They had started out as a barbecue restaurant, but the brothers found it took too much work to keep customers satisfied. The restaurant was packed but break-even was as good as it got. Maurice and Richard McDonald decided minimalism was the way to go. The range on offer was reduced, improving logistics and increasing economies of scale. This in turn lowered costs.

The brothers also instigated a Ford-style systematic assembly line to produce and serve the food, which they dubbed the 'Speedee Service System'. This system was based on the principle that no customer should wait for his or her food longer than 90 seconds. If for some reason a delay should occur the food would be given free of charge. Moreover, the food was sold at 50 percent less than any of their competitors' offerings.

Pioneering vision

Kroc had seen the future and he wanted to be a star in it. He is quoted as saying: "The two most important requirements for major success are: first, being in the right place at the right time, and second, doing something about it." The next day an agreement was signed. The brothers gave Kroc exclusive franchising rights as an agent to set up McDonald's restaurants.

Ray Kroc, now in his late 50s, forfeited the comfortable $12,000 ($70,000) a year income he was earning and the security that went with it. He would now earn 1.9 percent of the gross sales of franchises with the brothers picking up 0.5 percent. Each franchise would have a 25 year agreement (later extended to 99 years).

Kroc accelerated take-up by targeting entrepreneurs with an easy payment scheme. He encouraged landowners to set up McDonald's restaurants on their unused land. On April 15th 1955 Ray Kroc opened his first McDonald's franchise in Des Plaines, Illinois, followed in July by an outlet in Fresno, California.

Things did not go well. The French fries weren't as great as the ones produced by the McDonald brothers. Kroc had problems recreating the McDonald's taste, but he soon discovered the French fry secret. It was the searing heat of the Californian desert breeze curing the potatoes and turning the sugar to starch (just before eating) that made them taste so good. They had to be eaten soon after the curing process, and therefore kept hot and served immediately after cooking. It was all a question of 'just in time'. Kroc decided that salt would be added just before serving, whilst the chips were curing. From that point forward, they tasted consistently excellent.

By 1956 Ray Kroc had opened 12 restaurants across America. Sales for that year were $193,772 ($1 million). Things were going well, except for a slight personal issue – Ray Kroc hated the McDonald brothers with a passion. Whilst he was fanatical about opening restaurants (to his dying day) the brothers were stuck in 'California cruise control'. Kroc described the two brothers as not being on his wavelength and said he often felt like killing them. The brothers had a restaurant that Kroc wanted, but the 'comfortable' intransigent pair threatened to end the whole enterprise rather than give it up. They wanted to play hardball so Kroc simply closed them down by opening up a new franchise down the street.

The buy-out

In 1960, the annual sales total hit $37,579,828 ($200 million). The following year Hamburger University was founded by Fred Turner, who started out as a grill man. It was during this year Kroc realised he had created a beast, though it was not yet his beast. As soon as he realised this Kroc decided to not waste any time and called the brothers, asking how much they wanted for the chain and the rights. The brothers' reply was a staggering $1 million ($5 million) *each* after tax. Kroc dropped the phone and nearly fell off his chair. The deal was done but Kroc would eventually spend $14 million ($70 million) obtaining the McDonald's chain he created. From the financial trajectories he had calculated he believed it would take him until 1991 to pay off the borrowings; it also cost him his marriage of 39 years.

Kroc borrowed heavily to finance the deal and his company. A New York money manager got him a $2.7 million ($14 million) loan from a number of pension and college endowment funds, with interest payments determined as a percentage of McDonald's' sales plus 22.5 percent equity share. Despite all the borrowings the company was still financially anaemic.

McDonald's becomes a property company

Kroc and his team came up with an idea. A new venture, Franchise Realty Corporation, was launched. The entrepreneur bought up land, influenced by the time he had spent in Florida selling property. From now on, the McDonald's Corporation would buy a building and lease it to their franchisees with a mark-up of close to 40 percent. Franchisees would pay McDonalds either a minimum rate of return or a percentage of sales, whichever was greater. As sales grew so too did the property values and the rents the corporation could charge. It was a no-brainer. By 1964 there were 657 McDonald's restaurants and Kroc never looked back.

McDonald's was once described by Kroc as a massive real-estate company selling burgers to pay the mortgage. The property portfolio doubled and trebled in value over time. By 1985 McDonald's had a property portfolio worth $416 billion. It was this difference in perspective of the company that split Kroc and his main partner Harry Sonneborne, credited with the move into property. Kroc sold burgers and Sonneborne acquired properties. The two perspectives collided. Nevertheless, both men got rich.

In 1976 Kroc opened the 4,000th McDonald's in Montreal, Canada. He died on January 14th 1984, aged 83, survived by his third wife, having achieved his dream to make it big. He left behind him an estate worth $500 million, and was quoted as saying: "I was 52 years old. I had diabetes and incipient arthritis. I had lost my gall bladder and most of my thyroid gland in earlier campaigns, but I was convinced that the best was ahead of me." By 2004, there were nearly 32,000 McDonald's outlets globally.

BERRY GORDY 1929 –

"Create, Sell and Collect"

Henry Ford's motor town was about to become an assembly line of an entirely different sort: talent. Enter Berry Gordy Jr., the man who created Motown.

Born in the midst of America's Great Depression in 1929, Gordy was the child of entrepreneurs Berry Gordy II and his wife Bertha.

The couple had moved their young family from America's Deep South to Detroit, in the North. They weren't, however, in Detroit to look for work in the car factories. They were there looking for property to buy and would become the only black people in the neighbourhood to own a commercial building.

Family business

The family eventually moved to live on the more sedate West Side of Detroit. The industrious Gordy Sr. studied to acquire his contractor's licence and built a construction business on the fast-moving and dangerous East Side in 1935. Alongside his construction business the entrepreneurial patriarch worked at a local grocer. He was eventually able to purchase a commercial building with two apartments on the upper floors (where they lived) and a double-fronted grocery store on the ground level. Bertha named the grocery store 'Booker T Washington' after the legendary (Reconstruction era) black leader. After studying commerce at college, Bertha started the Friendship Mutual Life Insurance Company. It didn't stop there: the couple added property and a print shop to their business portfolio.

The East Side represented everything Gordy's family was not. Young Gordy's home was unified, disciplined, religious and organised. The East Side was simply hip and wild. The one thing both sides had in common was the art of hustling. Blacks needed to hustle. President Franklin D. Roosevelt's 'New Deal', which aimed to stabilise, reform and stimulate the US economy during the Great Depression, was largely inaccessible to black citizens. Many unions made sure new job programmes served white workers only. When companies tried to hire blacks the white workers went on strike, causing race riots.

In school Berry Gordy Jr. was the class clown, compensating for his academic under-performance. He learned how to entertain so well that even his straight-laced teachers cracked under pressure from his comic performances. Another strategy was learning the alphabet backwards. Its recitation was always useful in veiling his poor educational performance.

Hustlers and hustling

Eventually the dangerous East Side streets replaced fear in young Gordy's mind with excitement. He embraced the streets. The street hustlers generally lacked formal education, but teenage Gordy observed them with awe. Many of them were sharp, with powerful memories. They applied their talents to the three key ingredients of hustling: survival, moneymaking and the acquisition of women – in that order. One local numbers runner amazed Gordy. He couldn't speak for stuttering, but he could remember numerous combinations of the three or four-digit numbers of the close of the New York Stock Market on a given day, from the dozens of different players, without need of paper or pencil. The lottery game was popular among poor African Americans and became sardonically known as the 'Nigger Pool'.

Gordy tried various entrepreneurial schemes, like selling papers, gambling and a shoeshine stand, with limited success. The young hustler's primary incentive for money was the ladies. So, it was a toss-up between his love of boxing and singing. The two seemed to have cornered the market on beautiful women. Joe Louis and Sugar Ray Robinson were kicking up a rumpus and both fought out of Detroit, so boxing got the nod.

Gordy learned his trade in what would become one of the world's most prestigious gyms. He just happened to walk into 35 year-old Eddie Futch's gymnasium in Detroit.

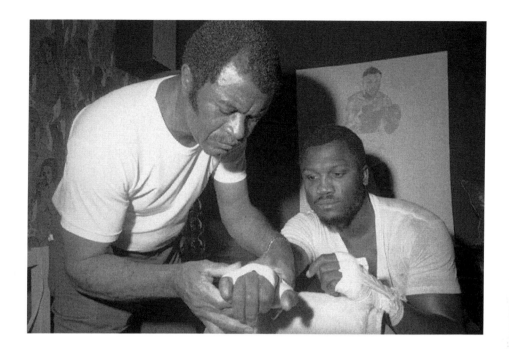

Futch would lead champions Joe Frazier, Michael Spinks and Larry Holmes to world titles, and he thought teenage Gordy was talented. Consequently, Gordy quit school to become a professional fighter, earning on average $150 ($1,000) a fight. On November 19th 1948, when Joe Louis topped the bill in the Olympic Stadium, Detroit, Berry Gordy Jr. made the undercard. He did just enough to get the points decision that night and put himself in the running for a title.

During a session at the gym he sat for a break. Looking up he saw a poster advertising a 'music clash' between Stan Kenton and Duke Ellington, juxtaposed with another poster promoting a boxing bout. The boxers on the poster were in their twenties but looked 50, and the musicians were in their fifties but looked 20. The struggle between music and boxing was over. Gordy hung up his gloves for good.

Korean war

Uncle Sam interrupted Gordy's bid to become a songwriter, dragging him off to Korea to serve in the army. He gratefully made it back to America and music in 1953, with the equivalent of an electronics degree.

Jazz was the black music of the 1950s. Gordy opened a jazz record shop called 3-D Record Mart with army buddy Billy Davis, who suddenly started appearing on the street corner dressed to kill. And that's where his end of the partnership went – on flashy clothes. Davis decided to pass on going into the music business with the young ambitious Berry Gordy so that he could dress well for a while: a decision he would regret for the rest of his life. Nevertheless, with the money Gordy had borrowed from his dad and his stubborn brother George, it was game on. They got the venture up and running, working out of the family store. Gordy Jr. also took another kind of partner around the same time. Thelma Coleman became Gordy's wife and the two lovebirds started a family.

The need to focus

In 1955, the business failed. The young entrepreneur needed to get a job to support his new family, which he duly did at Guardian Cookware, selling pots and pans. It was there he learned how to break down the selling process, a lesson he'd never forget. His father was with him on his first independent sale. After his performance his Gordy Sr. told him he was utterly ashamed. Gordy Jr. was *so* good he was able to overcome the poor man's every objection including being flat broke and having a large number of children to support, and moreover having a more-than-adequate supply of pots and pans. Gordy Jr. was able to persuade such a guy to sign up to purchase even more. His father tore strips off him and Berry Jr. resigned, immediately ashamed. It was at this time he began focusing on his song writing as a career.

Gordy's sister Gwen was a songwriter and entrepreneur, with a photo concession at the Flame Show Bar frequented by black stars like Billie Holiday and Dinah Washington. Gwen introduced Gordy (as a songwriter) to Al Green, a club owner and manager of singers, including a teenage kid called Jackie Wilson.

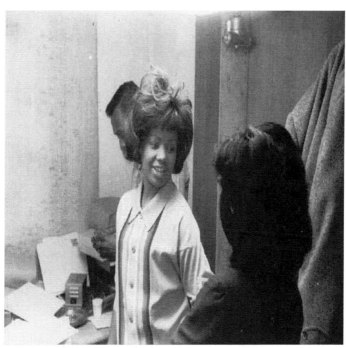

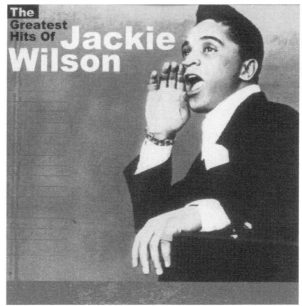

They struck up a collaboration and as a result Gordy Jr. registered his first hit *Reet Petite,* written by him and sung by Jackie Wilson, in 1957. It earned Gordy Jr. $1,000 ($6,000); he was now a professional songwriter. A string of hits followed, including *To Be Loved,* written the night Gordy Jr. was thrown out of the family home and sued for divorce by Thelma. It was sung by Jackie Wilson, a guy who never dropped a note. This became the standard of Berry Gordy's expectations when assessing artists – perfect pitch and holding a note.

He just happened to be working on a song in an office when a teenager called Smokey Robinson came in with his group for an audition. The group struck up, struck out and were shown out. But Gordy sensed something in them, particularly Smokey, and chased after them down the corridor. They all hit it off straight away.

Gordy cleaned up a song that Smokey had written which excited them both. The song was a catchy answer-tune, replying to a previous hit by The Silhouettes called *Get a Job,* and Smokey called it *Got a Job.* In 1958, Gordy hustled together Smokey's music, musicians, rehearsals, and a recording deal. It was a smash in Detroit but a dud nationally. Nevertheless, singers were now biting his arm off at the elbow for songs.

Divvying up the monies for tunes between himself and his co-writers left everyone on the bread line. Gordy asked for some of the action from the B-sides of releases but Jackie Wilson's people said no. Gordy's team pushed ahead and set up Anna Records, complete with a distribution deal. Gordy made a shock announcement: he had no intention of working in a 'strict' business partnership ever again after his experience with his very difficult brother. He would do his own thing and if they wanted to take the trip with him they could. But he was definitely doing all the driving. Bad experiences with trying to get paid for songs he'd written led to the impromptu entry into the music publishing business. Gordy waited for the money to roll in from his producer's cut of *Got a Job.* It did – all $3.19 cents ($16.54) of it. Smokey told Gordy: "You might as well start your own record label," and with that Gordy created Jobete.

Family funds

Gordy needed $1,000 ($6,000) to put out his first record under his own label. Everyone he approached turned him down. He was left with no choice but to apply for a loan from the dreaded 'Ber-Berry Fund': the collective savings of his entire family. This was no act of charity, however. Gordy's parents and siblings put the entrepreneur through the mill, demanding justification for every penny of their investment. Gordy eventually got the approval for $800 ($5,000) but the family contracted him to provide future royalties as lien.

A new and separate label from Jobete was required. The name needed to be something the buying public would be comfortable and familiar with. *Tammy* by Debbie Reynolds was a number one hit. So Gordy called his label Tammy, riding on the back of the already familiar title. But the name was already registered, so he altered it to Tamla. Gordy's first tune, *Come to Me* was a hit. United Artists wanted both the tune and him, so he hooked up a deal with the major corporation and went national.

Smokey wrote a piece for his group The Miracles; Gordy refined it and then negotiated a deal with an engineer who was also the studio owner's son. The mix was great, but Gordy thought a different approach was needed in marketing this latest release. The Tamla image was geared to individuals, and Gordy wanted a separate label for groups. Detroit was the home to Henry Ford and his motorcar factories, and was where he built his first car. The city was known as a 'motor town' as a result. Gordy, a fast developing marketer, chose the name 'Motown,' reflecting the hustling, bustling city of Detroit, which he loved.

But there were problems; the majors blew hot and cold on releasing and distributing his tune. From then on Gordy saw musical success as an impostor. All the fanfare of having a hit was nothing. Every release of a song was held hostage to fortune by single executives and whether they liked a tune or not. Greater control over the product was needed. His sisters wanted to go even further. But the budding entrepreneur continued to resist pleas for a social refinement department and the development of an etiquette programme for artists.

The Motown sound

Earnings from songs began to increase, along with the female attention Gordy craved. He bought a new two-storey apartment, turning the lower floor into a studio. It was all hands to the pump. Gordy used his electronics training, his family's building skills and the conscripted artists to create the studio. A big sign was put in the window that read 'Hitsville'. It was here the magic would happen. Gordy would control most of the creative process, as well as the periphery issues that gelled to create stars and hits.

The cheap studio sound was replaced by re-worked versions in a sophisticated New York studio. The strange thing was the public didn't buy the re-worked versions, only the old ones. They wanted that hollow, tinny and echoing sound produced by the rickety studio at Hitsville. The Motown sound had been born.

Integration era

The machinery for Hitsville was almost complete. Gordy's aura now attracted helpers, who became staff, and distributors were competing with one another to sell Gordy's records. Artists began seeking out this new Moses of music, one who could lead them out from obscurity. Smokey was already in the bag, and then came a smooth, cool and deeply mysterious guy called Marvin Gaye. In 1961, some skinny schoolgirls were signed, a year after they had auditioned and been told to come back when they finished high school. The lead singer was a child called Diana Ross. In 1963 Ronnie White of The Miracles brought in a youngster called Steveland Judkins. Gordy had his breakfast interrupted and was rushed downstairs into the studio to listen to the kid play bongos, harmonica and piano whilst singing. They signed him and decided to market the kid under the name Stevie Wonder.

Gordy fused together an amazing amalgam of talent. The Motown family sang the company song together once a week in the company meeting, with the entire rostrum of artistes and stars in attendance. They lived together, cooked together, ate together and made music together – and some even made love together.

Then came the Artist Development Department, created and driven by Gwen and Anna Gordy after finally obtaining their brother's approval. The sisters went to work producing human dynamite. The department was staffed with professionals from the modelling industry, finishing schools, and the promotions industry. They hammered artists into shape for an image-crazy world: how to walk, sit, get out of cars, eat and behave well were all taught, down to the last detail. There was a strict policy of no smoking in public. Berry Gordy's outstretched hand had now become a clenched fist that would fight for market-share in all demographic sectors of America's music spend.

During the mid1960s Gordy added 'Pay, Save and Reinvest' to his business mantra of 'Create, Sell and Collect'. He also added accountants Sidney Noveckto his professional and established firm, to manage the company finances and add backbone to the company.

By 1964 Motown Records was the largest and most successful independent record company in the US, selling black music to a predominantly white audience struggling with black civil rights issues. Gordy simply took the view that, regardless of race, everybody appreciated good quality music.

◼ New Album: Live recording of his speech to 200,000 Detroiters is presented in Atlanta to the Rev. M. L. King Jr., by Morton Records prexy Berry Gordy Jr. (l) as bias-fighting entertainers Lena Horne and Billy Taylor observe presentation of the first copy of new album.

Michael Jackson and The Jackson 5

In 1966 Gladys Knight and the Pips were signed. During 1967, Hitsville had 13 top-ten hits, allowing Gordy to move into a big house in Hollywood Hills, Los Angeles, California. The company continued expanding in 1968, with a new office in L.A. Soon after moving, Gordy was being harangued about a new group who were causing a stir. The kids were brought downstairs ready for presentation and the place was buzzing. Some staff knew what they were in for, having seen the kids perform previously. They performed and were mesmeric. Gordy walked over to them, unsmiling and unemotional, and said: "You keep working hard and we'll do the rest." The kids roared with joy.

The name given to them was 'The Jackson 5' and they were introduced to the Motown family at Gordy Manor, a three-storey mansion, with an English pub and an underground tunnel leading to the pool house, separate from the indoor Olympic-size swimming pool (the full-size bowling alley was also a favourite). Gordy, feeling the place to be ostentatious, never lived there but it was a great place for entertaining guests from out of town.

Berry Gordy's 'music machine'

The Best of Motown
2 CD
Billy Preston & Syreetha
Diana Ross
Lionel Richie
Stevie Wonder
Marvin Gaye
Michael Jackson
Smokey Robinson & the Miracles

Smokey Robinson, Michael Jackson, Diana Ross, Stevie Wonder and Marvin Gaye were some of the greatest pop artists that had ever lived, yet they represented a small proportion of Gordy's stars. He didn't go looking for them; they all came looking for him. Berry Gordy had created a 'music machine' that was a conveyor belt of cultivated creativity, production, appearance and personality. He controlled every aspect and made billions for Tamla-Motown Records, the music industry and America in general.

Gordy's first wife, friends, mother-in-law, bosses and teachers all thought he was a screw-up. Often the only difference between a screw-up and a genius is luck. Despite all this he knew what he wanted, was confident in his talent as a songwriter and had learnt the art of hustling (getting enough without having enough). Berry Gordy's mother taught him that everything learned can become useful and he made use of everything and everyone around him. He marshalled all he had learned from the Jewish junk traders who advised him as a young teenager, a stuttering numbers runner, and his unstoppable mother and father. Gordy used those around him to provide what he couldn't, to climb to the pinnacle of his industry and create history.

The entrepreneur had many affairs with beautiful women and was married and divorced several times, producing seven children by four mothers. His $800 loan created the largest black-owned business in the United States. In June 1988, Gordy reluctantly sold his business to a partnership consisting of Boston Ventures and MCA for $61 million ($90 million), with him retaining the ownership of the Jobete publishing catalogue. Five years later the company was sold for five times the original amount to Polygram Records. Gordy made sure he didn't undervalue Jobete (the publishing arm of his business) when he sold it to EMI Music Publishing (who outbid Michael Jackson) for $320 million.

DON KING 1932 –

"I'm one of the world's great survivors. I'll always survive because I've got the right combination of wit, grit and bullshit"

On March 31st 1949, Don King's school report read: "Donald King's mother came. Don will be eighteen next year and will not be accepted back September because of truancy and general bad behaviour." From the very beginning, Don King was a troublemaker.

Don was the fifth of Clarence and Hattie King's six children. His father died in a steel plant explosion when Don was only ten years old. His mother made sure the insurance money was used to improve the family's prospects by moving into a middle-class neighbourhood. Hattie was an entrepreneur, selling homemade pies and roasted peanuts. The whole family got involved with boosting sales. King would sell door-to-door and came up with the idea of inserting a prize draw number into each bag of peanuts. The chance of winning some money encouraged punters to buymore bags of peanuts.

During the early 1950s, King had a brief career as a boxer (brief because the rules got in his way). The street had regulations too but they were laws of the inner-city jungle, an environment that suited King's skills. After a year at Case Western Reserve University in Cleveland, King abandoned dreams of obtaining a university degree and tried on the university of the streets. Six-foot-two Don King became a stone-cold ghetto bad boy, running things.

Two dead – life in jail

King had an edge. He was a mathematical genius, a major advantage in a gaming environment. Donald the Kid, as he became known, developed and controlled a numbers racket. He, like the stuttering genius that had so impressed Berry Gordy, ran the numbers. But King was no street runner. He ran a clearing house from his club, the New Corner Tavern, in Cleveland. It operated like the UK banking system's APACS and BACS organisation, settling payments between the racketeers/banks and turning over $15,000 ($110,000) each day. Ironically, criminal success in the ghetto makes you a prime target for crime. A posse attacked King's base in 1954, in an attempt to rob the business. During the ensuing shoot-out King shot and killed one Hillary Brown. 'TeflonDon' got off with justifiable homicide.

79254
POLICE DEPT
CLEVELAND O
AUG 14 1954

From his vantage point as the main cog in the numbers business, Don King was able to hustle the hustlers. At 2pm each day he made his customary daily call to his broker, establishing the pre-close positions of the New York stock market. This enabled him to bet, using his 'runners' as takers. From these numbers and the proximity to the close of the market, he could establish probabilities. His complex calculations mitigated the risk from 600-1 to 200-1. He made a lot of money.

Getting paid sometimes proved difficult. Sam Garrett owed King $600 ($3,000). On April 20th 1966, King noticed Sam at a bar they both frequented and rushed him. King pistol-whipped Garrett to the ground then stomped him to death in broad daylight and in full public view. None of the onlookers dared intervene, as King was wielding a loaded pistol at the time.

In 1967, King was sentenced to life in prison. His attorney also represented Cleveland Mafia figures and he held a private meeting with the judge that sentenced King. The decree was commuted to manslaughter. It is alleged that $30,000 ($150,000) changed hands during the trial. Whilst in prison the entrepreneur managed to acquire a 40-acre farm in Ohio for $1,000 ($5,000). He studied and read furiously, particularly philosophy and the classics. Even today, King can quote famous Shakespeare pieces verbatim. He would later say: "I didn't serve time, time served me."

In 1971 King listened to the first of the three fights between Muhammad Ali and Joe Frazier from prison.

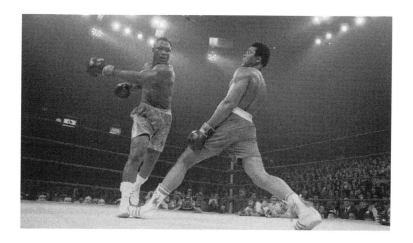

The third fight, in 1975, was put together by King himself, just two and a half years after he left prison. Held in the Philippines, with great media attention throughout the world, it was billed as 'The Thrilla in Manila', and is still considered one of the greatest fights of all time. In just four years, Don King would go from a jail cell to the domination of an entire industry.

Boxing's new era

Don King's path to riches began in 1972 when Forest City Hospital was under threat of being shut down. It served the – predominantly black – local community and King rode in as the black knight in shining armour. He was already involved with boxing at the time. Ray Anderson and Jeff 'Candy Slim' Merritt were two fighters he was able to secure under his management, after easing out the existing manger with some slick manoeuvring.

King booked singers from his club and asked his friend, the legendary performer Lloyd Price, to get his pal Muhammad Ali (who had the pulling power of the Pope and Michael Jackson combined) involved in a boxing exhibition bout to help raise funds. Ali was a sucker for good causes and agreed.

Don King was also able to lean on Price to get the mysterious and mercurial Motown star Marvin Gaye, a protegé of Berry Gordy, to appear. Knowing Gaye's curious disposition, emotionally intelligent King arranged for some guys to pretend they were photographers and go down to meet the singer off the plane with powerful flash photography equipment going off. Marvin lapped it up and got pumped up; the ruse ensured he didn't walk out of the low-brow event. With the help of Don Elbaum (a professional fight promoter) the boxing event broke all records for an exhibition bout. Don King had saved the hospital from closure. Ali suggested King get into the boxing promotion business. King never looked back. During a heart-to-heart with Elbaum, Don King threw his arms theatrically around the promoter and begged him to get him out of the numbers racket through the salvation of boxing.

Elbaum later introduced King to Ernie Shavers, reputed to be the hardest-hitting boxer in history. Entrepreneur Joseph 'Blackie' Gennaro and baseball pitcher Dean Chance had a joint interest in Ernie Shavers. Elbaum arranged for King to buy out Chance. After a grandiose speech by King during an Ernie Shavers investors meeting, King left with $8,000 ($30,000) to pay for his share and another $8,000 for ongoing expenses. Elbaum thought it was critically important that a black promoter fronted the business in the racially charged times.

In 1972 Elbaum continued elevating King, introducing him to a company called Video Techniques, providers of satellite technology and closed-circuit TV coverage for fights. Once again Elbaum made the point about the racial divide and a shift in black consciousness to a more strident nationalistic slant. Elbaum made the situation clear to the Video Techniques President, Hank Schwartz. If they harboured serious ambitions and wanted to assert themselves in the boxing game, they needed a smart black man to front it. It was essential to find someone who could get up close and personal to the prize catch (black heavyweight fighters). Elbaum told Schwartz that King was peerless in this task and that if he had any sense he'd employ him.

Frasier v. Foreman

Video Techniques covered 'The Sunshine Showdown' (Joe Frazier v. George Foreman) in Jamaica on January 22nd 1973. King took the opportunity to slink into champion Joe Frazier's camp. He volunteered for the responsibility of picking up the Frazier family from the airport and lugging their heavy bags around. King then watched the two-round fight virtually from Frazier's stool. King backed the wrong horse. Foreman dropped Frazier six times in five minutes, so King dropped Frazier too, and joined Foreman's camp. Even before the bell could be rung to herald the end of Frazier's unbeaten reign as a fighter and champion, King was in the ring celebrating with Foreman. The guys at Video Techniques looked on in awe as

King and Foreman left in a limousine on their way back to the hotel as an inseparable couple. Schwartz couldn't believe the audacity and sagacity of Don King.

The Jamaican government had financed the Video Techniques satellite feed and had a stake in its corollary broadcast rights. This was not lost on the precocious King. He learned at an exceptionally fast speed. Schwartz sat down with fighter and consummate gentleman Ken Norton, and signed him up for a promotion. However, signing his bad-ass opponent George Foreman was not working out. Bad-ass Don King was wheeled in. The supreme entrepreneur knew how to deal with bad boys, having already killed two of them. He knew he needed big upfront money in small bills, which he raised himself. King is alleged to have found Foreman at an airport urinal. It's rumoured he didn't bother waiting for the boxer to finish relieving himself before laying the money on him and getting him to sign the contract, mid-flow.

Muhammad Ali

King's fighters were losing their big fights. When Muhammad Ali called King to commiserate on the Ernie Shavers loss to 'the great white hope' Jerry Quarry in a one-round defeat, the entrepreneur seized the opportunity to charm Ali into letting him promote an Ali v. Foreman bout. He even went as far as to sprinkle the conversation with quotes from Islam in order to get Ali to agree to the idea.

King put all of this energy into selling the idea to Ali. He outlined his vision for an all-black event: black entrepreneurs as well as boxers, with the best black singers. This was music to Muhammad Ali's ears and impossible for the black icon to resist.

Unsurprisingly, Ali's existing promoters were not very happy about his new alliance with Don King. Entrepreneur Bob Arum (a white Jew) was Muhammad Ali's lawyer and occasional promoter.

Herbert Muhammad (a black Muslim) was both Ali's manager and the son of his spiritual leader, Elijah Muhammad, who was noted for vitriolic anti-white philosophy and anti-Jewish sentiment.

Nevertheless, Don King posed such a threat to their livelihoods that the two men joined forces against him. King, of course, did not take kindly to this attempt to unseat him. He ranted to Muhammad Ali that Arum had reneged on the Ohio closed-circuit rights for Ali v. Frazier II in 1974, and harped on about white 'blaxploitation'.

Arum underestimated King and thought he knew how to out-manoeuvre his competitor. He essentially told Herbert Muhammad to put the 'fruit' high up on the tree beyond King's reach. The requirement was for King to come up with a verbally agreed $5 million ($16 million), as part of a non-refundable advance down-payment. King was also required to produce a contract with Foreman's name on it. Arum knew King could never cover all bases. He thought Don King's idea for a 'Black to Africa' celebratory event was the stuff of fairy tales, but he failed to understand what kind of player he was dealing with.

King successfully put Ali off the idea of a fight organised by Arum and Herbert Muhammad worth $850,000 ($2 million), that could have jeopardised his proposed Africa event. He wooed Ali with his silver tongue, preaching to him about destiny and the greatest sporting event in the history of the world, with black gladiators returning home to Africa. King looked up to the heavens as though he had been taken over by a mystical apparition and then began to speak in hallowed tones as if unaware of his surroundings saying: "I feel we are just instruments in an overall plan."

Ali knew this was outrageous stuff but it was pure theatre. King was a man after Ali's own heart. With millions in the bank from the non-refundable deposit, it was a no-brainer. Ali went for it. The full-on promoter and mathematical genius was eventually able to put a complex multi-faceted deal together. This former convicted murderer and Cleveland street hustler had out-manoeuvred Bob Arum, a Harvard law graduate, member of the bar and former state prosecutor.

George Foreman's management company was in financial disarray and losing money. Many thought King was crazy to plan such an ambitious event. But Leroy Jackson, Foreman's manager, was negotiating to get Foreman to fight Ali and Frazier on the same night! What Jackson was attempting was lunacy. King knew how to get signatures from bad boys. He lay in wait for Foreman in a hotel car park, where he began his pitch:

"I can deliver [Ali]…monumental…reverberate around the world…Black Gladiators… inspiration to the downtrodden… proficiency… perpetuity… " It lasted 90 minutes. Foreman then turned to King and said, "I'm going to give you my trust. I've never done this before." He signed a blank sheet of paper. It was thought that acquiring a signature from George Foreman was going to be an impossible task. King not only got the signature; he got Foreman to sign a *blank* sheet of paper with a promise to fill in the details later! The boxing world simply did not understand what measure of a man was entering its commercial arena.

Trademark hairstyle

By the mid 1970s, King was a celebrity in his own right – he even had his own trademark hairstyle, called the 'crown'.

It was time to secure a venue for King's Africa event. It was actually King's friend Lloyd Price (author of the 'crown' hairstyle) who suggested Africa itself as the location. King travelled to the Congo, a country in turmoil and in need of distraction from its plight, to make a deal with the despot Mobutu. Booked to perform on the night of the fight were living legends like B. B. King and James Brown. King signed TV stations and auctioned the closed-circuit satellite feed. The entrepreneur held together dozens of disparate factions, all of whom had individual and separate agreements and rights to airing, filming or publishing of the greatest sporting event in history, known as 'The Rumble in the Jungle'. The promoter guaranteed an unprecedented $10 million ($35 million), split between the boxers. Muhammad Ali caused one of the greatest upsets in boxing history, having almost been written off by the popular press before the fight. The battle was a sensational exhibition of guile versus brute force. The event went beyond even King's expectation as a spectacle, and cemented his position as a one-man global force in boxing.

In 1976, King arranged for the heavyweight champion of the world, Muhammad Ali, to campaign on behalf of Judge Corrigan, the same judge who commuted his conviction for murder to manslaughter back in 1967. King got himself a pardon from lame duck Ohio governor James Rhodes in 1983. The entrepreneur had thought Rhodes' political campaigning worthy of financial support some years earlier.

King lost his grip on the heavyweight championship when next-big-thing Mike Tyson, managed by a competitor, became the youngest man to win the heavyweight title. But King did not rest on his laurels; he kept busy by promoting and managing Michael Jackson and his brothers' 'Victory Tour' in 1984, grossing $150 million ($250 million). King then brokered a product-endorsement deal for Michael to appear in a series of television commercials for Pepsi.

Mike Tyson

King kept a close watch on Tyson, and seized his opportunity to take control when Tyson's co-manager and friend Jim Jacobs died from leukaemia on March 23rd 1988. Remorseless, shameless and audacious, King gatecrashed the funeral (Tyson was a pallbearer).

Tyson's personal life was tumultuous at the time and King stepped in to help. Tyson's wife, who had access to his bank account, tried to secure a sack load of his cash, so King went into hustler mode to thwart her attempts. He also gave the young boxer a black revolutionary perspective on the history of 'blaxploitation' in the boxing industry. At 24 years of age, Tyson signed a four-year exclusive promotion deal with Don King. Game over.

Former great heavyweight champion Larry Holmes said of Don King: "I make more money with Don King stealing from me than with 100% from other promoters." Don King brought more money into the world of boxing than all his peers combined, and certainly attracted more in than he could ever take out. He received every business accolade that boxing had on offer.

Seth Abraham, former president of HBO Sports said of King: "He has the most brilliant business mind I have ever encountered ... Don King is formidable in his sleep."

Criminal Entrepreneurs

LUCKY LUCIANO 1897 – 1962

"The world is changing and there are new opportunities for those who are ready to join forces with those who are stronger and more experienced"

Francis Ford Coppola's film *The Godfather* portrays the alternative route to the American dream. The movie was loosely based on the life of a boy born in the village of Lercara Friddi, a stinking sulphur-mining town, close to Corleone in Sicily. The boy's name was Salvatore Luciana and he would grow up to become known as 'Lucky Luciano'.Luciano's father was a hardworking sulphur miner, who broke his back trying support his family.

Life was harsh, and his boy was up to no good, hanging out with the village's persona non grata. In 1906, Antonio decided to get his family away from crime-infested Sicily, moving to New York. But it was a case of out of the frying pan and into the fire. The Italians huddled into the big city amongst the other ethnic groups. Immigrants, however, faced an uneven playing field, with unequal access to legal opportunities and free access to countless illegal ones. Southern Italians and Sicilians soon dominated Italian Harlem and the neighbourhood became known as the Italian-American hub of Manhattan. Luciano's family settled into 'Little Italy'.

Juvenile and lifelong alliance

Bad boy Salvatore hit the ground running. The new arrival was arrested at the age of ten for shop-lifting. In 1911, he was expelled from public school and sent to a Brooklyn correctional facility where he served four months for truancy. One of Salvatore's earliest entrepreneurial accomplishments was the establishment of a protection service to other kids in the neighbourhood. The subscription fee was two cents per day. Non-payment resulted in a beating. It was this business that would bring Salvatore and life-long friend and business partner Mayer Lansky together. Lansky was a pocket battleship, a Jewish kid devoid of fear. They met in the streets, where Salvatore tried it on, pitching him his services. Lansky, despite his diminutive size and skinny frame, made very clear he was not the slightest bit intimidated, using the colourful language befitting of the streets. The young Sicilian admired the little battler's balls and replied: "Ok you get yours for free." Lansky told him to stick it where the sun don't shine. They were kindred spirits.

Salvatore gained experience with the Five Points Gang of Manhattan, named after the famous junction there.

The crew worked under John 'The Fox' Torrio (an organisational genius and gifted entrepreneurial gangster), client and colleague of George Remus, who also features in the 'Criminal Entrepreneurs' section of this book. Just as Paolo Vaccarelli (aka Paul Kelly and founder of The Five Points Gang) matriculated, Torrio (who left for Chicago in 1909) into the art of 'gansterpreneurship', Torrio would eventually nurture the youthful talent of Lucky Luciano and Al Capone (handed the reins in 1925) passing on skills and guidance. By the age of 14, Luciano had dropped out of school all together.

He got a job delivering hats for a Jewish hat maker, Max Goodman. It paid $7 ($115) per week. The logistics of delivering hats presented entrepreneurial opportunities. Salvatore began using the hat delivery function as a front for his illegal drugs sales and delivery business. Stealth was important to success and his drugs were hidden in the hat-boxes, so that he delivered both drugs and hats simultaneously.

Aged 18, Luciano, who by this time had inherited the nickname 'Lucky', was imprisoned for selling heroin and morphine. He was sentenced to six months. Though the gang had some protection from local politicians at 'Tammany Hall', as thanks for coercing voters on Election Day, they could not prevent his imprisonment. It was around this time he met Francesco Castiglia, better known as Frank Costello. Costello would become the most politically influential gangster of all time.

They met the night Salvatore's gang was thrown out of a theatre in East Harlem for rowdy behaviour. The two would also go on to become close friends throughout their lives.

After a six-month stint in prison in 1915, Salvatore was able to improve his drug business operations. His reputation caused him to change his surname from Luciana to Luciano in order to protect the family name back in the old country (his mother and father never visited him whilst he was in jail). He restructured his organisation's sales and distribution teams into a tiered system. Later he added leisure and pleasure facilitation. As with many big corporations the tiered system induced greater dependability and performance from his recruits.

Joining forces

In 1917 Luciano dodged being drafted into the US army to fight in World War I by intentionally catching the sexually transmitted disease chlamydia. He welcomed the federal government's ban on alcohol and by 1920 he and Lansky were distributing contraband alcohol to Manhattan speakeasies. Luciano always thought big. Whilst other players had to off-load shipments of booze on to small boats, he had contracts with shipyards allowing him to dock his loads. It was the contraband liquor business that gave him his first million. His success, Jewish connections, aptitude, and capacity brought him to the attention of the larger players in the market.

He relinquished his independent status in favour of absorption into Giuseppe (Joe the Boss) Masseria's operation in 1921.

The risk/benefit of competition with the big boys made the opportunity to join compelling. Luciano's career would see him establish an extensive arrest record and he was prepared to do what needed to be done to avoid jail time. In 1823 he was again arrested for dealing heroin.

He ratted out a Jewish gang in order to save himself. They had a trunk full of heroin in a basement, so 'Lucky' gave them up in exchange for his own freedom.

By now Luciano had combined forces with his new lieutenant, Frank Costello. Costello delivered business links to politicians, judges and police.

It was through Costello that Luciano became acquainted with heavy hitters such as William O'Dwyer (who went on to become Mayor of New York) and two Jewish entrepreneurial crooks, Arnold Rothstein (who fixed baseball's Black Sox 1919 World Series scandal) and his protégé Dutch Schultz (who had a pathological tendency towards violence).

The lynchpin in the hook-up with the latter two was John T. Noland, aka Legs Diamond. Arnold Rothstein provided funding and also hired the services of Luciano, Lansky and Siegal. Officials were the key to the smooth uninterrupted running of the business, which allowed it to become a more profitable and manageable operation.

In 1927 Salvatore created (with the assistance of the retired Johnny Torrio) an amalgamated number of Italian and Jewish alcohol distributors to combine as the 'Seven Group'. This provided greater market stability and penetration. The group was efficient and effective in taking over and developing markets in Boston, Cleveland and Florida.

The coup

Salvatore's approach (guided by Mayer Lansky) was very different from the bellicose Mafiosi. Violence became a less integral part of its functionality. Stability of supply generated an increase in profitability. The Italian mafia were impressed by Luciano's Seven Group and aimed to bring them under their own umbrella. In 1928, Luciano, a multi-millionaire by now, held a conference with his trusted young and ambitious associates to announce his plans. He outlined an audacious proposal to stage a coup to centralise command. Luciano continued developing his great vision of centralisation, creating a stable and profitable *syndicated* business spanning all of America. Inevitably the plan created powerful enemies.

In October 1929 Salvatore was at dockside inspecting a shipment. Major boss, Salvatore Marranzano's men pulled up and kidnapped Luciano, bundling him into their vehicle. They took him for a ride. His mouth was taped and he was beaten within an inch of his life and repeatedly stabbed with an ice pick. The henchmen cut his throat from ear to ear and dumped him in a ditch. Miraculously, and to the complete astonishment of all concerned, he survived, justifying the name 'Lucky' which he inherited from picking winning horses at the races. He now found himself in the middle of 'The Castellamarese War'.

1930s Castellammarese War

Joe "The Boss" Masseria
1887 – April 15, 1931

Salvatore Maranzano
July 31, 1886 - September 10, 1931

Lucky Luciano needed market stability and order. War was not good for business in the underworld. So, he threw in his lot with Masseria. Bugsy Siegal (an enforcer for Luciano) and some other assassins burst in on the restaurant where Luciano and Masseria were eating and assassinated Masseria in 1931. Luciano had delivered Masseria to Marranzano as a means of ending the bloodletting, which was so disruptive to business. Lucky was then installed as number two in the pecking order after Marranzano. He brought with him his business associates, producing a bigger, more capable and better-managed organization and acquired Masseria's lottery business. Lucky encouraged the Marranzano to develop into a national syndicate.

But Marranzano had another vision; he saw the mafia as a Roman Empire, with himself as Caesar. As a result, Marranzano planned to have (potential competitor) Lucky killed.

Luciano got his revenge in first and on September 11th 1931 he eliminated his boss and up to 40 Mafiosi executives. The program of 'removals' lasted only 48 hours from beginning to end. Luciano then established a federal national operation, managed from his Waldorf Towers apartment on 50th Street near Park Avenue in Manhattan.

His new structure allowed the free-enterprise spirit of America to thrive accompanied by systems and order. He created a low-profile organisation, removing problems that had previously beset the business, such as Al Capone (now in jail sentenced to eleven years). This federal conglomeration of families went from strength to strength. It even competed with US Steel (one of the largest businesses in the world) in turnover, employment and profitability.

Demarcation

A governing body called The Commission organised the smooth adjustment to post-Prohibition America. Luciano organised lines of demarcation with territories and operations. The business was segmented into respective profit centres: prostitution, gambling, racketeering, drugs and contract killings. The Murder Incorporated division carried out the orderly fulfilment of contract killings. Luciano also introduced a ban on the murder of members of the public. This reduced the attention the organisation drew to itself from the public, politicians and thus law enforcement agencies. The mafia were so well connected that FBI chief J. Edgar Hoover even denied they existed.

By 1934, Luciano was the *Capo di Capa* – Boss of Bosses. He lived the high life; always well dressed with a white handkerchief displayed in the top pocket of his jacket.

The war dividend

Lucky's luck ran out in 1936 when he was sentenced to 30-50 years in prison for pandering (i.e. sexual slavery) and extortion, after being prosecuted by Thomas Dewey. Luciano had introduced a flat tariff and worked the prostitutes through a six-day week.

A police raid of 80 separate brothels resulted in over 100 prostitutes being brought in for questioning. In jail, Luciano had everything he could ever want. He was let out after serving ten years, having negotiated a deal with the American Government.

In 1942, whilst Luciano was still in jail, French luxury liner the SS *Normandie* was being converted into a US troop carrier renamed USS Lafayette. The ship was destroyed by fire as a result of sabotage whilst docked in New York. Luciano controlled the docks and the US government asked for his help in ensuring there was no repeat of such an event. Lansky talked a reluctant Luciano into doing a deal. Luciano assisted *Operation Underworld* – code name for operations designed to sequester mafia assistance to counter Nazi saboteurs along the US Eastern seaboard. The US had suffered attacks by spies on shipyards during World War II. Luciano was now so powerful he was even able to offer the government and Allied forces local assistance during the World War II invasion of Italy. He ensured the government received total cooperation from the Sicilians and gained important intelligence for the US government. The fact that he had Dutch Schultz killed and denied Schultz's request for a permit to assassinate Dewey (Luciano prosecutor and with whom he negotiated his get of jail deal with) did not hurt. Lucky Luciano was at first transferred to a minimum security prison, then released from jail and deported to Italy as part of the agreement.

Birth of Las Vegas

The 'Havana Conference' was held in Cuba on December 22nd 1946, with Luciano in attendance. The top bosses were there ostensibly to see their old friend Frank Sinatra in concert. There Luciano reasserted his supreme control, aided and abetted by his mentor Mayer Lansky. Lucky insisted that the delegates each pay him financial tribute amounting to a total of $200,000 ($1.6 million). The Cuban Army had been running the Cuban casinos for a couple of years with no success. So, President Batista invited the 'specialist' in to improve the business. Various motions were passed and seconded. Luciano would go on to purchase an interest in the casino business, using the tribute money, and set up home in Cuba. The essentials on the conference agenda included the quelling of disputes that threatened to break out into wars. Competing groups were always vying for lucrative 'franchises' held by fellow syndicate members.

Mayer Lansky brought up the issue of the 'Siegel Situation'. Bugsy Siegel was now very popular in Hollywood and had an idea to construct a casino in a backwater called Las Vegas. He had a vision of Hollywood stars performing at his casinos, with him making money from the punters gambling after the shows.

He took over from property developer Billy Wilkerson, who had run out of cash building a luxury hotel.

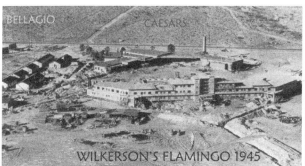

The syndicate invested heavily as shareholders, but Bugsy was skimming off the top. Contractors were also robbing the inexperienced entrepreneur blind. Luciano and Lansky (lifelong friends of Bugsy Siegal, who had saved both their lives on many occasions) got their friend a reprieve. But as soon as Bugsy Siegal completed the Flamingo and turned a profit, Lucky and Lansky could no longer justify sparing the life of a member who stole from his benefactors. On the night of June 20th 1947, at 10:45pm, Siegal was assassinated.

Not so Lucky

US drug agent Harry Anslinger got wind of Luciano's presence in Cuba and needed to get President Harry S. Truman involved to get Lucky deported. The Americans had to resort to a trade embargo to put pressure on the Cubans. However, Cuba was doing well out of Lucky Luciano's organised conglomerate and retaliated against the American embargo on shipments of medical supplies to Cuba. The Cuban President halted the shipment of sugar to the US, but eventually gave up trying to end the trade war and instead gave up Luciano, who was arrested and forced to travel back to Italy.

Severe restrictions were placed on Luciano's movements to avoid continued embarrassment to the Italian Government. Nevertheless, the entrepreneur was still able to run a casino business abroad. It was impossible to run the full operation from such a distance, but he kept his hand in where he could.

A significant deal was struck during the 1950s between the US and the Corsican Mafia. The Corsican operation was called the 'French Connection,' as depicted in the famous Gene Hackman film.

The connection was the smuggling of heroin from Turkey to France and then on to the US. Luciano, despite being exiled, had been able to corner the US heroin business via the French Connection. At home in Naples he was quite the celebrity. His iconic status in America and around the world did not diminish.

On January 26th 1962, Luciano met with a film producer who was organising the production of a film based on his life. Lucky Luciano suddenly keeled over and died of a heart attack whilst waiting to have a meeting at an airport in Naples. *The Godfather* was eventually made, and its depiction of a young man attempting to obtain the American dream using guile and sagacity was an instant global hit. The film is now regarded as an American classic.

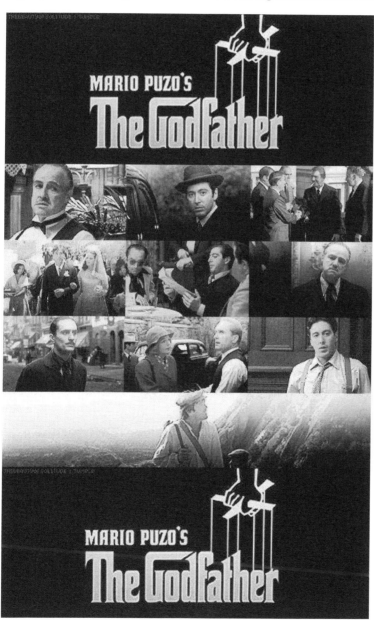

GEORGE REMUS 1876 – 1952

"The unwritten law will set me free."

In the late 19th Century many American men suffered from alcohol-related illnesses. Many of these illnesses proved fatal and a lot of children were forced to grow up without their fathers. Female reformers were concerned about alcohol's links to wife beating, child abuse, divorce and financial problems. Many labourers regularly became so drunk they couldn't perform their jobs properly. Absenteeism from work each week was very high as result of alcohol abuse.

Industrialists such as Ford, Rockefeller, DuPont, and the Pillsbury family were concerned about the impact of drinking on labour and productivity. The industrialists were dissatisfied. The Anti-Saloon League called Milwaukee's brewers "the worst of all our German enemies," and dubbed their beer "Kaiser brew." Others insisted that buying beer meant Americans were financing Germany, as all of the American brewers were actually headquartered in Germany. But America was about to change.

Prohibition

At midnight on January 16th 1920, the United States went dry. Advocates of Prohibition argued that outlawing drinking would eliminate corruption, end machine politics, and help Americanise immigrants. National Prohibition was defended as a war measure, and anti-German sentiment aided its approval. The change was well suited to George Remus, who had all the attributes to make a killing in such an environment.

He was born on November 14th 1876, in Friedeberg, close to the German capital, Berlin. Right from the start, baby George proved himself a survivor, with his three elder siblings dying as children. His father Franck Remus married above his station to one Maria Karg, whose father was a well-to-do entrepreneur who owned a mill. The family left Germany, emigrating to America when George was five years old. Franck dropped the 'c' from his name to avoid the anti-German sentiment which was then prevalent in the US. The family settled in Milwaukee, renowned for its tolerance and sense of enlightenment. It became known as the 'German Athens of America'.

Taking the reins

As a kid growing up in the US Remus was happy, but his world changed in 1890 when his father was crippled by auricular rheumatism and couldn't work. The family had moved to Baltimore before moving on to Chicago in 1880, where Remus's uncle, George Karg, had a pharmacy. The 14 year-old boy stepped up to the plate, supporting his folks. This included his sister Frances and brother Herman (the boy would die in 1913 as the result of being hit on the back of the head by a brick. It was unclear to the family how this occurred). Young Remus single-handedly kept the family's head above water by working in his uncle's business. George Remus entered the Chicago College of Pharmacy at the age of 19 after lying about his age to ensure entrance. When his uncle wanted to sell the business, Remus stepped up again, obtaining a bank loan to buy the pharmacy aged 21.

By now Remus had acquired a licence to practise pharmacology and *owned* two pharmacies. The young entrepreneur saw opportunities to expand the business. To begin with he became an optometrist. He came up with another money-making scheme. Doctors' fees were expensive, and many people couldn't afford a regular doctor. So, Remus slotted in (through the back door of pharmacology) as private de facto doctor. He was bright and intelligent with great self-belief and overpowering ambition. He sold prescriptions for glasses, did his doctor routine, ran two pharmacies, and now studied at night school to become a lawyer, completing the studies in half the normal period in 1900. The omens were good. Everything the entrepreneur had tried so far worked. It was around this time that Remus got married to Lillian Klauf in 1899, and had a daughter in 1900. George Remus was not to know that it would be marriage and divorce that would cause both his biggest downfall and his greatest achievement.

Defending criminals

In time he became a notable lawyer, and took great pleasure in defending the underdog. His speciality was the defence of murderers. The negative odds were more than counter-balanced by his natural brilliance. In 1901 Remus' first year of practice, he defended 18 individuals accused of murder. He spurned many opportunities to become District Attorney as it meant prosecuting, which would not bring out the best in him. Many of his clients were hung and Remus became a passionate anti-capital punishment campaigner.

Many states had introduced temperance laws prior to a nationwide blanket ban on alcohol. Chicago was one of the early instigators. The bootleggers of Chicago knew they could trust lawyer George Remus to get them out of trouble. The contraband alcohol industry grew rapidly, becoming more and more lucrative. One of his clients was a certain Johnny Torrio.

On Sundays, Torrio could be found at the local Catholic Church, acting the straight-laced businessman. During the week he pimped in his Chicago nightclubs and brothels. Torrio's young protégé was a young Al Capone.

Between 1900 and 1911 the annual per capita consumption of alcohol increased from 17.73 gallons to 22.81. These figures meant that brewers were generating close to $1 billion ($21 billion) in annual net revenue by 1911. Brewery was the fifth largest industry in the United States. Remus observed men with limited intelligence becoming rich overnight – and more than able to afford his high-priced defence fees. Remus was quoted as saying: "I was impressed by the rapidity with which those men without any brains at all, piled-up fortunes in the liquor business. I saw a chance to clean-up."

The Volstead Act, a law banning alcohol consumption nationwide, was ratified in 1919 and would become law in 1920. Remus knew the act Volstead Act backwards and was able to apply his sharp and discerning mind to identify its loopholes. It was time for a career change.

Remus sold his law practice after 20 years in the profession (retaining his much coveted bar membership) and got into the bootlegging business. He found a loophole in the act called Title II, Section 3, which stated: "That nothing in this act shall prohibit the purchase and selling of warehouse receipts covering distilled spirits on deposits in government bonded warehouses, and no special tax liability shall attach to the business of purchasing and selling such warehouse receipts."

The new bootlegger began by buying stores of barrels of whisky in 1919, hoping to sell them on again for a profit. When he got busted he knew Chicago was too hot and needed to move. He moved to the geographic location of Cincinnati, ideally suited to accessing America's bonded whisky stores, with 80 percent of them being within a three-hundred mile radius of 'Sin City'. He took with him a woman he had been fraternising with for years called Imogene Holmes. He eventually married her in June 1920, after he divorced Lillian and Imogene divorced her husband.

Bootlegging

Remus sank much of his life savings into the new venture. He hooked up with banker Oscar Fender, who was the manager of the department of savings at Lincoln National Bank, depositing $100,000 ($2.1 million). Remus initially began buying up almost worthless 'whisky certificates' perfectly legally, with a view to obtaining legal possession of impounded whisky. Section 6 of the Volstead Act permitted medicinal use of liquor and therefore the legal manufacture of liquor for such use. Remus began buying pharmaceutical companies with the aid of his legal adviser Elijah Zoline, who was on the payroll. These companies allowed him to obtain permits that could allow him to withdraw alcohol legally from government bonded warehouses. To keep the Feds off his tail Remus went about a programme of setting up and closing down these pharmaceutical wholesale businesses. The products found their way into nightclubs, speakeasies and into the hands of distributors. They were all labelled as 'Medicinal Whisky'.

When the law enforcement agencies caught on to the scheme, legislation was introduced to reduce the amount of medicinal alcohol that could be held by drug companies. Remus wasn't about to be defeated. He simply cooked the books to suit and staged robberies in order to mitigate the large quantities being ordered. The business was brilliantly thought out, well-drilled and expertly managed. The profits were amazing. Remus set about vertical expansion, making acquisitions up the chain, acquiring a significant number of distilleries. His first distillery was made with the backing of Lincoln National Bank with a down-payment of $10,000 ($210,000). He eventually bought out some of the country's most famous household whisky brands. Within three years Remus made a staggering $40 million (£400 million). By close of play he would be the biggest distillery owner in the US and known as 'King of the Bootleggers'.

Making friends

Whilst looking for a house he met real estate agent George Conners. The agent failed to find him a property but discovered, in George Remus, a mentor and friend. The two struck up a partnership immediately, and Conners went to work as a sales agent for the organisation. Conners was fiercely loyal and dedicated to Remus. Men like Conners became rich, working on commission, selling booze up and down the country under Remus's tutelage.

Remus purchased the Fleischmann Distillery, which produced a range of products, including yeast, vinegar, malt, syrup, gin and whiskey – included in the sale were 3,100 gallons of whiskey. Conners got it for $197,000 (£2 million). Remus discovered a secluded farm in an out-of-the-way location called Death Valley. If you didn't know it was there you couldn't find it. A hidden distillery was located at the end of the George Dater's 50 acres of land on Queens City Avenue. It was from a property based there that distilled whisky was secretly lowered from the attic via the dumbwaiter to the basement. From there it travelled through a tunnel 50-100 ft long and 6 ft down, to the transport vehicles that would whisk it away.

A dozen distilleries were bought out and acquired. The operation distributed alcohol nationwide to nine states and even beyond US borders. Remus never watered down the product. It was top-drawer stuff with a dependable delivery service. Staff levels rose significantly, to three thousand, with 12 lieutenants who managed procurement, distribution and public affairs. Remus bought a building and converted it into a fancy administration hub, which included a library and full-time chef. He also created a motorised distribution fleet, which included 147 transport vehicles. The whole thing operated 24/7. This in turn generated massive demand, resulting in the recruitment of an army of accountants. The operation was expanding at such a rate that a specialist called Harry Statton was brought in as a distribution manager. He moonlighted for Remus whilst employed during the day by a shipping outfit called American Express. Remus rewarded his best employees handsomely. Ernest Brady, who was responsible for transporting the Remus liquor across the Ohio River, received a salary of $208,000 ($4.5 million).

Putting money in the right pockets

Cops weren't the biggest threat to the operation. Remus kept them well paid and that kept them well away. Cincinnati's entire police force was on the Remus payroll (they were his principal overhead). Bribes went as high up as the White House, to the Attorney General. Jess Smith (who later committed suicide after being prosecuted for corruption) was the link to the anti-Prohibition president and Attorney General Harry Daugherty. He got $500,000 ($4.3 million) in all. Zoline provided the hook-up after the 1920 election. The bootlegger also had over one thousand salesmen in the field nationwide. Profits were enormous, with amounts of up to $2.7 million ($57 million) being banked in a single three-month period, but over a quarter of the profits were used to fund bribes for officials.

At the operation's height, annual turnover was close to $25 million ($530 million). Remus is quoted as saying: "Men have tried to corner the wheat market only to learn there is too much wheat in the world. I tried to corner the graft market, but there isn't enough money in the world to buy up all the public officials who demand their share of the graft."

George Remus became staggeringly rich and thought it was time to buy a multi-million dollar house. Both he and his wife were gifted swimmers and they installed an Olympic-size swimming pool in their newly bought and rebuilt mansion. Kids were given free access to the grounds. It became known as the 'Marble Palace'. George Remus was a wannabe socialite and began ingratiating himself into Cincinnati's elite. But later it would be clear as to why he needed the Cincinnatians on side. At his parties $100 ($1,000) bills were slipped under dinner plates. At one party female guests received a brand new car as they left and male guests received diamond watches. Remus, a non-smoking teetotaller, was rarely spotted on these occasions, instead spending much of the time in his library while the revellers got on with it.

Incarceration

Some estimate that by 1924 George Remus had made $80 million ($750 million), but it couldn't keep him out of jail. He was convicted after an investigation by out of town 'untouchables'. With all appeals exhausted, he gave his wife Imogene a big cheque, and put his affairs in order. He then made a catastrophic error when he signed over power of attorney to her before being chauffeured off to prison. In prison he settled down to bide his time.

Remus was put in a separate section of an Atlanta prison, known as 'millionaire's row', at a cost to him of $1,000 ($9,000) per month. It catered for couples (his wife would stay over for days) and was like a five-star hotel, with its own kitchen. Remus had three separate banquets during his time away, with over 50 'guests' present each time.

In 1925, Remus arranged for his wife to feel out Justice Department agent Franklin N. Dodge, to see if he'd play ball in trying to get him a pardon. She took the instruction too literally and fell in love with him. They did everything they could to take advantage of Remus' bad fortune. The pair emptied his accounts, sold his shares in distilleries and removed all the valuable objects from his house. Nothing was sacred. She arranged for the removal of Remus' initials on the cutlery and his silk pyjamas, amongst other things. She replaced them with 'FD'. The woman even tried to get poor German George deported. Imogene went all the way, arranging for a hit man to murder her unsuspecting husband, paying gunmen $15,000 ($300,000) of her husband's *own* money.

Remus found out his wife wanted a divorce a couple of days before getting out of prison, and took his frustration out on his jail cell. He left the prison straight for the mansion, having to break in as it was boarded up. With dedicated friend George Conners in tow, Remus crawled through a window and discovered chaos inside his once-beautiful home. Remus anxiously made his way to his treasured pool, then he burst into hysterical laughter, screaming: "She has not taken the water! I have the water!"

But he sat and cried and began a spiral into a very deep depression.

Murder trial

Dodge and Imogene got Remus sent back to jail. The conviction was linked to the original charge. On this occasion, Remus did hard time like any other con. George Remus was a short, stout Napoleonic figure, a powerfully built ex-swimmer and boxer who in 1907 set an endurance record for swimming in Lake Michigan, remaining in the water for nearly six hours during the winter.

Prison held no fears for the pugilist. He took his whipping quietly and did his time. But still waters ran deep.

On October 6th 1927 Remus had a date with destiny at the Domestic Relations Court to finalise the divorce. His wife was also due to appear. He spotted her cab on the way there and ordered his chauffer to chase Imogene's car. His driver forced her car off the road. Remus got out ranting and raving and waving a handgun. His stepdaughter begged him from the car to calm down, but he chased the fleeing Imogene and as he grabbed her by the wrist, she screamed:

"Oh Daddy, you know I love you. Daddy, don't do it! Don't do it!"

Remus drew her close, pressed the gun up against his wife's abdomen and shot her twice. He gave himself up later that day at a police station.

When Remus walked up to the desk he said, "I just shot my wife."

The officer asked: "Is she dead?" and Remus replied: "I hope so."

When asked, during the trial, had he attempted to effect reconciliation with his wife, Remus replied, "How could I? No sane man would."

The former defence lawyer who specialised in murder and divorce submitted a plea of 'insanity' to the homicide charge. The media attention was on the level of O. J. Simpson's trial. The only news that competed with Remus' trial was Charles Lindbergh's ticker-tape return from his solo flight to Paris. Remus led much of his defence; his performance was theatrical. He once bolted out of the witness stand, flailed his arms about like a fruitcake and promptly fell backwards, Charlie Chaplin style, with no attempt to break his fall, lying flat out on the ground. He was taken back to his cell and laid out with an icepack placed on his forehead. Moments later he opened his eyes and said to a familiar reporter leaning over him, "How did I do?"

The jury took 19 minutes to acquit him.

When the verdict came in the public gallery roared with delight, as if the home side had scored a last-minute winner in extra-time. George Remus eventually got back into the game (after a six-month stint in an asylum battling lawyers trying to section him) but things had changed again. It was a different terrain now, one unsuited to his talents. The business was in the hands of entrepreneurial predators who had a greater talent for killing than enterprise. Remus was a killer but he was not prepared to kill as a matter of course in business. The stakes were raised too high even for the fearless entrepreneur. He tried creating a business around patented medicines and developing apartment buildings, but there was no grand phoenix re-emergence. Had he avoided the prison term it is likely that Remus' life would have followed the path of his more successful bootlegging competitor Joe Kennedy (father of future president John F. Kennedy), who converted his criminal businesses into well-known legal entities.

Remus lived out the rest of his life in Ohio, with his new wife. He suffered a stroke in 1950 and died in 1952. At his heights his net worth estimated at $80 million ($750 million). It is said that F. Scott Fitzgerald met George Remus whilst staying at the Seelbach Hotel in Louisville, Kentucky. The novelist was said to be inspired by the entrepreneur to write his novel *The Great Gatsby*.

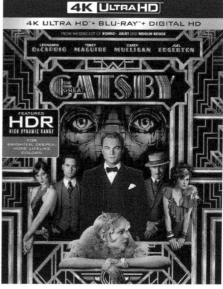

PABLO ESCOBAR 1949 – 1993

"I'm going to be big one day"

Columbian drug habits

Cocaine was first synthesised in the late 1850s and regarded as a wonder drug. In 1860 a graduate student at the University of Gottingen named Albert Niemann devised a technique for isolating cocaine, the active alkaloid of the coca leaf. Chemist Angelo Mariani started marketing a wine called Vin Mariani in 1863, which had been treated with coca leaves. A 'pinch of coca leaves' was also included in John Styth Pemberton's original 1886 recipe for Coca-Cola. Both produced a successful product. The synthesised stuff was sold over the counter at Harrods right up until 1916. The health warning read: "Could make the coward brave, the silent eloquent, and render the sufferer insensitive to pain." Pablo Escobar would ensure global demand was sufficiently satisfied.

In 1914, the Harrison Narcotics Tax Act outlawed the use of cocaine in the United States after learning of its detriments. But the genie was out of the bottle by then. The product delivered man's primary need – the feelgood factor. This could also be achieved quickly and comfortably. The product was a sensation. Improvements in science and technology, plus the Cold War (and political intrigue) would mean serious changes in the accessibility of drugs. Governments sought to take advantage of drug trafficking allies and overlook the activity of useful 'political agents' in their war against communism.

By the mid-90s, Colombia (because of its natural climate and geography) was on its way to becoming the world's leading producer of cocaine, responsible for three-quarters of the world's annual yield. The business was illegal with extraordinarily high penal tariffs. This meant the extremely profitable product produced enormous margins, concomitant with the enormous risks associated with its distribution. It was the perfect draw for entrepreneurs with a high propensity towards risk, sensation seekers and pathological killers. Pablo Escobar fit the bill. He had evolved in a cocaine-infested environment and was well adapted to the terrain. Escobar was born in Rionegro, Colombia, close to the industrial city of Medellín, in the Andes Mountains. His ethnic heritage was both native and European. The family eventually had to move into Medellín when his father left his farm to become a night watchman on the lookout for crime.

Starting young

The appeal of the streets offered immediate gratification compared to school. Consequently in 1966 Escobar became dedicated to his chosen career path as an entrepreneurial criminal and left school. The usual hustles were in play – contraband cigarettes, dodgy lottery tickets and the like. Escobar also worked for his uncle's tombstone business. The Panamanians created a steady demand for stolen tombstones. Escobar and his street-hustling team would steal them, sandblast them, and distribute them. The business was fruitful but wasn't going to make anyone rich. Car theft was standard matriculation. However, Escobar and his team had ideas about improving the returns on the business. They would blatantly pull over their intended prey in broad daylight. Within hours the car would be stripped to its constituent parts and sold piecemeal. No car, no car theft, no crime. In the video game 'Grand Theft Auto: Vice City', the airport is named 'Escobar International' after him.

Escobar's vehicle parts business created an opportunity for vertical expansion. Such was the fear of having one's car stolen by this team he was able to provide the market with protection from the car theft team. With only marginal increases in expenditure Escobar was able to significantly increase turnover and profitability by 'protecting' the cars that he had not stolen.

His attendance at the 'university of the streets' was supplemented by further education at the institute of further advancement of crime the local Medellín prison. The young hustler was inspired by the greater knowledge and enhanced connections gained from his time there. This was compounded by the inheritance of his mother's ambitious nature. He made his aspirations clear to her as a young man, announcing, "I'm going to be big one day." The opportunities for those with dark olive skin were more limited. 'European' Columbians invariably owned the large businesses and properties. With his heritage, Escobar was always going to be on the outside looking in. To have the things rich people owned he had to enter the businesses reserved for his class. Abundant opportunities awaited those with gumption and a high propensity toward risk. Escobar was able to secure a dealership distributing marijuana as a middleman. This was the traditional start-up position often following the consumption and appreciation of the product. The step up to coke was a smooth and logical transition. Higher market value and growing popularity were accompanied by improved margins and profitability.

Cool under pressure

The young hustler possessed a quality highly valued in his game: an extraordinary ability to stay calm when all around were losing their heads (literally). Regardless of the environment and circumstance, Escobar always stayed calm. This feature led to him rising in stature amongst his peers. As a promising entrepreneurial crime boss, Escobar instilled a sense of fear in everyone around him. Often any subordinates owing him money would be kidnapped and the outstanding funds demanded from the family. If he wasn't paid off, he murdered the kidnap victim. He sometimes murdered them even when he did get his money. This promoted swift payment of outstanding debts, which had a positive effect on cashflow, reducing opportunity cost.

In 1971 factory owner Diego Echavarria was involved in evicting villagers from their farms, having acquired the land for expansion.

The farmers had nowhere else to go other than the slums of Medellín. The industrialist was kidnapped and the $50,000 ($200,000) ransom was paid. Diego turned up dead in a hole close to Escobar's childhood stomping ground. From this point onwards, Pablo Escobar became a hero to the poor underclasses.

Diego Echavarría Misas

Escobar was the right man, in the right place, at the right time. Mid-1970s America had flung her doors open to the cocaine business. America was desperate to win the Cold War with the USSR and keep communism out of South America. The popularity of the drug permeated every level of American society. New demand was more than welcomed by ambitious narcotics dealers. The stakes suddenly increased. The wealth that could now be generated was enormous. Escobar assassinated cocaine boss Fabio Restrepo and took charge of his organisation's cocaine business. He inherited a well-oiled machine that knew the drill. In 1975 he began improving its logistics, distribution, and financing by partnering with established coke entrepreneurs the Ochoas brothers.

Vertical expansion

Large amounts of coca paste were purchased in Bolivia and Peru, processed and distributed to the valuable US markets. In the early 1960s, Colombian farmers grew and sold coca plants and extracts to outside interests, without knowledge of what the vegetation was used for.

Escobar decided that the best way to drive up profits and margins was continued vertical expansion. Thus, all aspects of the business would be under his control. He quickly took over the coca fields around Medellín, doubling the farmers' and workers' wages. The increased income and further inward investment buoyed the local communities' economies.

Escobar invested in technology, opening a new processing laboratory and facilities for processing the raw materials into the refined consumable product. Smuggler Fabio Ochoa was enticed on board, adding his smuggling routes as part of the distribution channel.

Escobar interrupted business to marry María Victoria Henao Vellejo in 1976. He was closing in on 30 and she was 15 years old, but very few people were willing to deny Escobar his prospective wife. The couple got special dispensation to tie the knot from a Colombian bishop. The business Escobar created grew exponentially. George Jung (a biopic of the drug dealing entrepreneur was released starring Johnny Depp, called *Blow*) was making $500,000 ($1.5 million) per week with Escobar as a distributor. His biggest problem was finding time to count his money. More importantly he ran out of places to store it.

Columbian economy

Escobar's exports brought much-needed foreign currency into Colombia in the form of US dollars. Additionally, he became fully entrenched in Medellín's community affairs. Their welfare was directly linked to Escobar's business activity. Both factors offered him protection against competitors and forces bent on undermining his operation. His mixture of particularly sadistic murders combined with 'spreading the love' in the form of money, jobs and protection, worked to great effect. Escobar had the emotional intelligence to recognise the importance of the carrot as well as the stick.

Escobar's contribution to the Columbian economy was extensive, allowing peasants to buy houses, cars and above all food. At his heights Pablo Escobar's Medellín cartel had revenues of $25 trillion ($70 trillion) per annum, and was the largest business sector in Colombia bar none. Escobar's export-derived revenue was so desperately needed in Colombia that laws were changed to maintain and fuel the export drive. Banks were allowed 'side windows', permitting an unlimited intake of US dollars to be converted into pesos. Highly speculative and ostensibly legal investment markets appeared. Thus, fresh new funding opportunities emerged to float coke deals. Investors rushed the 'Columbian Klondike'. By 1980, Colombian bank deposits in the four major cities had doubled from their 1976 levels. Escobar had single-handedly accelerated Colombia's GDP growth rate.

Making the Forbes list

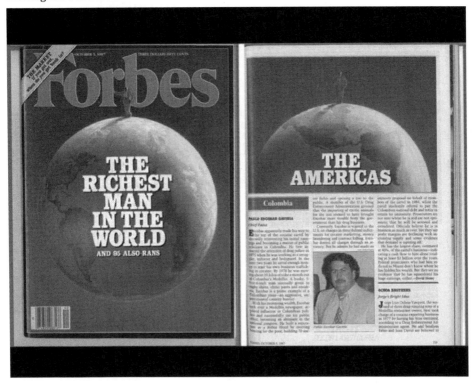

In 1989 Forbes magazine listed Pablo Escobar as the world's 7th richest man. In 1993, actor Johnny Depp lost his colleague and close friend River Phoenix when the young thespian died of an overdose outside Depp's LA nightclub The Viper Room. Both were massive Hollywood stars at the time. George Jung became one of America's richest men. Pablo Escobar's rise was driven by customers like River Phoenix and partners like Jung. As the wholesale price of the drug in the United States dropped, some of these savings were passed on to lower-level dealers and consumers. The standardised price of cocaine fell by more than 50 percent between 1981 and 1988, expanding the market significantly.

However, Escobar (a great movie buff) appears to have got carried away with his own epic drama, in which he had the starring role. He saw himself as a latter day Che Guevara. He had foreign diplomats killed on foreign soil, attempted the assassination of an American president, had officials killed by the dozen, taxed drug bosses at $100,000 per month, financed and equipped private armies to war with various leftist guerrilla movements who opposed him, and blew up a fully-laden passenger plane just to get to one particular individual. He upset too many people – he went too far.

Pablo Escobar loved the limelight and during a momentary lapse on a mobile with his son he made a critical error. The son required his responses to a range of questions put by a journalist. Escobar was on the run after a jail-break (he agreed to go to jail as part of a deal with the US and Colombian governments in 1991) and the predatory entrepreneur was now being hunted by a five hundred strong Search Bloc team (an elite government enforcement squad). On Thursday December 2nd 1993 he hung about on the phone for too long. They tracked him down, shot him to pieces, then put his body on display.

Pablo Escobar was an iconoclastic entrepreneur with the power to affect his home country's national economy. His business would devastate lives across the world. The biopic film, *Blow*, was directed by Ted Demme, who himself died of a cocaine-related heart attack. The movie's lead star Johnny Depp's best friend River Phoenix, died as a result of taking cocaine. The movie was a true story that showed how a small-town boy made $100 million selling cocaine. But Escobar would end up spending much of his life in a prison cell as a result of his career choice, with all his ill-gotten gains confiscated.

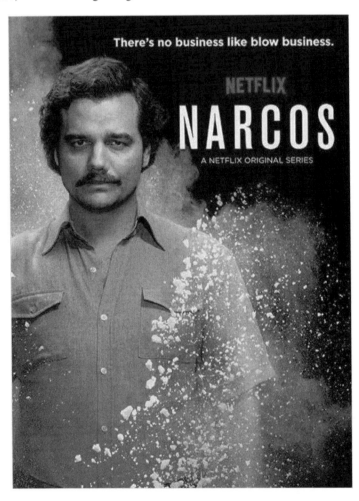

The Modern-Day Greats

MARTHA STEWART 1941 –

"When you're through changing, you're through"

Martha Stewart was born with a gift of moving the masses. She recognised, understood and took full advantage of the powerful American mass market that was trying to live up to the ideal image of family as portrayed by the mass media. Martha Stewart's hometown was Jersey City in New Jersey, USA. Her parents were Polish Americans Edward Kostyra and Martha Ruszowski. They christened their daughter Martha Helen Kostyra.

Mr. Kostyra was a strict disciplinarian whose flaming temper sometimes got the better of him. Martha never forgave him for kicking her in the back and onto the pavement for some minor misdemeanour when she was young. Edward Kostyra was competitive and always wanted his family to have the best and cleanest of whatever there was in the neighbourhood. Martha inherited his ideals, and a steely ambitious inner strength to go with them.

Early tutelage

Stewart's father worked as an editor for Transcription Broadcast Systems. They aired a very popular show called *My Favourite Husband*. Her mother was a former schoolteacher and now a stay-at-home mother. The future entrepreneur was already developing links to food, television and idyllic American family life. This combination would later manifest itself in her business concepts.

Mrs. Kostyra had five other children as well as Martha. All family meals were prepared by mother and the family *always* ate together. School was an escape from her father and chores, and Martha loved it. She was a little madam and as bright as a button, who had the teachers eating out of the palm of her hand. On one occasion Martha arrived home with a blue ribbon symbolising first place in a design competition. Her father was artistic and taught Martha things like how to arrange flowers. She would often help out by babysitting her siblings. In 1959 she graduated Nutley High School and wrote in her yearbook the motto: "I do what I please and I do it with ease."

Martha was 'hot', so she was easily able to find work as a model. She did TV ads for Breck hairspray, Lady Clairol, Lifebuoy soaps and Tareyton cigarettes. She also paid her dues working as a maid and cook for a couple of old ladies. She was a meticulous perfectionist and could clean and bake like a pro – all this whilst studying at college. There she discovered a love of chemistry, then architectural history and art. Nevertheless, like her mother, teaching was her great passion. Martha really loved learning – because she loved teaching.

Ambition on hold

She married a high-performing Yale law student – Andy Stewart – at the age of 20, after the couple met on a blind date. Unfortunately, this meant she had to leave college to become the sole breadwinner whilst Andrew finished his degree and masters at Columbia University, which he did in 1964. When he completed his studies Martha, the consummate homemaker, began finishing her own degree programme in history and architecture, which she did in six months. Within a year she became a mum, giving birth to daughter Alexis in 1965. Martha gave up modelling and was looking for what to do next. Andrew's father worked at the stock exchange and that's where Martha ended up in 1967. That year she managed to pass the broker's exam and registered with the New York Stock Exchange. The job she got paid on average basic rate of $100 ($400) a week. But Martha with her "I do what I please and I do it with ease" mantra moved her commission from the paltry to the exorbitant, ending up on a six-figure salary.

Dodgy dealings

The family had moved to New York, where Andrew was also doing well in the publishing industry. Their success was short-lived however, as the mid 1970s economic crisis set in. Martha had to deal with the hoo-ha that rippled into the brokerage business. The bosses at the brokerage firm accused her of kickbacks from furniture company Levitz for disposing of stock in the troubled business. She eventually threw in the towel and resigned aged 32. It wouldn't be the last time Martha Stewart would have problems at the stock exchange – there was much worse to come. The young couple decided to move out of the city and buy a farm in Westport Connecticut (a place where no state taxes were payable).

The catering business was her natural next step, since she had worked as a cook for the two old widows during her college years. She partnered with Ann Brody and then later Norma Collier. The hook on the business was that clients wouldn't know what they were getting until they tasted the food. They called the business The Uncatered Affair. The business took off and she ended up catering for movie stars such as Paul Newman and Joanne Woodward.

By 1977, Stewart was proving difficult to work with. Business partner Norma Collier found Stewart to be doing jobs behind her back and they parted company. Stewart moved on, managing Market Basket, a gourmet shop and building it up.

Martha Stewart was good to look at, meticulous and first-class at what she did. It didn't take long before she began being noticed. Magazines started featuring her in their publications. Andrew had become the president of a prominent New York publisher and her father was in the family entertainments business. Publishing her own periodical on domesticity was the logical next step for Martha, and she used her husband's connections to release *Martha Stewart Entertaining* in 1982.

It was a huge success. Martha Stewart went into overdrive with new books, videotapes and dinner music CDs – anything that affected the American family.

Gathering momentum

Her success in publishing led to invitations to appear on TV programmes. Once she had the confidence that her stuff could fly on TV she focused on the medium. But just as things were gathering momentum, having struck a chord of domestic bliss with the American people, her husband was caught having an affair with Martha's flower consultant. They split in 1987. It was the same year Martha did a deal to consult for major retailing corporation Kmart. A bitter divorce took place in 1990. She completed another major deal that same year, with global corporation Time Warner launching her *Martha Stewart Living* magazine.

MARTHA STEWART

Living

MARTHA STEWART LIVING January 2009 zesty citrus dishes closet solutions meringue techniques flowers by the dozen

Fresh
Thinking
NEW INSPIRATIONS
FOR THE NEW YEAR

Light, Bright, and Easy
CITRUS MARMALADES,
SALADS & SWEETS

Staying Healthy
MARTHA'S
TOP 10 TIPS

Space-Saving
CLOSET
MAKEOVERS

plus:
CLASSIC CASSEROLES
REINVENTED

BEHIND THE SCENES
AT LIVING

NUMBER 182

JANUARY 2009
marthastewart.com

As if she hadn't enough to do, Stewart found herself at the top of Mount Kilimanjaro in 1993: the same year the *Martha Stewart Living* TV show was launched. But this was what she was all about – climbing mountains both figuratively and literally. The entrepreneur of domestic bliss continued her climb and conquest, launching a line of products under the Martha Stewart brand, including gardening furniture for Kmart and a range of fabrics for major US retailers. She came; she saw; she conquered.

During 1997, Stewart's company Omnimedia made $25 million on a turnover of $120 million – twice the previous year's profits. Martha Stewart was gobbling market sectors and market share like Pac-Man. She was an all-American celebrity, a one-woman branding phenomenon. The founder of the cult of domesticity now had a couple of magazines, TV shows, 27 books in circulation, radio slots, newspaper columns, Internet sites and e-commerce plans in the pipeline.

No stranger to the stock market, Stewart took advantage of her knowledge and connections to float the company in 1999. In the midst of the dot-com era and the threatened 'new paradigm,' Stewart stayed one step ahead of the competition and raised $150 million worth of capital to launch her six day a week TV programme *Martha Stewart Living* via the Internet. By 2001, she was pulling in a salary of $2.7 million with a further $2 million hitting the bank in royalties. However, the great homemaking guru was about to find herself in big trouble. On December 27th 2001 Martha sold shares in ImClone.

Insider dealings

Coincidentally, the ImClone CEO was Sam Waksal, a close friend of Stewart's, who also offloaded shares. The following day the FDA announced it would not be rubber-stamping ImClone's new cancer drug. The situation instantly aroused suspicion and was investigated by the authorities. Nevertheless, the cougar of America continued her climb up the mountain, being elected to the board of the New York Stock Exchange.

Unfortunately, she lost her footing when broker Douglas Faneuil changed his original statement, which had cleared Stewart of insider dealing on the ImClone saga and now implicated her. She was indicted on nine counts of fraud. The love affair with the American people came to an abrupt end with a poll showing 50 percent in favour of the celebrity entrepreneur going to prison.

On March 5th 2004, a jury of eight women and four men found Stewart guilty of conspiracy, obstruction of justice, and two counts of making false statements.

She was sentenced to five months in an open prison, plus five months of home confinement, and two years' probation with a $30,000 fine. The total downside of her insider trading loss would have been $45,000 at most: for Stewart, who was worth over a billion dollars at the time, this was about a week's wages.

On May 21st 2004, Larry Stewart (no relation), was charged with two counts of perjury relating to Martha Stewart's trial. Stock in Martha Stewart's Living Omnimedia company leaped 23 percent on the news. But she was not exonerated.

On her release from jail the *Martha Stewart Living* group of magazines welcomed back their founder with open arms. She expanded her product range at Kmart and Sears. Daytime shows called *Martha* and *The Apprentice* were launched. Stewart also launched a 24-hour satellite radio network. Her talk show received multiple nominations in the Daytime Emmy Awards in 2006. In the same year she got into the real estate business, selling her own-brand houses.

In October 2005, Stewart released her latest book *The Martha Rules*, featuring her ten rules for entrepreneurial success. She offers the following guide:

1. Passion

2. Get a big idea

3. Teach so you can learn

4. Spread the word

5. Quality

6. Build a team

7. If the pie isn't perfect cut it in wedges (abandon the bad, "focus on the positive, stay in control, and never panic")

8. Take risks not chances

9. Make it beautiful.

10. Get a telescope, a wide-angle lens and a microscope for the long-term vision as well as attention to detail.

By 2011 she was inducted into the New Jersey Hall of Fame. The woman that has been struck by lightning three times, bounce right back.

Martha's net worth at the time of writing was estimated at $970 million and she continues to expand her business empire.

DONALD TRUMP 1946 –

"Sometimes by losing a battle you find a new way to win the war"

The Trump property legacy

The name "Donald Trump" is synonymous around the world with success, wealth and daring. Trump was born into an entrepreneurial family in New York City, his grandfather's name was Friedrich Trump. Friedrich was of German descent but passed himself off as a Swede, because the popularity of Germans in the US had not improved since John Jacob Astor's day.

De Young's   815 BROADWAY, N. Y.

Both Donald Trump's father and grandfather were property developers. Fortunately for Donald his father was a major success. Grandpa on the other hand didn't fare so well. After leaving Germany in 1885 he set up a property-based business on the main strip of a popular tourist spot in Alaska. He travelled the famous Chilkoot Trail, which led through the Coast Mountains to Bennett in British Columbia servicing the prospectors participating in the Klondike Gold Rush. There he set up the Arctic Restaurant and Hotel. In an article posted in 2015 Alexander Panetta of The Canadian Press wrote "In his three years in Canada, Trump opened the Arctic Restaurant and Hotel in two locations with a partner — first on Bennett Lake in northern B.C., and then moving it to Whitehorse, Yukon.

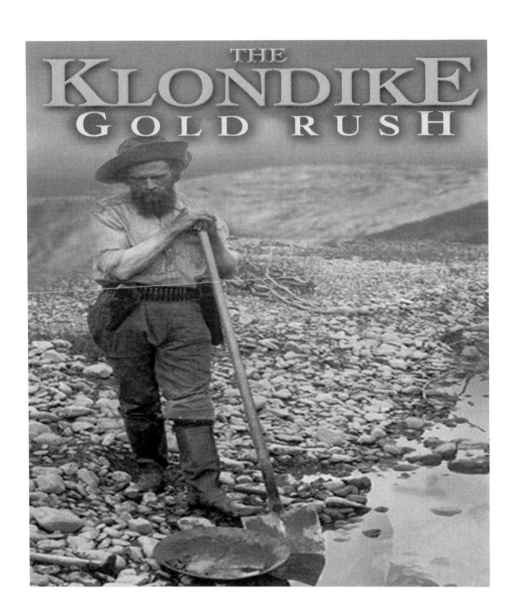

THE KLONDIKE
GOLD RUSH

Their two-storey wood-framed establishment gained a reputation as the finest eatery in the area, Blair said — offering salmon, duck, caribou, and oysters.

It offered more than food.

"The bulk of the cash flow came from the sale of liquor and sex," Blair wrote. She cited newspaper ads referring obliquely to prostitution — mentioning private suites for ladies, and scales in the rooms so patrons could weigh gold if they preferred to pay for services that way.

'He had made money; perhaps even more unusual in the Yukon, he had also kept it and departed with a substantial nest-egg.'- *Gwenda Blair, author*

One Yukon Sun writer moralized about the backroom goings-on: "For single men the Arctic has the best restaurant," he wrote, "but I would not advise respectable women to go there to sleep as they are liable to hear that which would be repugnant to their feelings and uttered, too, by the depraved of their own sex."

He worked hard, played hard and drank hard, dying when Frederick,

Donald's father, was only eleven years old. Frederick, as the eldest son, had to help make ends meet, supporting two other siblings. He did anything he could, including shining shoes, but found his calling on a construction site. Evening classes supplemented his on-site education as well as gaining him various building trade qualifications. By the age of sixteen Frederick Trump had built his first structure – a garage (for a neighbour). Thanks to guys like Henry Ford and Alfred Sloan of General Motors more and more cars were being bought. Consequently, more and more garages were being demanded. Frederick Trump decided to get into business selling and constructing prefabricated garages at $50 ($500) a pop. The business grew along with his experience. Larger and more ambitious projects were progressively undertaken, including the construction of affordable apartment buildings in New York City. Frederick began doing well enough to send his brother to college and then university where he earned a PhD in Physics. By the time Trump was born, his dad was well on his way to becoming a millionaire. The change that both he and his son were to benefit from was America's burgeoning population growth.

Positive omens

From very early on Donald Trump showed signs of the ruthless ability to zero in on a target, and pounce on it. On one occasion he and older brother Robert played with bricks, building little structures. Trump tended to build a little larger than his resources would allow (he would be accused of this throughout his career). So, he asked his brother to 'lend' him some of his bricks, which his brother duly did. Trump then glued his own construction together, which meant poor little Robert couldn't get his bricks back. But Trump did *finish* his building. It was a sign of things to come.

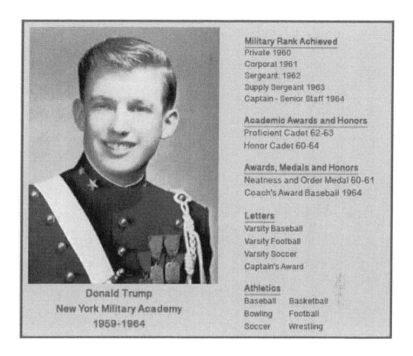

Military Rank Achieved
Private 1960
Corporal 1961
Sergeant 1962
Supply Sergeant 1963
Captain - Senior Staff 1964

Academic Awards and Honors
Proficient Cadet 62-63
Honor Cadet 60-64

Awards, Medals and Honors
Neatness and Order Medal 60-61
Coach's Award Baseball 1964

Letters
Varsity Baseball
Varsity Football
Varsity Soccer
Captain's Award

Athletics
Baseball   Basketball
Bowling   Football
Soccer   Wrestling

Donald Trump
New York Military Academy
1959-1964

Though Frederick was a fearsome father, the young Trump wasn't scared of him. At school Trump was aggressive and once dished out a black eye to a teacher who had upset him. However, he wasn't a vindictive fellow, just an alpha male type. His father knew just the place for him and, at 13, Trump was enrolled into military school. It was tough. Being hard was enough to survive but not to thrive; balance was needed. Having learned to combine aggression with guile, Trump made it to Captain before graduating in 1964.

After flirting with film school in California, Donald Trump attended Fordham University, later transferring to the prestigious Wharton School at the University of Pennsylvania. Whilst studying the theory of economics he also studied the newspapers hunting for opportunities.

He waded through the trade papers for foreclosures on properties in search of deals. Graduating in 1968 with a Bachelor's Degree in economics, Trump moved back in with his parents, working for the family property and construction business.

He loved the property game but his dad's clients were a bit too common for Trump, who had inherited his mother's love of pomp and finesse. Dodging bullets and knife thrusts on the rent-run was not his cup of tea. He had no intention of starting at the bottom.

Leg-up from father

Trump's first ever property deal was "Swifton Village" in Cincinnati, completed while he was still at college. He used his father's company and financial standing to purchase Swifton Village, an 'affordable housing' estate for $6 million ($19 million) when it had cost $12 million ($43 million) to build two years earlier. The property was immediately mortgaged for a similar amount with $100,000 ($300,000) left in the kitty for improvements. $800,000 ($2 million) was spent getting rid of the riff-raff and getting in a better class of tenant. Trump eventually sold it to the very *imprudent* Prudent Real Estate Investment Trust. They sent down a rep to survey it but he was more interested in lunching at a famous restaurant

Division of Engineering 10-21-53
Rhode Island Ave. — Looking north from Rockingham Ave. After Impr.

downtown. After lunch and a cursory 'once-over' of the site, he approved it. Trump then sold his estate for $12 million ($38 million) making a $6 million ($19 million) profit. It had 100% occupancy when the agreement was signed, however, by the time the deal had come through lots of tenants were about to pack their bags and leave as their tenancies had expired. The buyer had failed to specify a contractual requirement for full occupancy at completion with long-term agreements in place.

Trump now had his own money. He was constantly sniffing around Manhattan for property deals. Just as with the Swifton Village deal, he spotted another potential target in a newspaper

scouring. Penn Central Railroad was filing for bankruptcy. The trustees were raising cash by disposing of assets. The project Trump had in mind didn't pan out. However, Penn Railroad liked Trumps' high octane visionary style and turned him on to their Commodore Hotel building that was now up for sale slap bang next door to Grand Central Station. Penn Central hadn't yet put the Commodore Hotel on the open market.[1]

---

[1] Cornelius Vanderbilt had previously owned Penn Central and built the first Grand Central Station. The former main station was subsequently bought by P.T. Barnum and converted into the first Madison Square Garden. Trump was the latest in a sequence of great entrepreneurs to show an interest in the New York site.

No-one was looking at the Commodore building as it was fast becoming a slum and interest rates were going through the roof. The whole sector was in trouble.

The Japanese had risen as the top industrial country in the world and the oil crisis ensured the seventies would be a torrid experience for business in America. Trump saw it differently; he thought he could find the building a purpose that suited the changing times. He had picked up on the fact that well-to-do commuters were still flooding past the building from rich suburbs, heading for work. Frederick Trump, however, thought that buying the Commodore was akin to "buying a seat on the Titanic". Trump did his level best to get his grand schemes in the papers along with his own picture, drumming up support for his projects. Some worked, some didn't. An agreement was struck with Penn Railroad in 1974. But the deal hinged on Trump getting some major tax abatements from the city.[2]

He offered Penn Railroad $10 million ($27 million) for the Commodore building, pledging to pay a total of $6 million ($16 million) to the city in back taxes payable over forty years and tapered upwards. He also offered the city a capped profit-share. The council fought the deal, though yielded when Penn Railroad announced even greater loses at the Commodore and their intention to board up in six days. As floods of tenants began the exodus from the Commodore, Penn Railroad went out on a limb for 'the Donald' (as he became known). They loved him. It was his sharp and breathtakingly ambitious deals that led to him becoming known as a phenomenon or 'an experience.' His non-stop yapping kept them entertained. They refused to take anyone else seriously. No one had such vision and such energy. To do the deal $80 million ($220 million) was raised from two institutions with ulterior motives for seeing the neighbourhood rescued - they were situated close by the building being bought. After a long-drawn-out war with the city and competitors, the Commodore deal was sealed in 1976.

Donald Trump covered the old brick building in towering glass and bronze, bringing glamour to a dour and lame environment. The Hyatt hotelier group were brought in as partners to run the hotel.

---

[2] Donald Trump wasn't content with pursuing just one deal, even at this early stage of his career. He had a number of irons in the fire, including the Bonwit building, an eleven-floor structure on 57th Street and Fifth Avenue adjacent to the legendary Tiffany location. He was also eyeing up casinos in Atlanta during 1975.

Trump opened the Grand Hyatt New York (formerly the Commodore) as Hyatt's US flagship hotel in 1980. By 1987 profits were over $30 million ($45 million). Trump had a 50% share. 'The Donald' inserted a clause preventing Hyatt from opening hotels anywhere else in New York City without his permission: a caveat worth millions.

Aiming higher

Once Hyatt was in the bag the Bonwit building took centre stage. Trump had approached the owner Franklin Jarman. After the first meeting Trump was told to take a flying jump in the nicest possible way. But Trump was persistent and just kept coming up with new ways

of doing the deal. The Trump stayed on Jarman's trail for four years after his initial offer. Then one morning over breakfast, whilst reading the paper (scouring for opportunities as was his custom), he read that Jarman's company was in deep trouble and under new management. He waited for 9am to roll around and immediately called the new boss, a guy called Hannigan, who was a specialist at getting banks their money back. Hannigan was the new broom and knew exactly what Trump wanted. After all he'd read The Donald's dozens of offer letters dating back four years!

Hannigan wanted to sell and Trump wanted to buy. They shook hands on a deal. Had The Donald not kept up his persistent trailing of his prey, he wouldn't have realised it was injured and the opportunity would have gone begging. It was going to be a very large kill, but Hannigan suddenly refused to take Trump's calls. The Donald tracked him down. Hannigan told him the landowner of the ground the Bonwit building was standing on wouldn't play ball. Trump had made many contacts and luckily the owner of the land was one of them. He got a letter of intent before he left the meeting with Hannigan agreeing $25 million ($40 million) for the building and the remainder of the 29-year lease. This would be used to prevent Hannigan backing out of the deal. Donald Trump then went to work on the landowner – Equitable Life Assurance Society – the financier of his Hyatt deal. Equitable accepted a 50/50 partnership deal, which would see them grant a new lease and Trump build a major new iconic building on their site. To ensure he got the height of the building he planned, Trump needed to obtain the

building's neighbour Tiffany's 'air rights' (for overlooking their building). Trump showed Tiffany what a monster of a building the city would require him to build without their rights and the iconic beauty that he'd build if he got them. *His* ideal scheme would preserve Tiffany's legacy. Tiffany accepted his $5 million ($8 million) offer.

The market continued to improve and Bonwit's owners tried to renege and sell to oil-rich Arabs flush from OPEC shenanigans. The Donald waged a war of subtle threats (he was a military school graduate). With skilful use of the media he had Bonwit staff running like rats leaving the sinking ship, which brought Bonwit owners to their senses. They signed a deal in early 1980. The building became the greatest (and most visited) building in New York City. He called it Trump Tower. It is an unbelievable spectacle of glass and marble with an 80ft tall waterfall flowing in a monolithic atrium. It houses apartments bought by the world's elite and commercial tenants from the top draw of global retailing. Top-end private apartments were being sold for $10 million ($17 million) a throw. It was stars like Steven Spielberg and Liberace who bought Trump Tower apartments. Trump himself took an apartment on the top floor.

Money in casinos

In 1975 a news bulletin on Trump's car radio highlighted that a strike in Las Vegas had caused the Hilton group to wobble on the stock market. It didn't make any sense. A company with 150 plus hotels worldwide marked down because of workers in Vegas? The Donald smelled something in the air and decided to track it. On further investigation he learned that 40% of their profits came out of their gaming hotels based in Las Vegas. This was typical for such companies. The revenues from gaming were colossal. Trump went into the gaming business big style.

It wasn't all fun and games - Trump got into trouble. In 1991 the New York Times and The Wall Street Journal reported *The Death of the Donald*. Enemies were now brave enough to come out publicly to gloat. Ivana Trump asked for a divorce. Her claim was $1 billion; she got $125 million plus some major extras she was promised in the pre-nuptial agreement.

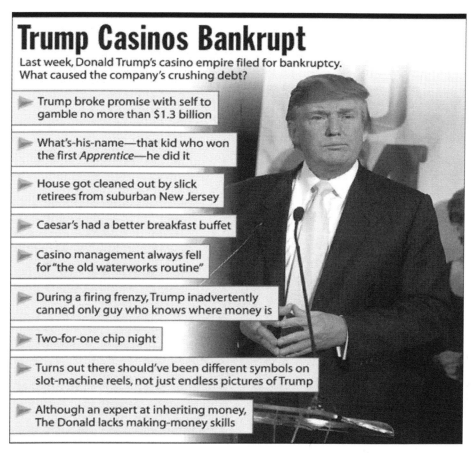

Trump Casinos Bankrupt

Last week, Donald Trump's casino empire filed for bankruptcy.
What caused the company's crushing debt?

- Trump broke promise with self to gamble no more than $1.3 billion
- What's-his-name—that kid who won the first *Apprentice*—he did it
- House got cleaned out by slick retirees from suburban New Jersey
- Caesar's had a better breakfast buffet
- Casino management always fell for "the old waterworks routine"
- During a firing frenzy, Trump inadvertently canned only guy who knows where money is
- Two-for-one chip night
- Turns out there should've been different symbols on slot-machine reels, not just endless pictures of Trump
- Although an expert at inheriting money, The Donald lacks making-money skills

Now for the first time in Donald Trump's career he was at risk of defaulting on loans. Desperate but yet successful negotiations with the banks were undertaken. The Donald subtly threatened to tie the banks up in bankruptcy protection litigation for years if they didn't cut

him some slack, plus a $50 million line of credit. It was a Trump triumph, but the entrepreneur had to restructure the casino business to survive. By 1995, the business was healthy enough to float on the stock market. Trump Hotels & Casino Resorts was snapped up by market investors, raising billon of dollars. It bought Trump time and reduced his enormous personal and corporate liabilities. However, in August 2004 after a long period of financial trouble and despite the flotation, Trump entered bankruptcy protection. In May 2005, Trump relinquished his position as CEO, retaining his role as Chairman of the Board. The company re-emerged from bankruptcy as Trump Entertainment Resorts Holdings.

The Donald is a star

In early 2000 The Donald was so popular that he seriously considered running for President as part of the Reform Party. Trump's deals and showmanship had made him a celebrity entrepreneur despite his very public reverses. His show *The Apprentice* with its catchphrase, "You're fired" was a sensational hit. Trump was paid $50,000 per episode, which totalled circa $700,000 in its initial season.

At the time of writing was on $3 million per episode, which adds up to $48 million per season. The new TV star was easily recognised with one of the most elaborate and ridiculous comb-overs ever seen. Interestingly, competition from Martha Stewart's version impacted negatively on Trump's ratings. The two great entrepreneurs vied with one another for ratings.

To this day, Donald Trump can command fees in excess of $5 million for a single TV commercial. He also rakes in millions from branded products ranging from suits to bottled water. He has numerous books on the market and launched *Trump Magazine* in 2006. He is a rarity – a man who does business in full view of the public and still remains a star.

ALAN SUGAR - 1947

"I don't think too many people would want my job. I'm a bit of a nutter"

In 1946, 38 year-old Fay Sugar was shocked to find she was pregnant again. She gave birth to her fourth and final child on March 24th 1947, a boy named Alan Michael Sugar.

The three-bedroom council flat occupied by Fay and Nathan Sugar and their four children was bursting at the seams. Coping was going to be a problem. Nathan Sugar was the world's greatest worrier. His hands were full even before Alan's arrival. He worked in the rag trade all his life, as did many East End Jews at that time. Queues of people harangued him, demanding clothes for their kids, but would he chance starting a business? Nathan was totally and utterly risk adverse, a doubting Thomas. The biggest risk he ever took was betting on horses. Neither of Alan's parents was big on business, religion or education. The greatest ambition they had for their children was gainful employment and that's what they achieved. No university grads, no highfalutin jobs and no careers in politics. They were just bog-standard regular people. This simple understanding about the mass market and ordinary people would stand Sugar in good stead.

The child-entrepreneur

As a child Sugar was not a great one for football or running with gangs. He was a quiet reserved kid who failed the eleven-plus exams but did well enough to enter technical school, where he enjoyed the practical hands-on lessons.

At his senior school, Brookhouse (a merged technical and secondary modern school) the only thing that got him going was business. He came up with an idea for a school magazine (as would Richard Branson few years later). Sugar needed start-up funds to launch it. As bold as you like, the young entrepreneur went straight to the headmaster for a loan – and got it. The estate he lived on was full of opportunities. Sugar thought his neighbours were bonkers allowing him to collect their empty bottles, redeeming them for a shilling (80p) at the local shop, which was less than two minutes away.

As early as 13 the young cub was learning what regular folk wanted. He launched his own budget soft drink business, providing the neighbourhood with his personal concoction of ginger beer. It wasn't enough to worry Coca Cola, Top Pops or Corona, but he realised if it was cheap enough and the product was inoffensive enough, there would be a market for it. A demonstration of Sugar's growing emotional intelligence was when he offered grandmothers portraits of their grandchildren photographed by him for half a crown (£2). The old dears couldn't resist it. He also worked repackaging black-and-white film. At eleven years old he was working for a grocer, boiling beetroot in a baby's bath before getting off to school.

Finding jobs came easily to Sugar; his natural enthusiasm and ability made him a catch for market stallholders and retailers. He also developed a reputation for being able to get hold of stuff, not unlike the great Del Boy Trotter with whom he had so much in common. Both traded stuff on the London council estate; one in Clapton, the other in Peckham.

Sugar would soon have a van just like Del Boy's. By the time he'd left school aged 16, he had O-levels and a bigger income than his anti-entrepreneurship father.

Sugar worked as a statistician for the government at Whitehall and then for a steel company called Richard Thomas and Baldwin. The job did his head in, but his Saturday job down Tottenham Court Road selling menswear was a joy. Tottenham Court Road has the biggest collection of electrical shops (all cheek by jowl) in the UK, a portent in Sugar's career. The Jewish kids had their own youth club in Stamford Hill where they all got together. It was here Sugar met TV repairman Malcolm Cross. Sugar could sell £5 notes for £5.50 so between the pair of them they came up with the idea of selling second-hand televisions.

Malcolm repaired them and Sugar sourced and sold them, usually for as little as a fiver (£60). One of Sugar's brothers was a mini-cab driver. One day he stopped for a coffee break at a stall in Stoke Newington, only to find an ad pinned up on a board for a second-hand TV with his mum's telephone number on it. Sugar was marketing the tellies as a one-off 'unwanted gift' all over North-East London. Their poor old mum was forever refunding punters after they'd turned up at the house demanding their money back.

Go into business

Malcolm's wife's name was Maureen and Sugar's girlfriend's name was Anne (she would later become his wife), so the soppy pair came up with 'MaryAnn' as the name of their new company. Sugar decided to quit his day job at Richard Thomas and Baldwin to go at the business full-time. His old man was not impressed. Nevertheless, Sugar rented a small storage room for the TVs and then got on his bike selling the second-hand recons. The venture lasted a year.

Teenage Alan Sugar knew that to sell you needed "wheels" as he put it. Sugar applied for a sales job selling tape recorders for a company called Robuk Electrical. The key to it was that the job came with a company van. One of Robuk's customers was Currys, and when the electrical retailer gave purchasing power to its branch manager it was Christmas come early for the young, hungry and ambitious Alan Sugar. He worked his tail off covering each of Currys' London stores, managing to sell a bundle of Robuk's tape recorders to every last one of them.

Come payday Robuk shafted him. Because he had sold so many they reckoned it constituted a bulk order and as such warranted a reduced commission. Sugar thought this was a diabolical liberty and promptly got himself an identical job with a competitor called Hendersons. Meanwhile Sugar's dad continued to pull his hair out over his son's reckless refusal to settle down in a secure job.

Hendersons were distributing masses of imported products from Japan. Sugar was on £20 per week (£250). Nevertheless, he demonstrated great entrepreneurial initiative, sourcing an out-of-stock product that was a major earner for his employer and even lining up a buyer. All Hendersons had to do was supply the purchasing monies, which they duly did. The teenager completed the deal, collected the cash and handed it in. Rather than offering him a partnership or promotion they lampooned him for not trying to get more out of it for the company. Sugar had enough of ungrateful bosses. He knew he could do better all by himself. So, he stepped out on his own.

He took the £142 (£1,500) out of his post office savings account, bought a minivan and spent the balance on goods for resale (the van would sport the number plate AMS 1; 40 years later the plate was on his brand-new Roller).

Young Sugar doubled his cash in two days. He had organised a meeting with another rising star, Gulu Lalvani, an Asian entrepreneur who went on to become a millionaire after setting up an import company called Binatone (a supplier of Hendersons). Sugar was intent on launching his own business but needed credit terms from companies like Binatone. Gulu didn't want to upset Hendersons and suggested that Sugar formally leave the company and take a two-week holiday before starting out on his own. Two weeks later Sugar returned, handed Gulu a post-dated cheque, backed his clapped-out van into the Binatone bay, loaded it and was on the road. Later that day he was back, demanding his cheque back and handing over the readies in its stead. He'd achieved a normal week's worth of business in one day.

With clear blue water in front of him, Sugar and his fiancée Anne Simons decided to marry, except Anne's family wasn't very keen. A struggling young businessman was not a secure proposition. The opposition to the marriage spurred the bloody-minded entrepreneur on. He made more money and eventually got the nod and tied the knot in 1968, aged 21.

He was now doing well enough from his home-based enterprise to move to a semi-detached house he bought in Redbridge, North-East London. He moved the business out of yet another newly bought house after it was burgled and rented a place near Islington High Street, later settling into a house in Chigwell, Essex where he lived for nearly 30 years. Anne's cousin recommended an accountant called Guy Gordon to help keep the business on the straight and narrow. The first major issue was the company's status. If the whole venture went pear-shaped Sugar could end up losing his house and the Simons' prognosis for the marriage would have been vindicated. Gordon recommended Sugar form a limited liability company.

Birth of Amstrad

On November 1st 1968, AMS Trading (Alan Michael Sugar) was created. The name was tightened up to the catchy 'Amstrad' shortly after he decided to badge his products. He listed AMS Trading's activity as importing. Sugar tried everything; he organised the repair of radios, bartered, swapped and even took an interest in an electrical retail business called Global Audio. In 1970 the youth market was getting into music in a big way. This was the year Richard Branson founded Virgin Records (and Virgin Mail Order). Kids were buying records, amplifiers, turntables and speakers. Music was a growing part of socialising and entertainment. Stereo equipment was what the new generation wanted and Sugar saw himself as the man who could get it for them – just as he'd got hold of all kinds of goods for the kids on the estate.

Stereo equipment coming out of the Far East was not supplied as complete units. Turntables, for example, came without their wooden bases or plastic lids. Sugar saw this as an opportunity and invested over £2,000 (£18,000) in getting an injection moulder to produce an Amstrad dust cover. He also bought wooden slats for the bases and assembled the whole thing to form a completed turntable. This appealed to both manufacturers and retailers. The stuff was cheap enough to undercut the market but just about good enough for it to compete. Amstrad was now a manufacturing company.

Getting Comet on board

Next were amplifiers. This meant getting his new Amstrad 8000 amp into the multiples. It was critical for Sugar to get his discount amplifier into Comet. After great perseverance they relented and agreed to meet. Comet's MD cut him dead from the very start, saying he was not going to buy any of Amstrads amps. Instead they wanted the young wheeler-dealer to source for them Garrard turntables, via the grey market (wholesalers).

Sugar agreed to procure them, complete the product using his dust covers and bases, then ship them to Comet with only one proviso.

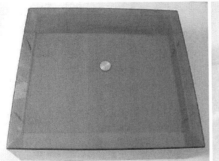 

The cunning opportunist said: "you've got to take my amplifiers." Comet begrudgingly offered a compromise – to include the amps on their product list. They'd only order when and if a customer wanted one.

Sugar promptly organised all his family and friends to go into Comet on an even geographic spread ordering Amstrad amplifier.

Within a couple of weeks, the call from Comet came through with an order for amps. They wanted seven. Sugar shouted down the phone "don't be so bloody stupid... it's one hundred minimum order" and slammed the phone down.

Then he began to plead with the phone to ring. It did, and he was in, shipping one hundred units to the major retailer shortly afterwards. By 1973, Amstrad was supplying to Comet regularly. Amstrad's profits in that year were £193,063 (£1.5 million) on sales of £1.3 million (£10 million). This compared with sales two years earlier of £207,534 (£1.5 million) which itself was double the previous year's takings.

The Amstrad amps were complete rubbish. Malcolm Cross, Sugar's old partner, who owned an electrical retail outlet in Stamford Hill, said he returned as many as he sold. But the amps, pitched at £17.70 (£140) resonated with the young kids and their disposable income. They were cheap, they looked pretty good, and they sold by the bucket load. Sugar grew the business, making improvements to existing product lines, which were always positioned to undercut the market massively. New and larger premises would be needed in time to come.

Sugar did a couple of significant things in the early-to-mid 1970s. He developed a relationship with a Japanese company called Orion, who supplied all manner of products which he badged and sold. Later he heard about a new factory that would manufacture 'Fidelity' TVs. He could now bring different components from Japan and have them assembled at the new factory.

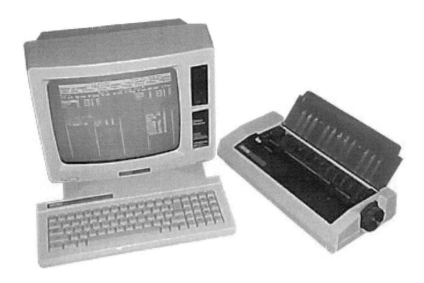

Sugar gave birth to a process known as 'the Amstrad effect'. He would first identify what was selling well, then copy it, stripping out the 'bells and whistles,' and aggressively source cheaper components, almost invariably from the Far East. The finished article always looked great, with lots of features. The product would be launched, undercutting its nearest rival by a mile, and Amstrad would end up owning the lower end of the market.

Next in line for the Amstrad effect was the 'stack system'.

Out in Japan in 1978, he discovered they were racking the turntable, amp, cassette deck and tuner one on top of the other and selling the composite. Amstrad launched its own rack system, going one better. The product had one housing unit, one power module, one lead. The whole idea was to remove duplication and save money, deploying components more cost-effectively. This meant fewer components, enabling Amstrad to achieve the critical price-point. Sugar called it the 'tower system'. They sold like hot cakes. Woolworth's were ordering them in their thousands. Rumbelows were selling a thousand a week. Sugar described an article written in the hi-fi Press at the time saying: "they thought what we had done was disgusting …We were attracting the truck driver and his wife. They saw this bloody big mug's eyeful in this whacking great big cabinet, with a beautiful front panel with knobs on … Plug it in and away you go."

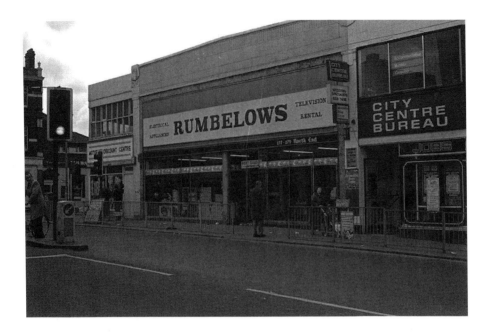

The following year Sugar turned down an offer for Amstrad. He passed on a £2 million (£7 million) windfall, including retention of a 25 percent stake. Turning down £2 million in cash meant he still didn't have that lump sum security that would see his family right if anything should befall him or the company. The growth of the business was financed from cashflow and short-term loans. It was now time to cash in some chips. In 1980, Amstrad was floated on the stock market. The offer was nine times oversubscribed.

Computers were next in line for the Amstrad effect. In 1979 IBM were putting the final touches to their first personal computer, due to be launched in the USA. IBM, supported by Microsoft, stabilised and standardised the PC business.

That was Amstrad's cue. They gave it the usual treatment, bringing PCs to the British mass market in 1984. Sugar stated in an interview: "They did exist, but they were £4,000 each. I made a commercial version for £400." Months later 37 year-old Alan Sugar received the title 'Young Businessman of the Year'.

In 1986, he tried to do a deal with Clive Sinclair for his computer interest. Sinclair's business was failing. Sugar put a £5 million (£10 million) offer on the table. Up until then the bankers (but not Clive) were haggling and holding out for more, playing hardball. Bloody-minded Alan Sugar told the bankers and creditors at an assembled meeting: "If you want it it's there if you don't I'm leaving and getting on a plane for my holidays – end of story." They took it.

Foray into football

In 1987 Amstrad continued expanding, setting up subsidiaries throughout Europe, Australia and America. Sugar tried something different in 1991, buying Tottenham Football Club, near his old stomping ground of North-East London. Even with Sugar sprinkled all over the club it was a bitter experience.

During the ensuing court battle with the popular football celebrity Terry Venables, Sugar was bundled out of court to avoid the anti-Semitic and raucous Tottenham fans who were all over him. He sold the club in 2001, describing it as "the biggest waste of time." In the same vein he told 10 Downing Street he couldn't make it to dinner because it clashed with his birthday. He also turned down Radio 4's *Desert Island Discs* and a David Bailey photoshoot. He wasn't impressed with pomp and ceremony.

Classic Sugar quotes

From humble beginnings, Alan Sugar has remained an unpretentious guy, who calls it as he sees it. He is quoted as having said: "The shareholders are looked after by me. And they should be very thankful. I run Amstrad as if it was my own. They get their accounts every year, their profits and dividends. And if they don't like it, they should sell their shares. But I'll run my company the way I want to. Not the way some twat in the City wants me to." When an insurance company representative criticised him over missing the shareholder's AGM he is quoted as saying: "He can go and f*** himself. He can stick his bloody share certificate right where the sun don't shine, as far as I'm concerned." It's also reported he sent a fax to a prospective supplier in China saying "Dear Mr. Ching Chang Chong, we received your video. It is shit." Alan Sugar doesn't take himself too seriously. He once said of himself: "I'm a bit of a nutter."

Amstrad experienced unbelievable growth during the 1990s. Post-flotation, Sugar raised over £9 million, disposing of his own shares and investing most of it into commercial property, (which he rarely viewed before buying). In 1988 the company was worth £1 billion (£1.7 billion). The company share-option scheme, instituted in 1985, created seven millionaires among Sugar's employees. Additionally, the lives of countless other staff members were changed beyond recognition as a result of their Amstrad windfall.

Alan Sugar (by now Sir Alan Sugar) widened his fan-base when he starred in the British version of Donald Trump's hit show in America, *The Apprentice*. The show is an unmitigated success. Sugar's fee goes to Great Ormond Street Hospital. He's quoted as saying: "I wish to avoid people saying, 'What's he doing that for? Hasn't he got enough money?' I really hate that feeling." In 2009, Sir Alan Sugar became Lord Alan Sugar and was appointed the British Government's 'Enterprise Champion'.

The Australian tycoon Rupert Murdoch has described Lord Alan Sugar as Britain's greatest entrepreneur. And all of this was achieved by that young entrepreneurial Jewish kid from North-East London, who failed the eleven-plus exams. He sums himself up by saying: "I was never going to be a rabbi or a priest, put it that way. I was a salesman."

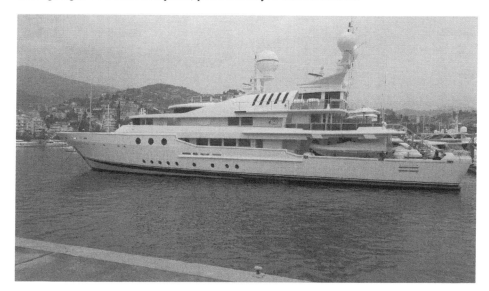

RICHARD BRANSON 1950 –

"A business has to be involving, it has to be fun, and it has to exercise your creative instincts"

Moulding of an adventurer

In 1954 a four year-old toddler was put out of a car and told to find his own way home, which was four miles away. He did. One cold dark January morning eight years or so later that very same kid had his sleep rudely interrupted. The sleepy kid was told to cycle the 50 miles from his home in Shamley Green, Surrey to Bournemouth to see a relative. He was given some sandwiches and told to find water on the way. Dawn was yet to break when he set out. As the young Olympian walked in the following day, from his amazing cycling feat, he expected a fanfare welcome. He received just a few pleasantries from his mum and was told: "The vicar is expecting you, I told him you should be home any minute now, so you'll be around shortly to chop some logs."

The little boy's name was Richard Charles Nicholas Branson (Ricky to his family). Though he had two of the most affectionate and caring parents a child could have, Richard's mum and dad weren't fearful of teaching their young cub by trial and adversity. His dad, Ted Branson, was a Cambridge-trained barrister and son of a knighted High Court judge. Ted's father was a cousin of Scott of the Antarctic. Richard's family were people of real character.

Money was always in short supply in the Branson household. Richard's entrepreneurial mother Eve Branson made ends meet by having foreign students to stay at their ivy-covered cottage in rural Surrey. She also had a cottage industry business selling tissue boxes to Harrods and waste paper bins to local shops.

Caught with pants down

At boarding school Richard was both short-sighted and dyslexic. At eight he still couldn't read a word. No one knew he was short-sighted, and dyslexia was hardly a common term in 1958. At prep school poor work meant a beating from the masters, and a weekly beating for Branson was standard issue. The flip side, however, was sports. Richard Branson was a veritable Daley Thompson. He was captain of both football and rugby teams, and would wipe the floor with the opposition come sports day. This did wonders for his reputation and was instrumental in 'bully evasion'.

Unfortunately, young Branson was bottom of every class and every subject. Forced to change school he left Scaitcliffe aged 13 to join Cliff View. At his new school they simply beat you till you got it right. For a short-sighted dyslexic this meant a perpetually sore arse. The backward eleven year-old sought solace in the headmaster's 18 year-old daughter. After being caught putting in some extra-curricular activity in her bedroom one night, randy Ricky was expelled. The discovery of his suicide note won him a reprieve.

Teenage entrepreneur

Three years after starting Stowe Public School in 1963 Branson started his first venture, which ended in disaster when rabbits ate the Christmas trees they had planted, and ruined the planned Christmas bonanza. The raising of budgerigars also failed to takeoff. After breaking his knee, Branson replaced the sports arena with the library. It was here he met the sophisticated *Private Eye* reader Jonny Gems, whose parents moved in highfalutin journalistic circles. This association with Gems led to an improvement Branson's English schoolwork – so much so he began nearing the top of his English class.

Branson's next venture was born out of dissatisfaction with the school rules and a new interest in journalism. The school's existing magazine was too timid for his ideas on school-rules reform. So, he and Jonny decided to launch their own inter-school magazine called *The Student*.Branson and Gems contacted MPs, sold ads, and travelled up and down from London.

After securing one-on-ones with 1970s A-listers such as Vanessa Redgrave, David Hockney, Mick Jagger and John Lennon, interviews were easier to get.

The headmaster's perceptive parting shot to Branson in 1967 was in writing: "Congratulations Branson, I predict you will either go to prison or become a millionaire." He was right – but on both counts. The magazine was launched in 1968. The following year, Branson was arrested. He had helped get a police officer sent down for planting drugs on a student. The police bided their time, waiting for an opportunity to avenge themselves. They got it when they arrested and charged Branson for indecency (they dug up an obscure 1889 statute) after his campaign in his magazine for an improvement in provisions to combat VD. A wave of interest gathered nationally, and the Home Office offered him a personal apology. But only one of the two charges was dropped and he was fined £7 (£63). The judge commented that the law was absurd. It was at this juncture that Richard Branson learned not to fear the establishment. He was yet to fulfil his headmaster's prophetic insight about going to prison.

The following year Branson had to cope with an attempted coup at the magazine. His best friend from infancy Nik Powell left a slip of paper at Branson's desk by mistake. On it were notes relating to ousting Branson as chief of *The Student* and turning the magazine into a cooperative where everyone was equal, with Powell installed as editor.

The note had been circulated without Branson's knowledge. When Branson looked up from the note on his desk the growing team he had assembled had their heads bowed, pretending to be working, and avoiding eye contact. Branson didn't have a clue as to the extent of the damage. When Powell walked in, foxy Branson put his arm around the would-be usurper and took him on a short walk and tried to bluff him. He told Powell the staff had approached him about the plot and they were upset at what he was attempting. Branson went on to explain that though they should always remain friends, but *The Student* was no longer the place for him. Powell, sad and embarrassed at his act of betrayal, stared at his shoes, said "sorry Ricky," then left.

The magazine had 20 people working for it now, all living and working at Jonny Gems' parents' place in Connaught Square near Marble Arch, London, down in the crypt. The costs were hard to control. Not only were there the magazine costs, but also the Student Advisory Centre, founded when Branson had great trouble finding an expert to perform an abortion after he'd made his girlfriend pregnant.

Gems' parents kicked them all out after they spread up from the basement through the house. Up until now money had been a side issue, but it was the lifeblood required to publish the informative magazine and provide facilities. Since Powell's departure the magazine was all at sea. A change of priorities was needed. Branson had to flip the script. He recognised he needed facilities and activities to provide money, and not the other way round.

The founding of Virgin Records

The government had removed the retail price maintenance agreement from the sale of records, yet record retailers weren't reducing prices. The decision was made to use the magazine as a vehicle to advertise and sell discounted records via mail order. The mail-order record distribution was started in the final edition of *The Student*. The record distribution angle brought in more money than the magazine had ever done before. With the flagging magazine having to close and the record business beginning, all that remained was to find the right name for the new company. 'Slipped Disc' was one suggestion. Another suggestion arose when a female worker commented on the lack of virgins amongst them even though everyone was a virgin to selling records. Branson knew it when he heard it and, in 1970, Virgin Mail Order was founded.

Tight-fisted Nik Powell was brought back, lured by a 40 percent stake to help run the new entity.

Next on the agenda was an appropriate site. John Menzies and WH Smith had sewn up record retailing, but their sites had no soul. A Virgin Record shop was to be a fresh and exciting place, an extension of *The Student* and the Advisory Centre where kids could hang out. Oxford Street was chosen over Kensington High Street.

Virgin's customers liked the familiar attitude and the informal atmosphere. The sites were a conduit for knowledge about the industry. Branson learned that big pop groups were still being treated as though they were being done a favour when it came to booking studio time. Musicians had to get their act together, get it done and get out of the studio on time. Branson thought – why not have a studio where artists could stay over for the week, and record at anytime of the day or night? On the strength of the Virgin records business he raised a

£20,000 (£200,000) loan from Coutts to buy an old 17th Century manor costing £30,000 (£300,000). Another £2,500 (£25,000) came from his parents and, unbeknownst to Branson, his aunt Joyce remortgaged her house for £7,500 (£75,000) to provide the shortfall. He got the house and begun turning it into a studio.

By 1971, Branson was desperate to raise funds (a Virgin Records store was due to open in Liverpool) when he was arrested then jailed (as his headmaster predicted), accused of smuggling records in through Dover customs.

The 21 year-old agreed to pay a £60,000 (£600,000) fine over three years with £15,000 (£150,000) upfront. Another jolt of reality was a woman landing at his and his girlfriend's feet as they walked down a road. She had jumped to her death from a high-rise building. After the two life-changing incidents Branson would always remember that life was about having fun.

In March 1972, Virgin Records banked £10,000 (£90,000) in its opening week. The shop-a-month programme Branson introduced during December 1972 had delivered 14 Virgin Record retail outlets. Virgin Records' discounting methods begin to make waves, so much so that music publishers refused to supply them. Branson, a true hustler, did a back-door deal with record retailer Pop In and operated using their account. Branson now had 20 stores and the recording studio was just about ready for action. Virgin was causing a stir and music magazines started to write articles about the new boys on the block. Record labels even approached Branson, requesting Virgin Records' support in backing their bands. Branson setup a separate company called Virgin Music, which was run by his cousin. The first artist signed to their label was weirdo and reserve guitarist Mike Oldfield. He couldn't believe

Virgin wanted to put out his tunes. The deal allowed Virgin to claim a 5 percent royalty on his sales.

Alas, Branson hadn't quite straightened out planning permission to record all night. A local man blocked the permission and Branson had to assemble an early-warning system, so that when the old boy was coming up the path to complain about the noise, a series of tin cans attached by string would alert everyone. When the tins rattled, all technicians, artists and musicians downed tools, ran into the living room and pretended to be having coffee. With Paul McCartney and his wife Linda now in the studio recording the smash hit *Band on the Run*, it could prove very embarrassing.

It turned out that every time a neighbour sought planning permission the old boy tried it on as a means of enticing a bribe. Branson rigged up a tape-recorder under his shirt and went to speak to Mr. Nasty. Branson's prey acted predictably, asking for money in exchange for stepping out of the way. Branson caught him and sent a letter outlining the ruse. The old boy was out-foxed and never bothered him again.

Virgin territory

In 1973, Mike Oldfield's album *Tubular Bells* was released, and sold over a million copies. Virgin made over £2 million (£15 million) plus the shop's profits, and continued to sign groups with excellent results. By 1974, Branson's aunt Joyce got her money back, plus an additional £1,000 (£7,000) in interest. *Tubular Bells* was the deal that would change Richard Branson's fortunes.

On June 22nd 1972, aged 22, Branson married Kirsten Tomassi, a woman he stole from a musician who was playing at the studio. Whilst on holiday in Mexico in 1974 they got caught in a storm on a small boat. They were with another couple, also tourists, at the time. The fishermen had had to be cajoled into taking them out. The weather didn't look good. The boat got caught up in a sudden storm. Branson and his wife couldn't convince the others to swim the two miles to the shore with them. The couple were in the water for two hours before making it back. They were the only survivors. That day they vowed to stay together forever as a result of their chastening experience.

The young couple were back in the UK no longer than a week before they parted. They went to dinner at a friend's house; dessert was a bout of wife-swapping. However, Kirsten did not want to swap back again, despite Branson's pleas. He trailed Kirsten and her newfound love around Europe, Paris, Majorca and then up into the Greek mountains, all to no avail. She had been lost just as she was gained.

By 1977, Branson's Virgin business was making a £500,000 pre-tax profit. Groups such as the Sex Pistols, Orchestral Manoeuvres in the Dark and The Human League were now on the books. Emboldened, Branson expanded into the USA. Virgin set in train the buying of houses in a number of US cities, with a view to creating recording studios. Branson was on a roll. The Venue, Virgin's first nightclub in London, was bought the following year. It was around this time that Branson tried to wangle a cheap holiday by pretending he wanted to buy a Caribbean island. This led to him offering a paltry £200,000 (£800,000) for Necker Island in the Virgin Isles. Its asking price was £3 million (£12 million). The offer was rejected. Later, the same vendor, hard up for cash, offered it up to Branson. The canny entrepreneur negotiated a further discount, and got it for just £180,000.

Book publishing was added to the portfolio of Virgin companies by 1979. Most of the books were biographies of rock stars, leveraging their already-contracted musicians. Branson himself was hard-pressed for money. By now, newly elected Prime Minister Maggie Thatcher's austerity measures were beginning to bite. Massive hikes in interest rates resulted. Virgin Records lost money for the first time. However, Richard Branson's reputation as an adventurous open-minded entrepreneur was well established by now. An American lawyer called Randolph Fields felt him out about collaborating on an airline venture. The sinister collapse of the entrepreneurial Laker Airlines launched by the late Freddie Laker had left a gaping opportunity on the Gatwick to New York route. Team Branson were violently opposed to it, but the entrepreneur loved it. He called Laker, called the competition, mitigated the risk and organised an exit strategy. Fields got edged out by Branson's foxy manoeuvres – he was given a £1 million (£2 million) parachute. Branson was left firmly in charge.

The founding of Virgin Airlines

Richard Branson was a real virgin in the airline business. The engine blew up on the first flight. It couldn't be insured, as it was an unlicensed test flight. A press photographer and other invited guests saw the blazing engine whilst onboard, but Branson charmed the photographer into ripping the film out of his camera and handing it over. Publishing those photographs would have ruined Branson's business.

There was a lot of desperate financial juggling and scurrying around trying to front the £600,000 (£1.2 million) for a new engine. Branson needed to go cap-in-hand to the bank for an extension on an overdraft. The bank said they'd see what they could do. The second test flight went ahead without a hitch and the licence was granted. It was 1984 and Virgin was in the airline business.

Branson had bought a house in Notting Hill and when he got home, exhausted from a long day of nerves and excitement, he was greeted by his bank manager from Coutts on the front steps of his house. The banker announced, out of the blue, they were about to start bouncing Virgin cheques – no extension. It meant the end of the airline and possibly the whole Virgin group. The business was to be strangled at birth. Branson, a man who never lost his temper, physically threw the banker out of his home and fell onto the sofa crying. He emptied all the overseas accounts, raising the £300,000 (£600,000) to keep them under the overdraft limit and honouring cheques. It was all last-minute high drama stuff. Nevertheless, the airline survived the early scares of childbirth and began to grow.

Branson realised the corporation had grown up. By the mid 1980s, Virgin was one of the largest privately owned businesses in Britain. Finance expert Don Cruickshank was brought in to rationalise the sprawling company. He reorganised the group's £3 million (£6 million) overdraft into a £30 million facility. In 1985 Virgin raised much-needed funds via a private placement. With pre-tax profits of £19 million (£36 million) and a turnover of £189 million (£378 million), the main rump of Virgin was floated on the stock market in 1986. The airline was held as a private concern. However, creative entrepreneurs and the City find collaboration difficult and the love affair soon ended. Branson bought back the elements floated in 1988, creating a new strategy to float, selloff and reinvest in a very selective and strategic fashion.

In 2002, Richard Branson was listed amongst the Top 100 Greatest Britons. In that year Virgin grossed over £4 billion. He currently has 350 companies, with dozens staring up all the time. When asked "How do you organise your day?" he replied: "A third of my time promoting, a third on new ventures and a third on fighting fires."

Having gone to the moon financially, Branson now wants to go there quite literally. He has teamed up with Burt Rutan, a space flight engineer, to create Virgin Galactic. The venture has been financed by Bill Gates's former business partner Paul Allen. Branson has signed a £14 million agreement for a new venture, taking tourists to space. His team was against it just like they were against Virgin Atlantic. But the excitement of pulling off such a venture is too much to resist for the entrepreneur who takes adventure very seriously.

STEVE JOBS 1955 –

"Remembering that you are going to die is the best way I know to avoid the trap of thinking you have something to lose. You are already naked. There is no reason not to follow your heart"

Ken Olson, President, Chairman and founder of Digital Equipment Corp., said in 1977:

"There is no reason [why] anyone would want a computer in their home." However, an uncertain future is seldom viewed in an undesirable light when the present feels so good.

Accessible technology like electronics has had the same profound effects as the discovery of flint. It cannot be monopolised and thus its applicability permeates and benefits every facet of human life. From time to time technology falls into the hands of a genius, just as flint surely did. It sometimes falls into the hands of a maverick, one who thinks outside the box, someone unconventional and unable to be satisfied. When this happens, the effects can be so far-reaching they become unimaginable.

Maverick child

Stephen Paul Jobs didn't always fit in and didn't always want to.

His father, Abdul-Fattah (John) Jandali, a Syrian Arab immigrant, came to America when he was 21, in 1952. He later rose to be Professor of Political Science in Michigan, Nevada, and Washington State Universities.

Steve's young unmarried European-American mother Joan Simpson later became a speech therapist. The couple did marry later and had a daughter, Mona Simpson (now a famous novelist) but eventually divorced. Steve was put up for adoption just after he was born. His adoptive parents Paul and Clara Jobs named him and brought him up in Mountain View, California.

The couple had some concerns about Stephen's schooling. The child always seemed bored and when he was eleven, he simply refused to go back to school. This contributed to his parents' decision to move to Los Altos, California. Stephen's new school was Homestead High, and part of what they offered was electronics tuition. At Homestead Stephen was known as a loner and had an odd way of looking at things – his own way. Things went from bad to worse as he developed into a delinquent schoolyard terrorist and was eventually thrown out of school. However, one perceptive teacher saw beyond the child's outward behaviour. Imogene 'Teddy' Hill was one of those special teachers. She bribed Stephen to work and in so doing lit the fuse to his mind. Money made young Jobs stretched himself and it became clear he was gifted. His class was once innocently asked what in the world they did not understand. Jobs's hand went up like a shot, "I don't understand why all of a sudden we're so broke!"

Paul Jobs was having problems at work. He had changed his occupation and was now starting from the bottom again as a machinist at Spectra-Physics, who at the time manufactured electronic equipment and gas lasers. Paul Jobs' work interested his son's curious mind. While still in high school, Steve Jobs attended lectures at Hewlett-Packard, acquiring a summer job at the firm. Having graduated high school in 1972, he enrolled at Reed College in Portland,

Oregon. Jobs lasted one semester. Most of his time was spent immersed in counter-culture and studying philosophy.

Self-discovery

He secured a job with Atari for six months, becoming a video-game designer. He told his line manager (who thought Jobs was a nightmare to work with) that if he passed out, the manager should "just roll me aside and not worry" explaining he was on a diet of water and air! After saving up enough cash he was off for enlightenment and self-discovery in India. When he arrived home, bald and dressed in sheets, in the autumn of 1974, he started frequenting the meetings of the Homebrew Computer Club.

It was the first of its kind. Homebrew began in March 1975, with members meeting in the garage of one of its affiliates in Santa Clara County, California. The philosophy behind the Computer Club was a place where like-minded individuals could meet and mess about with computers (what Napoleon Hill would describe as a Mastermind Alliance) but on a strictly non-commercial basis.

It was here that Jobs reacquainted himself with friend and future partner Stephen Wozniak, a mathematics fanatic (indeed most of Jobs' early team went to school together). Wozniak and Jobs were very different but had one thing in common: they were major pranksters. On their first meeting the pair traded stories of their pranks and hit it off. Their relationship to electronics was different: Wozniak was a geek in the extreme, and Jobs was an innovative entrepreneur. It was a precarious grouping. Jobs once told Wozniak that Atari had only given them $700 for some work they did for the company, instead of the actual $5,000 ($17,000). Wozniak got shafted, receiving only $350 ($1,200). He later said he regarded the matter as insignificant and unimportant.

Early hustles

Jobs' next venture's supply line came from the Cap'n Crunch breakfast cereal. The cereal came with a whistle and Jobs realised that the instrument had a similar frequency to AT&T's supervision tone for long-distance telephone connections. By modifying the whistle with a bit of tape one could reproduce the 2600 Hz access tone. An idea was forming.

Wozniak went to town building 'blue boxes' that allowed people to place long-distance calls for free using the technique.

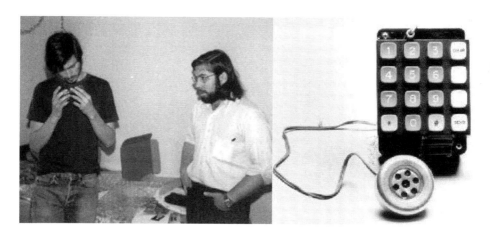

It was low-hanging fruit and didn't last very long before AT&T readjusted, but it was an early sign of the innovation that would one day propel the Apple brand into the super-cool league.

Founding of Apple

Wozniak had been working on his own personal computer and Jobs saw guys at the club surrounding him whilst he worked. Jobs saw the thirst in their eyes and had an idea of building and selling the PCs to Homebrew members, quenching their need.

Not being one to adhere to rules, Jobs disregarded the club's convention of a non-commercial ethos. He knew they wouldn't be able to resist their own personal computer. So, he and Wozniak (who was still at Hewlett-Packard) set about creating a computer in Jobs' bedroom. Their computer would be made with people in mind. Wozniak had to be dragged into the business kicking and screaming. Both Hewlett-Packard and Atari rejected Jobs' home computer, thinking the whole idea was ridiculous.

Designing a new computer was not cheap. It required the disposal of major assets to raise funds. Jobs sold his Volkswagen van and Wozniak sold his scientific programmable calculator. Combined asset disposals amounted to the $1,300 ($3,500) needed to finish the project. Most of the production took place on Jobs' bed and couch. It wasn't long before they had their first order from the Byte Shop, a computer store, who ordered 50 units at $666 ($2,000) a throw.

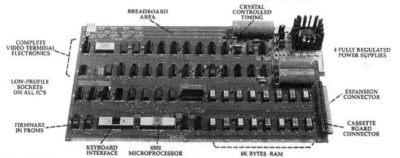

The price was tongue-in-cheek, reflecting the phone number of Wozniak's Dial-A-Joke machine, which ended in 666. Jobs named the new personal computer company 'Apple,' reminiscent of his halcyon days as a young apple picker in Oregon.

The product had no keyboard, no case, no sound and no graphics. Nonetheless, it was an improvement on what was already out there and soon they were flying out the door. After leveraging a deal to obtain much-needed credit facilities, operations moved from Jobs' bedroom to his parents' garage. The whole family got involved. Jobs achieved a first when he brought in marketers, advertising agents Regis McKenna. Adverts featuring Apple computers on a kitchen counter (suggesting pragmatism) began appearing with an emphasis on being about people and not computers. One of the earliest pieces of software written was a programme to balance chequebooks. The philosophy was "power to the people." In true Jobs and Wozniak fashion Apple Computer was incorporated on April 1st 1976, April Fools' Day.

By January 1977, a besieged Wozniak was forced to give up the day job at Hewlett-Packard. In addition to McKenna handling advertising, 38 year-old Mike Markkula was onboard full-time.

Markkula was a retired multi-millionaire, having taken advantage of stock options acquired as a marketing manager for Intel and Fairchild Semiconductor. Jobs sold them his vision of a personal computer for ordinary people. Markkula was convinced that the venture was worth coming out of retirement for. His $250,000 ($500,000) investment in the fledgling enterprise gave him one-third of the business. The core group then began assembling a team of marauding go-getters.

The company kept on improving its product, launching computer after computer. The new Apple II was the first personal computer to generate colour graphics and now included a keyboard, power supply and a well-designed case. It came equipped with two game paddles and a demo cassette, priced at $1,298 ($3,500). But customers still had to use their TV set as a monitor and store programs on audiocassette.

Then Jobs hit the market with the launch of Apple's Disk II, the fastest-ever mini-floppy disk drive. Two employees could knock out 30 of them in a day. The company grew at a phenomenal rate and Jobs floated it on the stock market in December 1980, raising over $100 million ($200 million). It was America's largest public offering since Ford Motors in 1956. The shares went in a matter of minutes. Steve Jobs became a multi-millionaire aged 23. During 1981, Apple's research and development budget jumped to $21 million ($42 million), three times the previous year's, with three thousand dealers worldwide and 2,500 staff. Apple was now a household name, with a leap in public awareness from 10 percent to 80 percent .

When the Leviathan IBM tracked them into the PC market, Apple used the event as a marketing opportunity via an ad in the Wall Street Journal which read: 'Welcome IBM. Seriously.'

Welcome, IBM.

Seriously.

Welcome to the most exciting and important marketplace since the computer revolution began 35 years ago.

And congratulations on your first personal computer.

Putting real computer power in the hands of the individual is already improving the way people work, think, learn, communicate and spend their leisure hours.

Computer literacy is fast becoming as fundamental a skill as reading or writing.

When we invented the first personal computer system, we estimated that over 140,000,000 people worldwide could justify the purchase of one, if only they understood its benefits.

Next year alone, we project that well over 1,000,000 will come to that understanding. Over the next decade, the growth of the personal computer will continue in logarithmic leaps.

We look forward to responsible competition in the massive effort to distribute this American technology to the world. And we appreciate the magnitude of your commitment.

Because what we are doing is increasing social capital by enhancing individual productivity.

Welcome to the task apple

Mackintosh was launched in 1984 and named hardware product of the year in 1985.

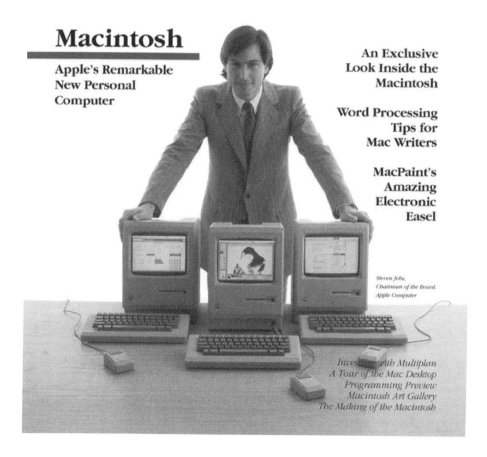

MACWORLD

Premier Issue $4.00
Canada $4.75

The Macintosh Magazine

Macintosh

**Apple's Remarkable
New Personal
Computer**

**An Exclusive
Look Inside the
Macintosh**

**Word Processing
Tips for
Mac Writers**

**MacPaint's
Amazing
Electronic
Easel**

*Steven Jobs,
Chairman of the Board,
Apple Computer*

*Investing with Multiplan
A Tour of the Mac Desktop
Programming Preview
Macintosh Art Gallery
The Making of the Macintosh*

Its users considered themselves almost a cult, thanks to Jobs' emotional intelligence in positioning the product. In just over a decade Jobs and Wozniak went from an electronics board in his bedroom to a $9 billion ($15 billion) business and billionaire status.

Time for a change

Despite the plaudits and Esquire magazine naming Jobs and Wozniak among the 'Best of the New Generation' there were new challenges. The business manager, Sculley, wanted cutbacks, including a major cull of burgeoning worldwide staff levels in light of a sales slump. Jobs and Sculley had a face-off. Wozniak left to avoid the conflict and started up his own home video business. Steve Jobs got up impromptu in the middle of a board meeting and announced phlegmatically: "I've been thinking a lot and it's time for me to get on with my life. It's obvious that I've got to do something. I'm thirty years old now." He promptly resigned there and then.

In 1986, Jobs bought a graphics-generating hardware company called Pixar from Lucas films. Its former owner was George Lucas: writer, producer, and director of the *Star Wars* franchise.

Lucas was at the time struggling to make headway with the company. In 1995, Pixar made *Toy Story*, the Academy Award-winning computer animation film.

It became the highest domestic-grossing film released that year and the third-highest grossing animated film of all time.

However, Jobs' real passion was his new start-up, NeXT Computers, on which he began work almost immediately after he resigned.

Steve Jobs' new *"machine for the '90s"*

The NeXT computer

- 25-MHz 68030 · Optical Drive
- Math and Digital Signal Processors
- 8 Megabytes of RAM
- Windowing Unix

He threw in a massive $7 million of his own cash and future presidential candidate multi-billionaire Ross Perot contributed $20 million. Quixotic and irreverent, Jobs was now out to obliterate the Apple product with his own new state-of-the-art personal computer.

Returning to Apple

It never happened: by 1996 Apple were begging Jobs to come back. They bought his businesses for $402 million and installed him as the ICEO (Interim Chief Executive Officer) on a nominal salary of $1 per annum (though he was gifted a $46 million jet in 1999 and almost 30 million shares between 2000 and 2002). The company had their backs against the wall and Jobs was up for the challenge of turning them around. The first thing he gave them was the iMac, morphed from a machine being developed at NeXT. The eye-popping product was launched on May 7th 1998. It was awesome and an immediate hit. Aesthetically, the iMac was unique with its translucent 'Bondi blue' plastic, egg-shaped body. Jobs realised that people need to like the machines they work on, and made sure Macs were recognisable computers as well as machines that delivered.

Next came iTunes in 2002. Apple had acquired the rights to distribute millions of published songs digitally.

Today his iPod dominates the digital music-player sales. At the time of writing they had over 90 percent of the market for hard drive-based players and over 70 percent of the market for all music players, achieved from a standing start. When Jobs started Apple, he created a complete revolution in personal computing. When he left they fell into disarray. Upon his return, Jobs revolutionised the personal entertainment business. In 2005 the Apple share price doubled in a six-month period.

The unconventional entrepreneur lives in a relatively modest house for a man worth $3.3 billion. He has displayed his true colours throughout his career. He tore strips off Bill Gates and Microsoft decrying: "they just have no taste." He also condemned them for lacking originality and culture. He later apologised to Gates for his comments, admitting they should have been made in private.

Great inventions are not enough, as Matthew Boulton had demonstrated centuries ago. Great entrepreneurship is needed to power great inventions.

When fire was first 'invented' there were probably guys standing around thinking "now that's a bloody dangerous idea." Had Steve Jobs been around he would have thought "forget warm meals, we can take over the world with this." Steve Jobs' total disregard for the restrictions imposed by conventionality led him to become a multi-millionaire at 23 and billionaire before 30 – all without actually inventing anything. He revolutionised his industry – twice! – with the pure force of his peculiar maverick character.

When Dean Kamen's revolutionary Segway scooter was to be launched, he tried to involve Jobs. Jobs told Kamen: "I think it [the design] sucks. Its shape is not innovative, it's not elegant and it doesn't feel anthropomorphic." The Segway is universally understood to be a great invention – only nobody wants one.

BILL GATES 1955 –

"People always fear change. People feared electricity when it was invented, didn't they?
People feared coal, they feared gas-powered engines"

Bill Gates, born in the same year as Steve Jobs, knew the future would welcome a product that made doing tasks easier. Like Jobs, Gates recognised that electronics would change the world. Gates is spoken of primarily as a software man. But his amazing products have obscured his entrepreneurial savvy, and his ability to hustle like a P. Diddy or an Alan Sugar. Had he not had these qualities, who knows what the PC industry would look like today. No doubt it would be rather fragmented.

It's his ability to hustle that has seen him benefit himself, dominating his industry. The flipside of this is that his domination provides a ubiquitous uniform platform. So much so that we can go around the world with our portable memory sticks, stick them into virtually any computer and continue working on the same objective. Gates knew the world was forever changing and recognised it was about to take a leap forward when the release of the first PC was announced. He didn't cause the change (he in fact had to be shown it), nor could he stop it, but he knew he could shape it 'in his own image'.

William Henry Gates III (who was actually the fourth William Gates) was born in Seattle, Washington. He was from a long line of high-achievers and geared to greatness from very early on. The original Bill Gates I was an aggressive entrepreneur, running a transport wagon business. He arrived in the booming city port of Seattle from Pennsylvania in the 1880s. Gates then followed the gold rush to Alaska, making money out of the hopeful prospectors. Once back in Seattle he launched a second-hand furniture business. This entrepreneurial trait would feature generation after generation among the Gates family.

First deal

Gates' great grandfather was a state legislator and mayor, his grandfather the Vice-President of a national bank, and his father a wealthy and prominent lawyer (and a giant, at 6ft 6 inches tall). His expressive mother, former teacher Mary Maxwell Gates, served on the boards of non-profit organisations, banks and educational institutions. The 'happy boy' (as he was known in the neighbourhood) was grilled on his times-tables by his father every day on the way to school. Gates' business career started early. The young entrepreneur's first deal was with sister Kirsti for the use of her baseball mitten. Gates produced a draft contract and had it signed prior to her being paid the $5 (£24) fee. Academically the gifted child made mincemeat of his peers. But he had to be sent to a psychologist after stressing out his parents. The psychologist told Mum and Dad to forget it – it was his way or no way. His parents recognised quite early on what they had in their midst and shipped their precocious child off to Lakeside, a private school known for its edgy scholastic grit.

Unruly child

The school provided direct access to new machines called computers. Young Gates bunked off lessons, handed his homework in late and often not at all.

In many instances he was ahead of his study group so was relieved from class. But he could always be found in the computer room – where there was a *real* challenge. Lakeside did a deal with a company called Computer Center Corporation in 1968. The company had just opened in town and offered Lakeside students free computer time. Gates and his classmates spent ages in the facility making a mess of the mainframe. They knobbled the security codes, reorganised the files and caused the computer to crash continually. Consequently, they all got banned – but they also got jobs.

The Computer Center recognised their computers' inherent weaknesses exposed by the kids and got them to help sort it out, paying them in computing time. The kids formed Lakeside Programming Group, and on the November 18th 1970 they got their first order. Information Sciences Incorporated (ISI), a company from Portland, Oregon, wanted a computerised payroll program. Gates was kicked out of the project as surplus to requirements. The group made a mess of the project and crawled back to Gates begging for forgiveness and assistance. He used this opportunity to implement his non-negotiable terms for returning to the fray. Because of the potential royalties payable the group became a legal entity.

The school administration offered Gates the job of computerising the school's schedule. He asked his pal and fellow computer nerd Paul Allen to help him. TRW, a defence contractor, heard what Gates and the Lakeside team had done for the Computer Center and employed them to do the same for them.

Gates, aged just 16 and still at school, decided to go his own way, setting up Traf-O-Data in 1972 with Allen.

They created a computer that measured traffic-flow. The duo set up pressure-sensitive hoses across roads and every time a vehicle rolled over the hose it registered and was counted by the computer. The data was then transferred to paper tape, and processed. They made $20,000 ($73,000) from various government and state departments, but lost much of their business when clients found out their age.

When Bill Gates went to Harvard they had to pack it all in. He scored 1590 on his entrance exams, a one-in-a-million result. The almost perfect score estimated his IQ at 170. But he was still trying to work out what to do with his life. The Schumpeterian thinker remarked about this period of his life saying "I was definitely always pushing us out into those frontiers of 'What should we do?'" He was curious, adventurous and hungry. Allen by now was tugging at Gates' coat to forget Harvard and set up a computer company, but Gates' parents wanted him back at school. Allen kept banging on about exponential phenomena in computing. Gates' response to Allen at 16 was: "Oh, exponential phenomena is pretty rare, pretty dramatic … Are you serious about this?" Gates still wasn't quite ready. In between programming sessions he played poker to combat boredom.

Then one day in December 1974, Allen stopped off to buy a magazine. His jaw hit the ground when he saw the front cover of *Popular Electronics*: it was a picture of the Altair 8080 accompanied by the headline: "World's First Microcomputer Kit to Rival Commercial Models." It was exactly what he'd been trying to convince Gates to build.

Launch of the PC industry

Allen (who hung around Harvard) bought the magazine and made for Gates' dorm. He knew he had just witnessed the first spark that would ignite the world's personal computing explosion. Change was on the way. It was bad news someone had got there first, but first is not always best. Gates sat quietly thinking, rocking backwards and forwards as he had done since a small child (and still does to this very day). It was time. He called Altair's producer MITS and blagged a meeting, telling them he had a great new software programme he had just written, right up their street. Nothing could have been further from the truth. Gates got his invitation to meet and immediately started to write the programme. His team not only had to write, but also load and test the newly written programme and it was for a computer they didn't have access to.

Allen altered a computer owned by the college to simulate the Altair machine. Gates helped co-write the programme and a couple of months later they flew in and met with MITS, seeing the 8080 for the first time 'in the flesh'.

They tested the programme on the Altair. It didn't work. They reloaded it paused for a while as it whirred away. It loaded, and worked like a dream. Everyone sat there, amazed that it was working, including Allen (who worked for MITS for a while). The deal with MITS for supply of their programme (called Altair Basic) was sealed. It was a version of a John George Kemeny and Thomas Eugene Kurtz creation completed in 1964.

The founding of Microsoft

Later that year Gates dropped out of Harvard and in 1975 the duo started a company called 'Micro Soft' (short for 'Microcomputer Software'), and later changed to 'Microsoft'.

Gates moved the company to New Mexico, setting up their first office in Albuquerque, close to MITS' head office. At this stage staying close to the money was imperative. He nevertheless still needed a loan to cover the cost of his lodgings. It was later in Albuquerque that young Gates got himself arrested and jailed in Mexico, for racing his Porsche 911 in the desert.

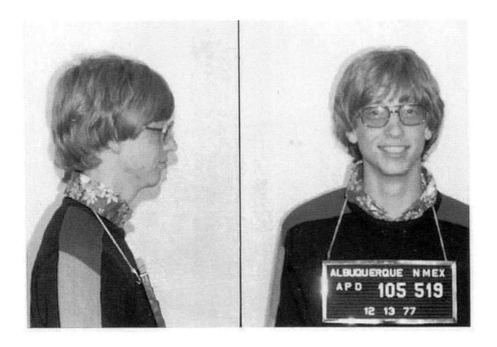

Gates began pressing home his advantage of being one of the very first companies to produce a viable software product for PCs. Unfortunately, the original basic tapes were stolen and Gates began a lifelong war against piracy. Once he'd been able to overcome this blip he kicked on with a Basic for Tandy/Radio Shack, and another for Commodore and the Apple II by 1977. Apple got a graphic-orientated version, which they called AppleSoft.

Opportunity comes knocking

IBM was just about the most admired company in the Western hemisphere and beyond, referred to affectionately by all as 'Big Blue'. Thomas Watson Jr., head of IBM, led the leviathan of the electronics and computing industry. IBM was so huge that if they had a bad day at the stock exchange, so too did the stock exchange. When they came calling you dropped everything you were doing, cleared your diary and called home to tell the family you'd hit the jackpot.

IBM rang Digital Research Inc (based in Seattle, as was Microsoft at this time) and said they were flying in to do a deal on the software Digital were developing. They spoke with Dorothy McEwen, Digital's attorney, secretary and the wife of Gary Kildall their developer and founder (they later divorced). She asked when they wanted to meet. They were already on their way.

Gary Kildall was the software industry's leading man. He developed a clever piece of software for the next generation of computers featuring floppy disks. His software allowed stuff to be written to and from the floppy disk and the hard disk. Rather than follow through, he started dithering about the meeting, saying he was focused on other projects. IBM wanted to get their hands on the operating system he was creating. Microsoft was developing software with the upcoming IBM PC in mind. It was 1979 and IBM was desperate, needing to remedy a disastrous attempt to steam into the PC market. They needed a decent operating system, yesterday. Microsoft by now had a turnover of $80 million ($162 million) and 80 employees, but Gates couldn't deliver all IBM wanted in time. It was then that Gates turned them on to Kildall to take care of the operating system.

When IBM arrived they found that Gary Kildall couldn't be bothered to turn up and Dorothy McEwen refused to sign an NDA (non-disclosure agreement) so no meaningful discussions could be had. Kildall harboured issues surrounding potential royalty payments on offer and alternative ideas of rolling out his technology. IBM was not happy. Gates, who accompanied the IBM team to the meeting, decided to take the IBM guys back to *his* place. He assured IBM they need not worry; he could hook them up.

Gates called in a guy called Tim Paterson, of Seattle Computer Products, who was working on a competing operating system for a client who was fed up waiting for Kildall to get his act together. Gates' offices were close by. Paterson's version was a bit of a turkey but Gates bought the rights of the programme for $50,000 ($100,000), never letting on about the IBM hook-up. Between Microsoft and IBM the turkey was plucked and cleaned. Now they had a watered-down version of Digital's Direct Operating System. It was christened the 'Quick and Dirty Operating System' or 'QDOS'. Gates then convinced IBM to let him retain sole rights of the programme, threw in a modified version of their 'Basic', tied the whole thing together with a bit of cunning and the entrepreneur was laughing all the way to the bank.

Gary Kildall had missed that random once-in-a-lifetime collision with good luck. Seattle Computer Products sold its creation for a song and IBM didn't have the rights to the software. But Gates, a true player, a true hustler, had it all. He not only helped write the programme, co-ordinate and negotiate with all parties involved, he was also astute enough to retain all rights to the creation. Paterson ended up leaving Seattle Computer Products for Microsoft. In future, when Gates came to dinner, they'd all count their spoons.

Microsoft was asked by IBM for a hard-disk version. Gates gave them one and promptly rewrote the floppy-disk version. Now Kildall had no case for plagiarism and suing IBM was out of the question. The market had already become used to Microsoft's version despite Digital's stuff having more features. Digital's versions were not fully compatible with the IBM architecture that dominated the market. Microsoft was able to marginalise Digital's releases by some sharp marketing practices (so a Justice Department investigation found). Digital's version was hammered when Microsoft released version 5.0 and 6.0.

Riding the bear

From this point on Microsoft had its feet firmly under IBM's table, referring to the situation as "riding the bear."

Microsoft software was so prolific even the violently competitive Steve Jobs asked Bill Gates to assist on Apple projects. The PC market had to come to terms with the new power – Bill Gates and Microsoft.

Microsoft sales reached $150 million ($236 million) in 1984 and the company was valued at around $300 million ($472 million). The following year Microsoft launched the iconoclastic and now ubiquitous Windows operating system, jam-packed with features. By 1990, Windows would sell millions upon millions of copies every month, each retailing at $150. In 1995, Gates launched Windows 95. By then the anticipation of any new Microsoft version was just as hotly anticipated as the release of a cinema blockbuster movie. The release was widely featured in the press and even on news programmes.

Microsoft went to the stock market in 1986 and Gates became a billionaire aged 30. The defining moment for him as a great entrepreneur was when a global anti-trust suit was lodged against him. He was now in great company such as Fugger, Astor, Penney and Rockefeller. The only difference was Rockefeller had the US sewn up; Bill Gates stitched up the whole world.

At the time of writing the Microsoft cases are ongoing. A threat to break up Microsoft (the fate that befell Rockefeller's Standard Oil) is no longer realistic after Gates stepped down from CEO to Chairman and became Chief Software Architect. Steve Ballmer, who has been with Gates since his Harvard days, took over at the reins. Paul Allen had long since resigned to make the most of his tens of billions after becoming gravely ill.

World domination

Gates' house in Seattle cost nearly $100 million and is a techie's paradise. He can run a bath to an exact temperature whilst travelling home on the motorway. He has digitally-ordered copies of the world's greatest paintings upon his walls. Whatever smells and colours he or his guests prefer are pre-programmed to be emitted as that individual walks through the door. And it's all ecologically friendly.

Gates has spent $27 billion on good deeds such as fighting infectious diseases, funding vaccine programmes, amongst other things, via the Bill & Melinda Gates Foundation. His spending makes him the greatest philanthropist of all time, despite it accelerating (at least publicly) after billionaire Ted Turner goaded him into spending more on charity.

Microsoft Operating Systems feature on 95 percent of the computers sold globally. Their headcount is over 60,000 staff worldwide. The turnover (at the time of writing) amounts to $40 billion; profits are in excess of $12 billion. Microsoft continues to go from strength to strength. Forbes Magazine regularly lists Bill Gates as the world's richest man. On February 13th 2009 he was listed by them as having a net worth of $40 billion. He sells 20 million shares each quarter (at circa $27 a share) diversifying his equity portfolio by investing in divergent sectors like mining and airlines. Gates knows the world is forever changing and diversification allows the entrepreneur to take advantage of the future as well as protecting himself from inevitable change. In the future Bill Gates via his Bill and Melinda Gates Foundation will save more lives than any human in history (primarily in Africa) with their mantra of 'every life is of equal value'. This makes him the greatest entrepreneur in history in my book (excuse the pun). The Gates and Warren Buffett founded the Giving Pledge. Billionaires co-opted to give away the bulk of their fortune to charity before they die.

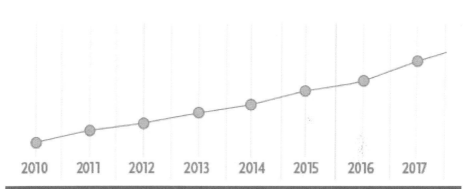

2010   2011   2012   2013   2014   2015   2016   2017

As of 2017, there are a total of

170 PLEDGERS

RICARDO SEMLER 1959 –

"Trying to grow bees in the sky"

Sometimes in life someone comes along who is successful not because of his adaptation to change, but because he is the force of change itself. These are true revolutionaries. Business has had many rebels but none like Brazilian entrepreneur Ricardo Semler. A rebel without a cause at first, Semler was destined to become a rebel entrepreneur.

He was born in São Paulo, Brazil. Both his parents were Austrian immigrants. His father was Antonio Curt Semler, a dentist with strong ideas about each generation bettering the last. Ricardo's grandfather wanted Antonio to become a physician. Antonio rebelled, acquiring a degree in engineering instead. When DuPont were offering jobs in Argentina in 1937, Antonio didn't need a second invitation. He was off. He later visited Brazil, prospecting for opportunity. By 1952 the adventurer had made up his mind. São Paulo was the place for him to unleash his dream.

Ricardo's mother, Renee Weinmann, and her family were chased out of Shanghai, China, where they had an export business. Mao Zedong purged the country of foreigners and the Weinmanns ended up in Brazil. Antonio was introduced to Renee who was teaching English privately, to wealthy clients. They were soon married. Though the marriage produced a daughter Antonio desperately wanted a son. It was just after the marriage that Antonio produced his invention, a piece of apparatus that extracted lubrication oils from vegetables. His forward planning required a son and heir to take over his yet-to-be-built empire. He really didn't have two pennies to rub together at the time, but he had plenty of confidence.

The need for an heir

Antonio Semler worked furiously on both projects, producing his machine and then an heir. Ricardo was born eleven months after his sister. The contraption was made on top of the dining room table (the lubrication oil extractor machine, that is). At the time they all lived in a poky two-room apartment. Antonio went into business with his invention, creating a company called Semco around it. By the late 1960s Antonio's view of Brazil was vindicated. The country was growing at a heart-stopping 7 percent per annum. The government decided they wanted Brazil to be shipbuilders next and started the Five Year National Shipbuilding Plan. Semco and Company took a slice of the action. With help from British manufacturers they began turning over millions. It was militarist Carl Phillip Gottfried von Clausewitz who said: "There are very few men, and they are the exceptions, who are able to think and feel beyond the present moment." Antonio Semler was one of those rare visionaries, with the strength of character to act on what he saw as the coming future. He got it right and the company grew into a major exporter, with factories dotted about Brazil. His teenage son Ricardo was a first-class bum, who loved frolicking around on his guitar (he was tone deaf), but when it came to business he could really rock and roll.

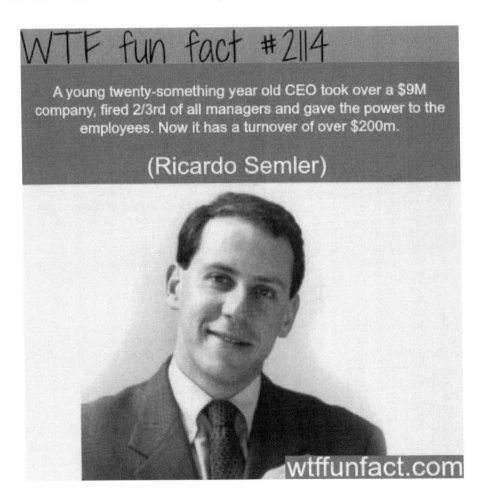

WTF fun fact #2114

A young twenty-something year old CEO took over a $9M company, fired 2/3rd of all managers and gave the power to the employees. Now it has a turnover of over $200m.

(Ricardo Semler)

wtffunfact.com

His earliest venture was the reorganisation of a lunchtime snack stand at his school. He increased the operation's hours, played suppliers off against each other, and put a halt to freebies. The budding entrepreneur made a little money and promptly invested it on the stock market. He made enough to fly all those involved off to a holiday resort.

After leaving school Semler was enrolled in Brazil's top law school, scraping through with Ds. Though he had spent many summers working at Semco as a child, the heir apparent now began his role as an apprentice CEO. His father, Antonio Semler, was a priggish, rigid and circumscribed sort of man. Work, home meals, golf and Rotary Club meetings were attended at the same time, on the same day, in the same way, without variation. Formality was everything. No first names were used throughout the company and many of his colleagues and employees feared him. Hence, Antonio had some trouble dealing with his young rebel son's informal and laid-back approach to business – such as holding meetings with his feet on the table and telling staff to call him Dickie!

His own man, with his own ideas

In 1980, it became clear to Semler that he was ready to run the show. However, he and his father were on a collision course. Their styles were diametrically opposed and the problem was further compounded by a serious slump in the Brazilian economy. Semler took advantage of some PricewaterhouseCoopers studies carried out for Semco on potential takeover targets. After conducting his own investigations he got very excited about buying out Brazil's largest ladder manufacturer with money borrowed from his father. On the day Ricardo Semler was to sign the papers his father called him into his office. The two discussed the way forward but the younger Semler was adamant their styles were incompatible and that his father was urinating into the wind. Antonio Semler's game all along was to wait and see how serious his son was about going his own way. When the ageing founder realised his son was to go it alone, he offered him the reins and a controlling interest in Semco, as well as the position of CEO. Twenty-three year-old Semler was shocked, but he took it, plus the $30,000 ($65,000) his dad put on the table to give up his pipe-dream. By 6pm on the following Friday, Ricardo Semler had completed a purge of 60 percent of the company's top managers. Some of these men had been with Antonio Semler when he was starting out, and Semler had not informed his father of his intentions. However, these were the men who had opposed and resisted his suggestions to diversify away from shipbuilding all along. They weren't about to put their life and soul into new plans for revolutionary change. The process was no different to Lucky Luciano's removals in late 1931, when setting up the National Crime Syndicate and dismantling Marranzano's top-down authoritative Julius Caesar model.

Luciano

Profaci   Mangano   Capone   Bonanno   Lucchese   Magaddino

The revolution begins

On the Saturday after the purge, Semler employed a short-tempered man, "with enough energy for an entire executive board." The new right-hand man was Ernesto Gabriele, a man who offered his resignation as the opening gambit in resolving issues. He picked up languages like a three-handed shoplifter. Gabriele had worked at a high level in major companies all over the world, and was a little crazy – definitely a rebel. After Ernesto, Semler employed Harro Hyde, whose clothes appeared to have been stored in a damp, dark closet. He shook up the sales department. Ernesto introduced a raft of documents and schedules, accounting for everything that moved in Semco. Over the next two-year period Hyde and Semler visited 60 countries marketing their products. They managed to reduce their dependency on maritime manufacturing to 60 percent, taking on compressors, oil filters, soup mixers and grinders. Whilst Brazil was becoming a basket case, Semco, with its new controls, bizarre personalities in management and the removal of formalities, were freed from a self-imposed maritime prison and started to make inroads into new markets.

Things were going so well that they hit the acquisition trail with a budget of $500,000 ($900,000). The criteria for interest were that the company must be a market-leader in its field with some synergy, and be technologically advanced. PricewaterhouseCoopers, which had been on a retainer with Semco since Antonio's days, were given the task of locating such a business. Semler continued his breakneck tour of visiting potential acquisition candidates, pushing himself so hard that he fainted during a factory visit. Eventually they decided on a business called Merck. The price was $3 million ($5.5 million). Semco had $500,000 (£9.25 million), as $300,000 had already been spent on acquiring a subsidiary called Flakt, who were to take over Semco's maritime business and merge it with their own shipping, refrigeration and offshore drilling divisions.

Semler offered Merck a cash payment upfront (which Semco would effectively take from Merck's own bank accounts), with the balance payable over five years, plus 25 percent of the profits. They went for it. As they assembled at the offices of Merck's lawyers, riots and shots rang out from protestors and police battling in the streets below. The mêlée resulted from the recent economic announcements from the Brazilian government.

The only new addition to Merck's successful management team was a short obese guy called Antonio Carlos Iotti. He was well-known for refusing to perform tasks he was instructed to undertake when he disagreed with them, even when threatened with the sack. Once again, Semler had recruited an incurable rebel. Gabriele, who had introduced timesheets, schedules, passes and accounting for everything that moved, got into a dispute with the board. The dispute involved the Semler family. It led to Gabriele leaving in a flood of tears. Sadly, he died shortly afterwards in a car accident. Hyde was doing fantastically well but got headhunted. The key factor in this switch was that he would be better able to look after his chickens! "No one could replace Harro." But a human resources and training guy named Clovis was brought in. He was a badly dressed ex-lecturer and ex-Ford executive, labelled subversive by the Generals running Brazil. This made him a rebel and thus an attractive acquisition to maverick Semler.

Whilst visiting a factory abroad Semler fainted again. Later that day, whilst resting in an office, he passed out yet again. His third spell of unconsciousness for the day took place at the hospital. Semler eventually gave the doctor a list of ailments which included permanent throat infection, back rash, rapid heartbeat, and on and on. The doctor had never seen such an acute case of stress in a 25 year-old.

"Why did running a large factory-based business have to be this way?" Semler asked himself. Change was needed. The maverick who refused to surround himself with conventional upper-tier managers decided to go to war on the causes of his stress. He wanted the company to become a more relaxed environment. He decided to go to war on convention. The idea was to create a company of happy individuals whom an employer need not be suspicious of, who had satisfaction and were *self*-driven. This left no place for Fernando and the like. They were bounced.

Trying to grow bees in the sky

Semler decided 'imposed order' was an enemy. Clovis, the political subversive, agreed, and became Semler's partner in crime. Checks on clocking-in times were banished, along with the management dress code. Factory workers were polled on colour schemes for décor and overalls. Semler's idea took on a revolutionary feel as he attempted to bestow his philosophy upon his management team. He believed that the way things look must not be muddled with the way things are, that effort and results must not be confused, and that quality and quantity were not always related. And that uncertainty shouldn't mean working harder.

Plants appeared in the offices; partition walls were removed; and the horrid locker room was redesigned by the staff, who also cleaned up the factory.

A food committee was formed to introduce better and more affordable meals: the lower the wage, the lower the price of the food. There were democratic weekly meetings for elected leaders. The cafeteria was the venue for a weekly chat between staff and managers over lunch, resulting in the formation of factory committees. Staff were free to do what they wanted so long as everyone agreed.

This powerful new culture revolutionised everyone's sense of responsibility toward the business. Management began getting tip-offs of pilfering, saving the company thousands. Freedom spilt over into other plants. Staff reorganised the dishwasher line making it more efficient, saving the company thousands yet again. Another group's improvements to the meat grinder section allowed for a cheaper cost of production, making the line more profitable. A pre-welding process idea from the factory floor saved $27 per unit. Blue-collar workers put out scoreboards to log competing output levels. Staff on the factory floor contributed to the reduction of inventory (just as Fernando had required but under duress). The struggling were completely turned around.

In 1985, Semler tried to pacify middle managers, who described his new corporate culture as "trying to grow bees in the sky." Semler adopted the remark as the title for their weekly meetings! All the organisational charts and the company manuals were rounded up and replaced with a single instruction: "Use Your Common Sense." Semler resolved a strike by getting managers and workers to sit down and admit to what each party had done wrong. By 1986, Semler's huge, sprawling company was divided up into small cells, with each unit managing itself. Productivity improved significantly. Semler felt it was now time to introduce affirmative action for women, and Semco grew into an autonomous and invigorated company performing very well.

Ricardo Semler kicked on, dividing the electronic side of the business from the main hub and bringing in Joao Fiasco to organise it. Fiasco (his real name) recruited 30 kids from the plant then checked through inventory, revealing, among other things, three years worth of redundant circuit boards and obsolete transistors, none of which had ever been returned to suppliers for credit. A 'just-in-time' stocking system was introduced, freeing valuable capital. Defective inventory was cut from 40 percent to 1 percent. Semler adopted the dictum of General Motors' Alfred Sloan: "What's the worst that could happen if I threw this out?"

Time-consuming memos were reduced to a single A4 page, written in newspaper style headlines. The maverick boss also introduced a profit-share scheme, with all employees equally catered for. Although 30 percent of middle managers left between 1985 and 1987 as a result of 'the lunatics taking over the asylum', unit costs came down and production soared. By 1987, Semco had made $2.2 million ($3 million) over an 18-month period. Semco now had one of the highest growth rates in Brazil. Semler's time at work had been reduced by 70 percent and his salary details were made available on request. The company was increasingly beginning to run itself. All the stress that had caused him to faint years ago was gone. In 1988, Semler went off to the Caribbean for a well-deserved holiday with his wife. He brought with him a collection of books including *The Prince* (Machiavelli) and *Malcolm X* (the autobiography).

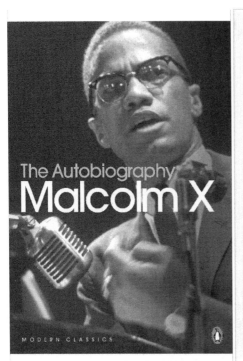

Whilst on the beach he found himself drawing circles in the sand and came up with an idea of a circular staff structure. All hierarchical titles were to be removed and everything was to be decided within three circles of people. Decisions must be made within two meetings. Positions were limited to four types and employees could choose their own job titles for their business cards. They would also be allowed to name their own salary (with certain issues considered) and the balance sheet was also to be posted on a public notice board.

Best-selling author

Ricardo Semler decided to write his memoirs after staff started to describe working at Semco as 'paradise'. He accepted $2,000 ($3,000) for his life story, called *Turning the Tables* in a book deal. His lawyer negotiated a far-sighted contract, with escalating royalties for every additional 100,000 units. No one expected the book to sell more than a few thousand copies but Semler felt he'd stick in a caveat just in case. The book sold over 400,000 copies, including a 200-week stint as a bestseller, and became Brazil's greatest selling non-fiction book.

Semler was named Brazil's Business Leader of the Year in 1990. In the same year, *America Economia* (the Latin-American equivalent of the *Wall Street Journal*) named him Latin American Businessman of the Year. However, in 1991 Semler suffered a reversal in fortunes: sales melted by 40 percent, largely thanks to the decision of the Brazilian president, Fernando Collor de Mello, to introduce restrictions on liquidity. He told people they couldn't take their money out of the bank – a sure-fire way to cause widespread panic!

The emergency measure that was ostensibly intended to combat hyperinflation resulted in large swathes of banking deposits being converted into government bonds. Companies were failing at an unprecedented rate. Semco's exceptionally good treatment of its staff was to save the company, just as Konosuke Matsushita's 'family business' ethic had saved him half a century before. Semler offered the staff greater control of the business in exchange for salary reductions. They took it. Profit-share rights were forfeited, and staff reduced overheads by delivering goods themselves after work or off-shift. Workers cleaned bathrooms and offices, taking over as many outsourced jobs as possible. The staff action was so effective the company was back on track after three months and salaries were restored to normal.

In 1993 Ricardo Semler released another book, called *Maverick*.

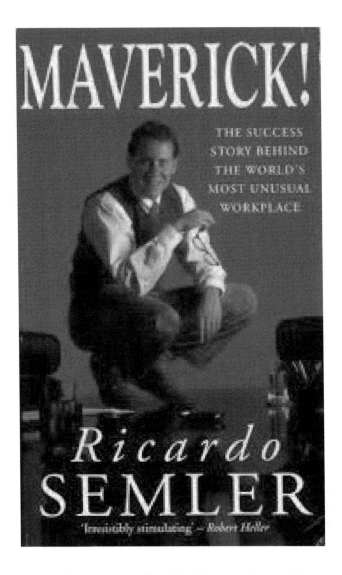

MAVERICK!

THE SUCCESS
STORY BEHIND
THE WORLD'S
MOST UNUSUAL
WORKPLACE

Ricardo
SEMLER

'Irresistibly stimulating' – *Robert Heller*

Time magazine featured him among its Global 100 Young Leaders profile series, published in 1994, while the World Economic Forum also nominated him for an award. In the late 90s Semler was lecturing and speaking at functions around 20 times a year (he charged a fortune in order to dampen demand). Semco expanded, becoming a conglomerate. From 1990 to 1996 Semco's sales grew from $35 million to $100 million.

In 1998 Semco registered 500 percent increased profits. Startling growth continued into 2004. Since Semler took over from his father turnover had risen from $4 million to $160 million. Under his leadership, Semco grew by 600 percent, productivity by 700 percent and profits 500 percent. Staff numbers increased from 100 to 3,000. The defining feature of Ricardo Semler and Semco is their 2,000-strong job application backlog. Staff turnover is just 1 percent, proving that rebels can also be excellent entrepreneurs and employers.

P. DIDDY 1969 –

"You're not what you were ten years ago. It's just a natural evolution and having wisdom"

One of the ways a youngster can generate some independence and extra money is by doing a paper round. It isn't an easy job, but for a hard-working kid, not shy about getting out of bed at unsociable hours, it can work. Sean Combs was that kind of child. His whole career would be characterised by never accepting what was on offer if it wasn't good enough. He knew instinctively that he could rely on his own ability. His secret weapon was to out-work the competition.

Those doing the paper round would get a taste of what was to come. When Sean saw a better paper round available he acted straightaway. He was the living embodiment of the maxim 'losers *let* things happen and winners *make* things happen'. Having identified one of the easier routes held by an older kid, he negotiated a friendly takeover by offering the previous incumbent the opportunity to participate in the revenues generated from the cushy round: "I'd split the money with him 50-50," he explained, "It was a great deal for him." Sean was on the road to big things. "I was making $600 a week by the age of 13. That's when I got the bug, when one plus one equalled two for me."

Sean may be known by many names – P. Diddy, Puff Daddy, Puffy, etc. – but the significance of his many names reflects something overlooked. He moves with the times, constantly evolving, never stale, always learning and adjusting. Very few that started out in the hip-hop industry have stayed at the top of the game for so long. He is not the world's greatest producer, rapper, dancer or financier. He's not a musician. He is an aggregation of all of these aspects of the business and that's why he is the leader of the hip hop industry, which earns over $100 billion a year in music sales, making it the world's biggest music genre. P. Diddy created and leveraged a street-cred brand into a mini conglomerate. He is a business mogul – one who strides over the whole industry, not limited by lack of talent to any one area.

Single mother

His mother Janice Combs was from the same generation as Earl Woods, Richard Williams, Joseph Jackson and Mathew Knowles (the parents of Tiger Woods, Venus and Serena Williams, Michael Jackson and Beyoncé respectively). It was a generation inspired by Martin Luther King and emboldened by Malcolm X. These parents had one thing in common: they suffered the indignity of Jim Crow as they grew up. They became steeled by the experience and aggressively pursued for their children the opportunities that Jim Crow had denied the young talents of their generation, as well as those before them.

Janice Combs was a beautiful up-and-coming model, married to Melvin Combs, a well-known local hustler and poser who had a reputation as a 'Robin Hood' character. Their son, Sean John Combs, was born in Harlem, New York City, on November 4th 1970. But tragedy was just around the corner. In 1973, when Sean was only three years old, his father – a limousine chauffeur was shot and murdered by a drug dealer in a New York City park, whilst sitting in his car. The assailant was never found.

Young and ambitious

It was clear by all accounts that Sean was switched-on, but he was taught the hard way. He came home one day screaming that he had been robbed. His mother Janice immediately set about teaching the young child how to street-fight, right then and there in the kitchen. Later, when his skateboard was stolen, Janice refused to let him into the house until he came back home with it; it was the same brand of tough love shown by the young Richard Branson's parents. Sean was smart enough to employ the services of an older and bigger kid to take care of the problem.

Harlem

What Mecca is to Muslims and Jerusalem to Christians, Harlem is to African Americans. The area has been considered the epicentre of African-American culture for the last 100 years and it was Sean's hometown. Black entrepreneur and property developer Phillip Payton (who founded the Afro-American Realty Company) was the son of a barber who fought the bar on blacks moving to Harlem and escaping the dilapidated tenements that hemmed them in the decaying parts of the city.

By 1920, Harlem was known as an exclusively black district. Absolutely every great black star, from Joe Louis to Michael Jackson, frequented Harlem. The famous musical showcase of the Harlem Apollo bolstered the town's international fame as a hotbed of talent. Rejection or acceptance at this venue was crucial proof of concept. If you could make it there you could make it anywhere. Harlem was the political epicentre of black America, and was home to modern-day black revolutionary thinkers such as Marcus Garvey, Clarence 13X and Malcolm X.

It is no surprise that Harlem was the birthplace of hip-hop. During the early 70s the streets of Harlem were filled with a new phenomenon – kids talking over music in time to the beat. The 'hip' word for impressive jive talking was 'rapping,' hence the name of the new trend. The one thing that never suffered through lack of money and resources in the black community was the music. During World War II the Caribbean suffered restrictions, but the islands were flooded with an abundance of steel drums, supplying the military with oil, among other things. This led to the birth of the steel band. Poverty always seemed to enhance musical creativity in the black community. The often-impoverished community frequently improvised, replacing expensive instruments with human imitation and interpretation, as well as makeshift instruments. The percussion and bass in this case were replaced with a series of a capella sounds called 'beat-box'. Now everyone could get musically involved at some level or another.

The founding of hip-hop

In 1969, the entrepreneurial DJ Kool Herc began using the Technics SP-10 turntables produced by Konosuke Matsushita (Panasonic).

They were the first commercially available direct-drive turntables. Herc began to use his fingers to stop, drag, and thrust vinyl records back and forth on dual turntables to create weird but innovative sounds – a practice called 'scratching'.

The direct-drive belt allowed the smooth physical handling of the rotating plate that spun the vinyl disc. Herc made it *hip* to be *hopping* from one turntable and/or record to another. It became known as 'hip-hoppin'. They combined this 'rapping' and 'scratching,' creating a fresh new musical genre, which we know today as 'hip-hop'. This phenomenon gave Herc's sound-system greater financial pulling power, making his own paid-entrance parties more profitable.

Sean Combs was surrounded by the whole movement as an impressionable child. A group from Sugar Hill (a neighbourhood in Harlem) released a record using as the background rhythm the hit single *Good Times* by popular pop-soul group Chic, in 1979. The release was entitled *Rappers Delight* and the band was called The Sugar Hill Gang. It was a sensation.

The dam had been breached and rap slowly seeped into mainstream music. Critics denounced it as a fad and gave the new genre a three-year life expectancy. To blacks it did not matter as it was simply about expression in a country that wasn't listening. What the music boffins didn't factor in was America's secret weapon – entrepreneurship. Young and hungry 'guerrilla entrepreneurs' – men like Andre Harrell, Russell Simmons and Sean Combs – would fight for markets by whatever means necessary. They recognised the changing habits of the market-herds and their changing palates. These entrepreneurs were different; they loved business as much as they did music. The combination was dynamite and inevitably headline-grabbing. This generation had, as Malcolm X put it, "lost all fear of the man." The old "keep your head down" mantra was replaced with "hold your head up."

The young Sean Combs was there in Harlem, right at the beginning, coming in at 4am off streets dominated by the new hip-hop genre and lifestyle (then, presumably, going out on his paper round shortly afterwards). Janice moved the family out of the daunting town of Harlem in 1982, as Sean reached his teens. She settled her young son and his sister Keisha in a middle-class suburb of Westchester County, Mount Vernon, NYC. Janice desperately wanted her son and daughter to have a quality education in congenial surroundings. Sean was enrolled at Mount Saint Michael Academy, a private secondary school in the Bronx. Janice worked flat-out to pay for private education for both her children. The young widow held down three jobs: she was a day-care centre teacher, a school-bus driver and an attendant for children with cerebral palsy. Sean's grandmother Jessie Smalls became his primary carer. Janice slaved hard but wasn't broke. The single mother was high-class with expensive taste. She held her head up.

At school Sean became a member of the football team. He often profiled bigger than he actually was by puffing up his chest, gaining the nickname 'Puffy'. After leaving Mount Saint Michael Academy in 1987, Sean was accepted at the prestigious Howard University in

Washington, D.C., known as 'Black Harvard'. He also attended St Charles Borromeo, where he took a course in business administration.

It didn't take long before Puffy was staging rap parties and concerts at the university. An enterprising diversification came in the shape of distributing term-papers and providing a shuttle service to the airport. After a student uprising Puffy had some commemorative posters and t-shirts made up and sold them on campus. As far as he was concerned he was surrounded not only by students but also by consumers. Puffy's entrepreneurial ambitions were now beyond his ability to be patient. He formulated a plan. From *his* vantage point black music was only half the story; the real commodity was the entire black scene.

Sean took advantage of his contacts. Heavy D (who went on to become a major rap star) was a friend from Mount Vernon, NYC. He hooked Puffy up in 1990 with 'hip-hoppreneur' Andre Harrell, founder of Uptown Records. Sean begged Harrell to hire him and he took the train every week from Washington, where he was studying at university, to New York to work his shift. Harrell became Puffy's mentor.

To his mother's utter dismay, Puffy dropped out of Howard and moved in with the affluent Harrell. Sean watched and learned from the two hip-hop industry leaders.

Workaholic

Sean Puffy Combs was the only teenager ever to be employed at Uptown Records. His work rate was staggering, averaging an 80-hour week. He'd take notes furiously, watching everyone like a hawk, listening and learning. The juvenile intern was talent spotting, organising, promoting and matching artists to musical ideas. Puffy held together not only put the music but the whole package. He directed the videos, produced the tracks and selected the wardrobe. He majored in remixing releases, allowing hits to be recycled and sold again and again to the same customers. Music tastes were becoming fluid and less staid. His productions flew in the face of the black community's disdain for watering down R&B. Sean would often use classic pop music riffs as a twist. It worked. Artists like Jodeci and Mary J. Blige were going pop and platinum. The 20 year-old minion sprinted up the ladder to become Vice-President within 12 months.

During 1991, Combs suffered his first failure when his celebrity basketball tournament at City College – an Aids fundraiser – ended in a stampede leaving nine kids dead. Harrell later reprimanded Combs for getting carried away with his success, and it soon became clear the two alpha males could not continue working together. It was Harrell's herd and Combs got the boot.

Combs took the rejection hard and fell into a depression, locking himself in his apartment – but it did not take him long to get his head together, lick his wounds and push on with the dream. The young entrepreneur's next move was solid. He founded Hip Hart Beat Records with JC 'Big Balla' Sledge. The partnership was short-lived, although the two men remained friends. Puffy decided to pursue his own vision of what he believed America wanted to see and hear next. Working from his apartment, he founded a new label, which was aptly named Bad Boy Records. Within weeks Bad Boy signed a $15 million deal with global music distributor Arista.

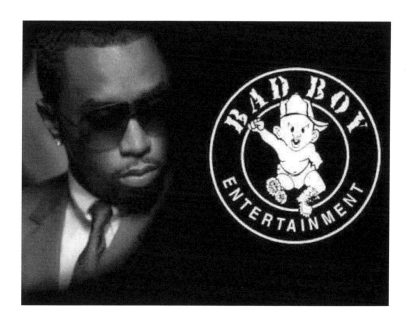

The entrepreneur took the major distributors across the Rubicon. He gave the predominantly white middle-class youth market intimidating but (generally) safe black pseudo-gangsters, edgy singers and rappers, all of which the rebellious youth market identified with.

Combs soon realised that he was dealing with a commodity. He discovered 'black oil': found underground, full of energy, created by the huge pressure heaped on the black inner-city overtime. It produced a product with currency. Within the following four years the young entrepreneur sold over $100 million worth of edgy black music. Lines of demarcation evaporated as hip-hop culture blurred the traditional racial divide amongst the youth and music market segments. They now had fashion, language and attitude in common. The much debated cross-over issue simply became an irrelevance. Major corporations flocked to the hip-hop artists as their route to penetrating the urban market segment. The multi-billion dollar global distributors never looked back.

Life imitating art

The hip-hop genre was powerful because of its close proximity to raw street life. But at times it was impossible to separate the street from the art. At 12:20am on the morning of November 30th 1994, hip-hop artist Tupac Shakur was shot five times in the lobby of a Times Square recording studio, but survived. It just so happened that Combs and his artist and close friend The Notorious B.I.G. (Biggy Smalls), were in the building at the time. Tupac accused Combs and B.I.G. of attempting to murder him. Tupac's manager was Suge Knight, owner of Death Row Records in California. During the Source Awards some months later Knight took a pot-shot at Combs, publicly announcing: "If you don't want the owner of your label on your album or in your video or on your tour, come sign with Death Row."

Combs's gracious and classy riposte was to appeal for peace. Despite the public derision the entrepreneur's response was to be magnanimous, applauding his accuser's entrepreneurship and highlighting the need for peace among fellow black artists, producers and entrepreneurs. He encouraged them to celebrate their black entrepreneurial achievements. Throughout the late 1990s the so-called 'West coast-East coast feud' rumbled on. Knight represented the West coast and Combs managed the East coast contingent. During the following month of August 1995, Jake Robles, Knight's close friend, was shot and killed at a party in Atlanta hosted by Janet Jackson's long-term partner (and later husband) Jermaine Dupri. The shooting took place in front of Knight and Combs who were standing together in conversation at the time. Knight blamed Combs' entourage. The anniversaries of both shootings were to prove eventful. Tupac suspected that his friend Randy 'Stretch' Walker was responsible for his attack. On November 30th 1995, the anniversary of Tupac's shooting, Stretch was gunned down and killed.

Almost a year after the murder of Knight's friend Robles, a face-off took place in a car park during the Soul Train Awards in LA. Guns were drawn all round. It was described as being like the final scene in Will Smith and Gene Hackman's film *Enemy of the State*, featuring dozens of men in a room at close quarters pointing guns at each other and arguing. However, they all thought better of it and the weapons were put away.

The deaths of Tupac and Biggie Smalls

The battle wasn't over yet though. On September 7th 1996, Tupac Shakur and Suge Knight attended the Mike Tyson v. Bruce Seldon fight (a Don King promotion). After leaving the venue together Suge Knight and Tupac were attacked in a drive-by shooting by unknown assailants.

Knight was shot in the head but survived; Tupac, who was hit several times, later died in hospital. The grapevine held Combs and B.I.G. responsible for the hit. Within six months B.I.G. was assassinated in a drive-by shooting following the annual Soul Train Awards in LA.

Combs was present but fortuitously decided to travel in a car behind B.I.G.'s ride and watched helplessly as his friend's life ebbed away. Combs rival Suge Knight was suspected but not charged with what is believed to be a tit-for-tat murder.

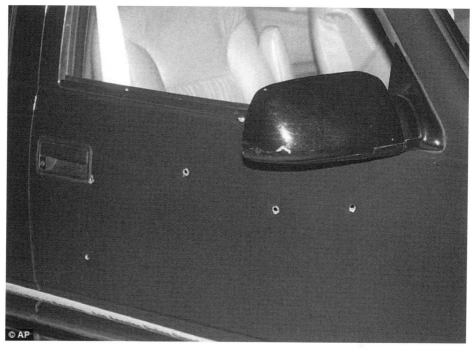

© AP

Significantly, Combs continued to thrive whilst Knight's career faded. But as the market continued to grow the feuding became extraneous. Young men and women in the business grew so staggeringly wealthy that business imperatives superseded small-minded street issues. In 1998 Combs led the way, manufacturing sweat-suits, hats and t-shirts, driving forward as an entrepreneur.

Combs had a global hit with the single *I'll Be Missing You* (a hip-hop version of Sting and the Police's original), his own performance to commemorate his friend's death. The album released that year was his biggest ever. Combs later named his son Christopher in honour of his fallen friend.

Despite his desire to focus on business, Combs got into yet more trouble. In 1999 on April 15th, Interscope Records executive Steve Stoute put Combs' image in a video without his permission. Combs gave him a slap (allegedly with a chair, a telephone, and a champagne bottle) and was convicted of harassment. They're still good friends though.

The man who had called his business Bad Boy couldn't steer clear of trouble for very long. In December 1999, he was charged with shooting up a nightclub, for concealing a weapon and bribery. It all went wrong when a punter took issue with the club's preferential treatment of Combs and made his feelings known by throwing a drink over the music mogul. Shots went off in the resulting mêlée. Combs had his latest squeeze and soon-to-be superstar Jennifer Lopez with him. His protégé, Jamal Barrow, aka Shyne, aged 22, was charged and sentenced to ten years for injuring three people using a firearm. Combs got off, having hired O. J. Simpson's lawyer, the late great Johnnie Cochran, to defend him. He did lose Jenny though; she waited until St Valentine's Day to end their relationship. It was showiness at its best.

Unstoppable drive

Arista also decided to get rid of the 'bad boy' and his label (whilst holding on to what they thought would be the next big thing – Faith Evans). The entrepreneur came back harder, signing an even bigger and more lucrative distribution deal with Universal. Sean Combs became immersed in a re-branding exercise, changing his name from 'Puff Daddy' to the less imposing 'P-Diddy' (a name Biggy Smalls coined in jest).

Whilst on trial for shooting up the club, the entrepreneur worked on a clothing collection, spending much of the time with a design team. 'Sean John' (P. Diddy's first and middle names) was the brand name chosen for his new line of ghetto-fabulous fashion. In 2004, the entrepreneur opened a Sean John boutique on Fifth Avenue with America's glitterati in attendance. His role models were Ralph Lauren and Martha Stewart, of whom he's reported to have said: "Those are the templates."

Combs hired former Ralph Lauren executive Jeffrey Tweedy as Vice-President of the Sean John company, having secured a $100 million investment in the clothing chain from supermarket multi-billionaire Ronald Burkle. The CFDA (the fashion industry equivalent of the Oscars) awarded Sean John 'Menswear Designer 2004'. Not content with just two hugely successful businesses, Combs subsequently opened a chain of restaurants named Justin's (after his eldest son). Next up was a licensing agreement with Estée Lauder to create a line of fragrances under the Sean John brand (Unforgivable was the number one selling US fragrance of 2006).

Continued expansion

At the time of writing , Combs' business interests are extensive, including the energy boosting 'Diddy Drink' and a limited-edition S.U.V. Navigator, tricked-out with a Combs-designed interior, as well as endorsement deals with global brands such as Gillette. His advertising company, Blueflame Marketing & Advertising, is another recent addition to his portfolio of businesses. All this is supplemented by the $10 million he's made as a rapper and actor. Given his Midas touch, it was no surprise when the entrepreneur began producing films. Bad Boy also produces programmes for TV and video such as *Making Da Band* (a reality TV show) and *Bad Boys of Comedy*, and latterly the hit programme *Run's House*. Movies were also in the pipeline at the time of writing.

Daddy's House

Combs sold a 50 percent stake in Bad Boy to Warner Music Corp. in 2005 for $35 million. He remains the company's CEO. The move positions the company to benefit from the new digital revolution now underway. He felt it was time to give back, launching the charity Daddy's House, funding social programmes based in Harlem, including a high-profile drive to encourage the youth of America to vote. Combs' personal net worth is estimated at $350 million (he has made comments about such figures being bandied about), but whatever the real figure, it's likely to increase substantially, given the rate at which the entrepreneur continues to expand his business empire.

Printed in Great Britain
by Amazon